Richard Petrillo

About the Author

David J. McLaughlin is a well-traveled writer and photographer with an abiding interest in New England. His book, *The Unfolding History of the Berkshires*, released in 2007, has been praised as a "literary treasure-trove," "informative and fun," a "captivating guide," a "rich resource of photographs, maps and information," and a "work of art." *Inside the Berkshires* extends the author's coverage of this favored region by presenting 16 captivating journeys of discovery through all 32 of the towns and cities of Berkshire County, Massachusetts.

David was born in Boston and grew up in Montague, in the western part of the state. He is the author of six other books and over 40 articles on subjects ranging from motivation to medieval history. With Laren Bright, he co-authored three pocket-sized books in the *Pathways to the Past Series* from Pentacle Press:

Around the Quabbin (2005), *Exploring the Upper Pioneer Valley* (2006), and *Along the Mohawk Trail* (2006). His distinctive history of the California Missions, *Soldiers, Scoundrels, Poets & Priests* (2004 and 2006), is in its second printing.

Inside the Berkshires and *The Unfolding History of the Berkshires* are the result of three years of research and travel that began in 2005. During this period David has visited the Berkshires a dozen times, often for extended stays. He contributed many of the photographs contained in these volumes. In addition to a sharp photographer's eye, he has an uncanny ability to capture the essence of places he visits by establishing warm connections with the long-time residents of a region and drawing out their personal histories and esoteric knowledge of the area.

D1056726

Table of Contents

< Jim McElholm

Preface

Because there are many traditional guides to the part of Massachusetts known as the Berkshires, we have endeavored to make this book more of an insider's look at the region's natural wonders and manmade marvels. We have focused on the lesser-known aspects of the area—including some behind-the-scenes information on the more famous attractions. We've included an abundance of colorful photos to further enhance your experience of the region as you read about it and to impart some of its essence that words simply can't convey.

The Berkshires had a relatively unique evolution, with successive waves of development. This created the rich tapestry of historic buildings, cultural attractions, and communities we now enjoy, nestled in a landscape that looks much as it did when the literary giants of the 19th century began to extol its natural beauty.

A Brief Look at the History of the Berkshires

The Berkshires was one of the last major sections of New England to be colonized, largely because of the area's geographic isolation and relatively difficult terrain. As the 3D map that accompanies this book makes visually clear, the Green Mountains, the Hoosac Range, and the Taconic Mountains form what came to be called "the Berkshire Barrier." As the English pushed westward beyond Plymouth Plantation, they naturally favored the lush farmland along the Connecticut River over the rocky, hilly land further west. The Dutch, who founded Fort Orange (Albany) in 1624, were close but they also had fertile and more accessible land to settle in the Hudson River Valley.

The first English settlement in the Berkshires, in Sheffield, didn't begin until 1725, well over a century after the Pilgrims landed in Plymouth. Even today, Berkshire County is one of the least densely populated parts of Massachusetts. This area, with less than 12 percent of the state's land, has almost 25 percent of its state park

THE MOUNT

acreage. Preservation-minded citizens have set aside even more land as wildlife sanctuaries, land trusts, and special preserves, and many of the house museums and performing arts venues have extensive grounds that add to the region's pastoral feel.

Settlement of the region was further delayed by Indian hostilities, fueled by rivalry between the British and the French in King George's War (1740–1748) and the French & Indian Wars (1754–1763). With the eventual arrival of peace, however, the area grew rapidly in the 1770s, as the table on page 9 shows.

The topography and early isolation encouraged ties that extended well beyond the distant capital of Boston. The Hudson River was a short wagon ride from major industrial centers, and thus much of the commerce flowed north and south. Later, with the arrival of the railroad, summer visitors from all the population centers of the Northeast, particularly New York, poured into the Berkshires. Stockbridge and Lenox became the "inland Newport" in the Gilded Age,

leaving a rich legacy of mansions, several of which—The Mount and Ventfort Hall in Lenox and Naumkeag in Stockbridge—are now major attractions for all to marvel at and enjoy.

The Berkshires region has benefited immensely from those who moved here to enjoy the area's beauty and openness. The Sterling and Francine Clark Art Institute was established in the Berkshires by a New Yorker, Sterling Clark, and his wife. Ted Shawn, the founder of Jacob's Pillow Dance Festival, came to the Berkshires by way of Los Angeles and New York. The famous sculptor Daniel Chester French had a summer home in the Berkshires for 34 years and left us Chesterwood. The largest collection of Norman Rockwell's illustrations and paintings is at the Norman Rockwell Museum in Stockbridge, where he made his home starting in 1952 and where he is buried.

The Berkshire towns and countryside were also shaped by the nature of the industrialization of Massachusetts that began in the 19th century. The early mills were water powered and manufacturing plants were placed

Kevin Sprague

along the major rivers. The Berkshires became an important center of paper and textile manufacturing, concentrated in the Housatonic section of Great Barrington, in Lee and Dalton, and of course in Pittsfield and Adams (which included North Adams until 1878). Later waves of large-scale manufacturing—electrical machinery and plastics, for example—were naturally attracted to the existing centers, particularly Pittsfield, the county seat.

One consequence of the manufacturing era was the inflow of European immigrants into the Berkshires. This not only created a more diverse, culturally rich population; these newcomers—many with a different religious tradition from that of the early Protestant settlers—created magnificent churches whose spires still dominate the skylines of the major towns and cities.

Preserving the History

Berkshire towns have revitalized with new purpose many of the mills that were a legacy of industrialization. North Adams has become a vibrant center of the visual arts with the creation of the Massachusetts Museum of Contemporary Art (MASS MoCA) in the former Arnold Print Works (and, after 1942, the Sprague Electric Company complex). More recently, former paper and textile mills have been developed to house art studios and other talent-intensive businesses. Some of the most attractive Victorian Age industrial architecture has been turned into housing, like the Berkshire Fine Spinning Mill complex

in Adams. Many Berkshire towns have proved adept at turning what could have become eyesores into something special. When word circulated in the small town of Becket that the 300-acre Hudson Chester Quarry, which had closed abruptly in 1960s, was slated for reopening, the citizens of Becket acquired and preserved the property, which is now a marvelous place to hike on discovery paths sprinkled with old abandoned machinery, presenting views that rival a modern art museum display.

Unique Journeys for Every Interest

One thing I have learned in three years of crisscrossing the Berkshires is that there is much to surprise and delight in every part of this favored land. Wandering the same countryside once populated by the likes of Herman Melville, Nathaniel Hawthorne, Edith Wharton, and Norman Rockwell is a special treat. Consider each journey I propose here to be a flexible blueprint that you can shape to fit your particular interests. There are those for whom the early meeting houses and preserved commons are the essence of colonial America, and seeking out these gifts from the past is a top priority in any trip. Others are fascinated by the Shakers, whose presence we trace in a special journey. Railroad buffs won't find a better area than the Berkshires in which they can marvel at the tunnels, granite bridges, and rolling stock from the time when the iron horse transformed the country. The cultural attractions which flowered and multiplied in the 20th century are a staple of any visit. Of course, God was here first, and the natural wonders abound, from the highest mountain in Massachusetts to abundant waterfalls, unusual geographic formations, and the rolling hills of the Berkshire Barrier, which, ironically, are now as heavily forested as they were when the Europeans first arrived. Enjoy your trips and let me know what you discover that I might include in subsequent editions.

— *David J. McLaughlin*

< *FIVE THOUSAND NAUTICAL MILES*, AN ACRYLIC ON CANVAS BY MELISSA LILLE | This talented artist displays her work at the Kolok Gallery in North Adams.

Population Trends in Towns of Berkshire County

(Towns listed by date of incorporation)

Town	Year of Incorporation	Population				
		1800	1850	1900	1950	2000
Sheffield	1733	2,050	2,769	1,804	2,150	3,335
Stockbridge	1739	1,261	1,941	2,081	2,311	2,276
New Marlborough	1759	1,848	1,847	1,282	989	1,494
Great Barrington	1761	1,754	3,264	5,854	6,712	7,527
Pittsfield	1761	2,261	5,872	21,766	53,348	45,793
Sandisfield	1762	1,857	1,649	661	437	824
Tyringham	1762	a) 1,712	821	386	235	350
Beckett	1765	930	1,223	994	755	1.755
Williamstown	1765	2,776	2,626	5,013	6,194	8,424
Lanesborough	1765	1,433	1,929	780	2,069	2,990
Richmond	1765	1,044	907	679	737	1,604
Lenox	1767	1.014	1,599	2,942	3,627	5,077
Peru	1771	b) 1,361	519	253	143	821
Windsor	1771	961	897	507	372	875
Alford	1773	518	502	272	212	399
Otis	1773	1,102	1,224	476	359	1,365
West Stockbridge	1774	1,002	1,613	1,158	1,165	1,416
Egremont	1775	835	1,013	758	731	1,345
Hancock	1776	1,187	789	451	445	721
Washington	1777	914	953	377	281	544
Lee	1777	1,267	3,220	3,596	4,820	5,985
Adams	1778	1,688	6,172	11,134	12,034	8,809
Mount Washington	1779	291	351	122	34	130
Dalton	1784	859	1,020	3,014	4,772	6,892
Cheshire	1793	1,325	1,298	1,221	2,022	3,401
Savoy	1797	403	955	506	291	705
Clarksburg	1798	253	384	943	1,630	1,686
Hinsdale	1804	b)	1,253	1,485	1,560	1,872
Florida	1805	c)	561	390	479	676
New Ashford	1835	380	186	107	118	247
Monterey	1847	a)	761	455	367	934
North Adams	1878	d)	d)	24,200	21,567	14,681
Total		33,633	50,118	95,667	132,966	134,953

Sources: U.S. Census Bureau population data; David Dudley Field's *History of the County of Berkshire*, published in 1829; official town histories; State of Massachusetts records.

Notes:
a) Until 1847, Tyringham and Monterey were one town named Tyringham; 1800 census data includes the populations of both towns.

b) Peru (then called Partridgeville) included most of present-day Hinsdale in 1800.
c) Florida was part of several communities until 1805. Its population peaked during the construction of the Hoosac Tunnel.
d) North Adams was part of Adams until it was incorporated as a separate town in 1878.

How *Inside the Berkshires* Helps You

MAKE THE MOST OF YOUR TIME IN THE BERKSHIRES

We have organized this book into 16 "journeys of discovery" for you. Each journey can easily keep you fully engaged for a day or more, or you can sample each area in a short "orientation" drive and cover a lot of territory very efficiently. *Inside the Berkshires* also can be used as a comprehensive inventory of Berkshire attractions, from which you can develop your own itinerary or short list of things to do and see.

Accommodations

You will find that where you stay in this accommodation-rich region will influence your level of satisfaction. The Berkshires is an area where you can be in the countryside, a charming small town, or a bustling city and still get almost anywhere within an hour. Recognize, though, that dining, shopping, and nightlife are concentrated in a few towns and the county's two cities.

There are over 5,000 hotel and inn rooms available to Berkshire county visitors, in all price ranges and offering all levels of elegance. If cost, location, and modern amenities such as TV and Internet access are paramount, you will find plenty of motels (and some hotels) typically located in or near the major towns and cities—along Route 7 in Great Barrington and Lenox, for example. Other choices range from sumptuous former Gilded Age mansions and upscale resorts that offer every imaginable service to small B&Bs where you'll share a bath, watch TV in the parlor, and hope the weather is cool enough to make up for the lack of air conditioning. Some venerable properties are also somewhat dated (in other words, they creak and groan). The Berkshire Visitors Bureau has a robust lodging service that contains every type of accommodation. You can access the Bureau via phone at 1-800-237-5747, ext. 506; by email at lodging@berkshires.org; or online at www.berkshires.org.

To provide a maximum of color photos and historical information, *Inside the Berkshires* only highlights lodgings that we call "accommodations with a past"—unique places we have flagged with a symbol. These places (most of which like to call themselves "inns") have three things in common: 1) a fascinating history that is usually reflected in an 18th- or 19th-century building, 2) the kind of authentic furnishings and/or expansive grounds that can enhance any stay, and 3) a reputation for superb service. We have selected 21 places in 10 towns for your consideration. Although most of these are "upscale," the level of amenities varies, and not all offer full-service dining. Check out their Websites carefully before you book.

Other Resources

We have made a special effort to facilitate your exploration by including the full street addresses of all attractions for travelers with car navigation systems. You will also find that each chapter contains town maps that show the location of places we discuss. We strongly recommend, however, that you stash a comprehensive county map in the car (such as the spiral-bound *Arrow Street Atlas of Western Massachusetts*) in case you decide to explore the back roads. We have also included scores of phone numbers and Website addresses to assist you in finding current information on festivals and parades and for up-to-date listings of special events and exhibits at the region's museums, theatres, and performing arts venues.

As you travel, you will find plenty of locals eager to help. In season, all the major towns have an information booth or visitors center staffed by knowledgeable personnel. These places and plenty of other outlets carry brochures and other free handouts to guide you through their slice of the region. If you want detailed listings and critics' reviews of local places, we particularly recommend *Berkshire Living* (a glossy, full-color magazine), *The Berkshire Eagle* (the county's newspaper of record), *The Advocate* (a free weekly newspaper), *The Berkshire Record* (a Southern Berkshire weekly), and *The Artful Mind* (a free monthly focusing on the arts scene). Also, we invite you to check out our Website, www.berkshiretimelines. com, where we post restaurant reviews,

reader commentary on attractions and accommodations, and other information you will find useful for enhancing your experience of the Berkshires.

We hope you enjoy this historically rich and naturally beautiful region, whether you travel there physically or experience it only through *Inside the Berkshires.*

Jim McElholm

FIRST TOWNS

Sheffield, Mount Washington, and Egremont

This opening journey takes us into the first towns of the Berkshires. The chapter tells of their founding and the momentous—or sometimes mundane—events that shaped their character. It gives context to the legacy we now enjoy over two centuries later.

In 1722, over a century after the Pilgrims landed in Plymouth and at a time when settlements covered much of New England, the general court of Massachusetts approved a petition to establish the Upper and Lower Housatonic Townships in the southwestern quadrant of Hampshire County. Dutch settlers from the Hudson River Valley had already built farms in what is now Mount Washington,

Egremont, and Sheffield as early as 1692, but this region was and would remain sparsely populated for decades. Some 40 years later, in 1761, when Berkshire was split off from Hampshire County, there were still only around 700 families in the entire county.

Sheffield, which lies on a fertile flood plain created by the Housatonic River, is easily reached today on Route 7, which cuts through the middle of the town. In the years when Obadiah Noble (who hailed from Westfield) and the other early settlers arrived in 1725–26, this was the frontier. But by 1733 Sheffield had enough inhabitants to be incorporated, winning the designation of the first Berkshire town.

SHEFFIELD STONE STORE >
David J. McLaughlin

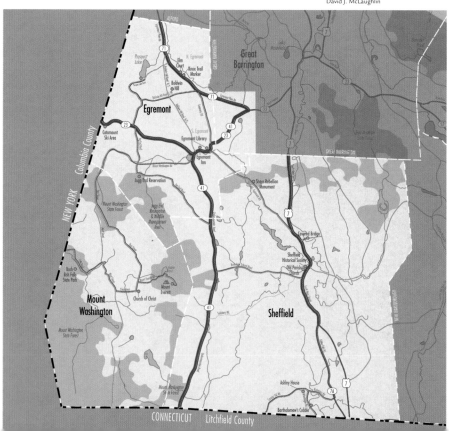

SHEFFIELD TOWN CENTER

Sheffield

Hamilton Child, author of the *Gazetteer of Berkshire County*, published in 1885, described **Sheffield** as "beautifully diversified by mountain, hill, and verdant valley … forming bewitching scenery that is charming in the extreme." The description is still apt in the 21st century. This historic town has compelling attractions: a vibrant village center that retains its charm, the oldest house and the earliest original church in the Berkshires and the county's only covered bridge, a unique

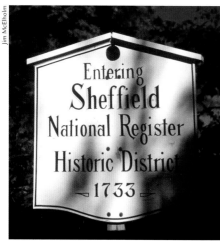

HISTORIC DISTRICT

complex of 18th- and 19th-century buildings managed by the town's Historical Society, and, to the south, in the village of Ashley Falls, Bartholomew's Cobble, where abundant wildflowers, the largest collection of fern species in North America, and 5 miles of trails invite visitors year round.

Most of these attractions are on or near Route 7.

As you head south on Route 7, keep an eye on the left-hand side for the access road (Covered Bridge Lane) that leads to the only remaining **covered bridge** in the Berkshires. At one time Massachusetts had over 100 covered bridges, but sadly, unlike nearby Vermont, the state exerted little effort to preserve these historic structures.

The bridge, called the Upper Covered Bridge in the 19th century when there were two covered bridges in town, extends over the Housatonic River. Be sure to walk south, along the river, to enjoy the best view of the entire bridge.

A great trip for those with a canoe or kayak is to paddle down the Housatonic from here. Bartholomew's Cobble is about 9 miles south of the bridge.

As you drive south on Route 7, a sign alerts you to the beginning of the Historic District.

Jim McElholm

SHEFFIELD BRIDGE SEEN FROM RIVER BANK
The Sheffield Covered Bridge is 93 feet long.

David J. McLaughlin

Town Center

The historic center of Sheffield lies on the west side of Route 7. It has a distinctive collection of 18th-, 19th-, and early 20th-century properties that add up to an inviting whole.

The **Old Parish Church** is the oldest church building in the Berkshires, built in 1760.

The Congregational Society of Sheffield was organized in 1735.

The clock in the tower of the church was added in 1876. It was paid for by the Grand Army of the Republic and the Women's Relief Corps as a memorial to George F. Root, a native of Sheffield who wrote *The Battle Cry of Freedom* and other popular Civil War songs.

< OLD PARISH CHURCH | In 1819–1820, the church was moved back from the center of what is now Route 7 to its present location. At that time the building was enlarged and modified to a Greek Revival style.

SHEFFIELD HISTORICAL SOCIETY COMPLEX | This nonprofit organization was founded in 1972.

Sheffield Historical Society

Just north of the church is a cluster of antique buildings managed by the **Historical Society of Sheffield**, a particularly active group of volunteers that has acquired and preserved some of the most important historic structures in the county's first town.

The **Dan Raymond House**, a brick colonial, was built on this site in 1775. It functions as a museum and houses the society's main office. Other buildings include a carriage house that contains an exhibit of agricultural tools; an unusual early 19th-century double-chamber Greek Revival smokehouse; the Parker L. Hare law offices (c. 1820), and my favorite, a Victorian vegetable-growing house.

In 1999 the society acquired the oldest commercial building in town, known as the **Old Stone Store** (a photograph appears on page 13). This handsome building, constructed of stone obtained at the local Hewins Quarry, now serves as a community information center and museum. The society's research shows that over more than a century and a half this store, built in 1834, was a butcher shop, a billiard

hall, a barber shop, a millinery shop, a harness maker's workshop, a drugstore, a café, and a wine store and liquor outlet. It was also the location of the town's first telegraph office.

The **Mark Dewey Research Center** has an extensive collection of town documents, family files, house histories, cemetery records, and photographs, including over 1,000 glass plate negatives. The center is housed in a former hatter's shop (built in 1816) where Dewey and three young apprentices made hats and caps.

Fortunately for all of us who love historic buildings and want to know more about the area's history, the Sheffield Historical Society is staffed throughout the year. On Mondays and Fridays between 1:30 and 4:00 P.M., knowledgeable volunteers are stationed in the Mark Dewey Research Center to answer questions and assist with regional genealogy.

Sheffield Historical Society
159-161 Main Street
Sheffield, MA 01257
413-229-2694
www.sheffieldhistory.org

Sheffield is home to the **Berkshire Choral Festival**, founded in 1982 to "provide choral singers with the opportunity to rehearse and perform masterpieces of the choral repertoire under the direction of world-class conductors and with the help of a professional musical staff." The organization offers week-long programs each summer, with four held at the Berkshire School in Sheffield and three others at international destinations such as Canterbury, England, where the participants sing at the Canterbury Cathedral. For additional information, check out their comprehensive Website (www.berkshirechoral.org) or call 413-229-8526.

PAINTED PORCH COUNTRY ANTIQUES

There are several other "must see and enjoy" attractions in Sheffield. In the southern part of the town, near the village of Ashley Falls, are the Col. John Ashley House, the oldest house in Berkshire County, and Bartholomew's Cobble, a natural attraction you simply don't want to miss.

As you head south it will be obvious that Route 7 itself is an attraction because of the many antique shops and other inviting stores located along this main road. The author of *Antiquing Weekends*, Gladys Montgomery, has written that "Sheffield may have more antique stores per capita than any other town in New England." While some will enjoy stopping at stores randomly, if you want to find authentic items of interest in Sheffield and the many other Berkshire antique venues, you should do your homework. Check out the Berkshire County Massachusetts Antiques and Art Dealers Association (www.bcaada.com; 413-229-3070), founded in 1973. Their members include 52 of the most reputable dealers in the county. Incidentally, the treasure trove of worthy stores continues along the northern reaches of Route 7, well into the southern part of Great Barrington.

KUTTNER ANTIQUES BUILDING

The historic **Sheffield Grange** is along Route 7. The National Grange of the Patrons of Husbandry was founded in 1867 to bring rural people together and help rehabilitate the South after the Civil War. The concept rapidly expanded all over the country in successive decades. The Sheffield Chapter was chartered in 1900.

As so many other social venues developed and the membership aged, most of the granges ceased operation. The Sheffield Grange building, the site of a popular dance festival for 30 years, is being sold, although the organization is still active.

To get to the **Ashley House**, take Route 7 south until it intersects with Route 7A, about a mile from the town center. Then follow 7A for about half a mile and turn right onto Rannapo Road. In another 1.5 miles, turn right onto Cooper Hill Road, where the Ashley House is now located. In 1929 the house was moved to the present site by an Ashley descendant, Harry Hillyer Brigham, and his wife, Mary, a professional architect. The Trustees of Reservations took title to the property in 1972.

COL. JOHN ASHLEY HOUSE | The house has been carefully restored and contains authentic period furniture from the 18th and early 19th centuries.

Col. John Ashley House

The Ashleys were a prominent New England family. John, a Yale graduate, was hired in 1832 to survey the Lower Housatonic Township. Over the next several decades he became the wealthiest and probably the most influential man in Sheffield. According to historian Myron O. Stachiw, by 1760 he owned "more than 3,000 acres with sixteen dwelling houses" and "he was operating a store, sawmill, gristmill, potash works, cider mill, tanneries and ironworks." Ashley, who saw military service during the French & Indian Wars, served as town selectman from 1740–1783. He was also a justice of the peace and advanced the funds to build the first county courthouse, in Great Barrington, the initial shire town.

ASHLEY HOUSE INTERIOR VIEW

The structure that is now one of the most important house museums in the Berkshires was built in 1735 at the time of Ashley's marriage to his Dutch bride, Hannah Hogeboom. It has the same directional orientation as it did on its original site so that the "front door" is on the west side and does not now face the street.

Though the house itself is quite interesting, the real attraction of this museum is what you can learn about events that shaped the history of the area.

Col. Ashley was one of the authors of the Sheffield Resolves, a series of resolutions that forcefully stated the rights of the American colonists in relation to the English crown. This statement of grievances was written in January 1773. Later that year, on December 16, the Boston Tea Party helped spark the American Revolution.

Col. Ashley, then in his 60s, was cautious about splitting from England, but once the die was cast he supported the cause of the new republic with his usual vigor and entrepreneurial skills. The Salisbury, Connecticut, iron furnace owned by Ashley produced cannon, swivel guns, and ammunition for the Continental forces. However, at age 67, he was too old to join the Continental Army and participate in the actual fighting.

During a visit to the Ashley House you will also hear the inspiring story of Elizabeth Freeman (called Mumbet), an Ashley slave who sued for and won her freedom in a celebrated 1781 court battle that took place in the courthouse that Ashley himself helped finance. The Great Barrington Court of Common Pleas held for Mumbet, deciding that slavery was unconstitutional under the new (1780) Massachusetts Constitution. Col. Ashley initially appealed the decision but dropped his suit when the Supreme Judicial Court of

MUMBET | The original of this painting is in the Massachusetts Historical Society Museum.

Massachusetts found for another slave, Quok Walker, in a similar case.

For the rest of her life Mumbet worked as a free domestic for the influential Sedgwick family of Stockbridge. Theodore Sedgwick had represented her in the court case.

The Ashley house is open Saturdays and Sundays, 10 A.M. to 5 P.M., from Memorial Day weekend to Columbus Day. Guided 45-minute tours are available.

Ashley House
Cooper Hill Road
Sheffield, MA
413-229-8600
www.thetrustees.org/pages/
252_ashley_house.cfm

BOSTON TEA PARTY

Currier & Ives

Paul Rocheleau

ROCK FORMATIONS

Bartholomew's Cobble

Bartholomew's Cobble is a 329-acre reserve located along the Housatonic River. In 1971 it was designated a National Natural Landmark. Since 1946, when they acquired the site, Bartholomew's Cobble has also been managed by The Trustees of Reservations.

The reservation is located on Weatogue Road in Ashley Falls. From the Ashley house, double back on Cooper Hill Road to where it connects with Rannapo Road, then turn right on Weatogue. The site's parking lot will accommodate 30 cars.

Bartholomew's Cobble is named for two rocky knolls that rise above the Housatonic River. Ledges Interpretive Trail takes you through this woodland community. If you hike (an easy to moderate trail) to the top of Hurlburt's Hill (1,700 feet above sea level), you can enjoy a panoramic view of the Housatonic Valley northward.

The cobble is home to the greatest diversity of fern species in the country. It also has more forest types than anywhere else in the Berkshires and just about every kind of tree you can find in the county (red cedar, oak, pine, birch, hemlock, maple, and hickory). My favorite time to visit is in the spring. In April and May there are abundant wildflowers. My birding friends tell me that the annual bird migration also peaks in May.

Bartholomew's Cobble is open daily year round, from sunrise to sunset. The museum and visitor's center is open from 9:00 A.M. to 4:30 P.M. each day but closed Sundays and Mondays in the winter months, from December to March.

Bartholomew's Cobble
Weatogue Road
Sheffield, MA
423-229-8600
www.thetrustees.org/pages/
277_bartholomew_s_cobble.cfm

Paul Rocheleau

On to Egremont and Mount Washington

The two towns to the west (Mount Washington) and northwest (Egremont) of Sheffield, along with Great Barrington, were all part of the Upper and Lower Housatonic Townships established by the General Court of Massachusetts in 1722. However, each evolved in a distinctive fashion.

Both towns can be reached from Sheffield by taking Berkshire School Road West about 2½ miles to pick up State Highway 41 North (also called Undermountain Road). This leads directly to South Egremont in a little under 4 miles.

Mount Washington

To reach the town of **Mount Washington**, make a sharp left on to Mount Washington Road before you get to the center of South Egremont. Follow this road 3.3 miles into Mount Washington State Forest, where it turns into East Street. The center of town, such as it is, is another 4 miles further along (the town hall is at 188 East Street).

You may decide to save remote Mount Washington for a special trip, particularly if you are an outdoor enthusiast. Tucked in the southwest corner of Berkshire County, it is surrounded by towering mountain peaks and forests, much of it state parkland. The longest waterfall in Massachusetts and the second highest mountain in the state (Mount Everett) are here. You can easily spend a day in these hills.

This border town has always been the most remote of Berkshire communities and, at 22.2 square miles, one of the smallest and least densely populated towns in the state. The population topped out at 450 in the 19th century, when the town had daily stagecoach service. The number of residents gradually declined until there were only 34 who lived here year round in the 1950s. The population has climbed partway back in recent years and reached 146 in 2007.

Jim McElholm

FALL FOLIAGE

The town was originally known as Tauconnuck (or Taghconic) Mountain, since it was part of the Taconic Range that rises between the Housatonic and Hudson Rivers. The successive applications submitted between 1775 and 1779, when the town was finally incorporated, include a plaintive statement about the area's isolation. The 1776 petitioners pointed out that this area was separated from Egremont and Sheffield "by a long and steep precipice" and that the connecting roads were "at all times extremely rugged, and at some seasons almost wholly (sic) impassable."

ALONG THE HOUSATONIC RIVER >
Darlene Bordwell

Jim McElholm

CHURCH OF CHRIST | The church is only open during the summer months.

The Town Center

The most prominent building in the center of town is the **Church of Christ in Mount Washington**, organized in 1874. The church is located in front of the small **town hall**, where voters still use an 1873 voting machine. The **Mount Washington cemetery** is the oldest in the Berkshires.

Mount Washington was well known for its wild blueberries in the 19th century. In 1940 a Harvard Business School professor, Robert W. Austin, began a commercial blueberry operation here. **Blueberry Hill Farm**, at 100 East Street (www.austinfarm.com/history.htm), offers several varieties of organically grown high-bush blueberries.

Mount Washington is known for far more than blueberries, though, and has a fascinating history.

The town was at the epicenter of an extended boundary dispute between Massachusetts

and New York State. Robert Livingston, who established Livingston Manor in the Hudson River Valley in 1682, claimed large portions of the Southern Berkshires under the 1705 Patent of Westenhook. He sent tenant farmers into the area and charged early English settlers rent for the use of lands they felt they had been given by the Massachusetts Colonial Legislature. As late as 1755 one of the settlers was killed by Livingston's agents and six farms were burned. The boundary line between the states wasn't finalized until 1787. The final boundary (20 miles east of the Hudson River) left Mount Washington (barely) in Massachusetts.

However, governance of the area still wasn't fully settled. Mount Washington included an isolated hamlet called Boston Corner. It was so hard to reach that it became popular with horse thieves and any promoter who wanted to duck the law. In 1853 Boston Corner was the site of a celebrated boxing match between John Morrissey and "Yankee" Sullivan, even though bare-knuckle boxing was illegal in Massachusetts. The match went on for 37 rounds, and word of it spread far beyond the town. Shocked by the adverse national publicity, Massachusetts issued warrants for both fighters' arrest and soon reactivated a dormant petition that transferred Boston Corner to New York State, which it did later that year.

Jim McElholm

BLUEBERRY HILL FARM

Outdoor Pleasures

This southwest corner of the Berkshires offers spectacular scenery. Mount Washington has a cluster of parks that are important target destinations for hikers, mountain bikers, campers, and every stripe of outdoor enthusiast. The most popular destination for the average tourist is **Bash Bish Falls**, located in the state park of that name within Mount Washington State Forest. Bash Bish is the highest waterfall in Massachusetts. It is actually two waterfalls that drop 80 feet in a V shape into a pool below. The falls are most dramatic in the spring.

Bash Bish has been a favorite subject of painters and photographers since the 19th century. John Frederick Kensett (1816–1872), an influential member of the Hudson River School, painted Bash Bish Falls at least five times.

To reach the falls from the center of town, turn right onto Cross Road, then right onto West Street and continue for 1 mile, then turn left onto Falls Road. The trailhead is about 1.5 miles down on the left. There are two parking lots (the lower lot involves less climbing).

Mt. Washington State Forest extends over 4,169 acres and offers 30 miles of trails. The second highest mountain in Massachusetts, Mount Everett, is located within the town of Mount Washington. In season there is road access to and parking available for **Guilder Pond**, which is a great spot to visit in the spring when the mountain laurel and azaleas are in full bloom. You can hike (about ¾ of a mile) to the summit from there. On a clear day you will be treated to panoramic views of Massachusetts, New York, and Connecticut from the 2,624-foot summit.

BASH BISH FALLS

Henry Dondi

Egremont

Egremont, the last town in this journey, is easily reached by returning to Mount Washington Road, which cuts through the bottom third of Egremont, where Route 41 N leads to the village of South Egremont. Coming from the east, Maple Avenue/Egremont Road in Great Barrington forks outside the center of town. Routes 41/23 (also called South Egremont Road) connect with South Egremont, while Route 71 (also called Egremont Plain Road) takes a more northerly path into North Egremont.

The road system and the hilly topography shaped the way this area was settled as two separate villages, beginning in 1730, and help explain the unique role that Egremont played in the history of the region. From the early days much of the traffic between New York and Massachusetts passed through Egremont. The Twelfth Massachusetts Turnpike, built in 1801, linked the town to the New York State border. (The toll for a man and horse was 4 cents, rising to 25 cents for a four-wheeled two-horse carriage.) These roads evolved into the old Albany-Hartford turnpike.

OLD MILL | The Old Mill is a restored grist mill and blacksmith shop in South Egremont, now an inviting restaurant.

By the early decades of the 19th century Egremont had over a dozen taverns and hotels. One establishment from that era is the **Egremont Inn** *(10 Old Sheffield Road in South Egremont). The Inn dates to 1780, when Francis Haere, an emigrant from Ireland who fought in the American Revolution, built a tavern along the stagecoach route. The Egremont Inn offers*

Jim McElholm

EGREMONT INN SIGN

20 rooms on the top two floors, with sitting rooms and a restaurant on the first floor. www.egremontinn. com | 413-528-2111 INN

The arrival of the railroad in the mid-1800s and development of the interstate highway system a century later diverted much of the east-west traffic elsewhere, but Egremont has remained an attractive stopover and vacation destination as well as a great place to live in the verdant Berkshire Hills. These days Egremont's 1,000-plus residents enjoy a quiet community known for its innovative school system, extensive recreational facilities, and effective public services. The dual centers remain, each with its own post office and store that carries essentials, but serious shopping requires a jaunt into nearby Great Barrington. The town area covers 18.96 square miles.

Shays' Rebellion

Just over the town line in north Sheffield, on the Sheffield-Egremont Road, is a monument that commemorates one of the most serious challenges to the new government of the United States: **Shays' Rebellion**. Egremont and the southern Berkshires played an important role in this conflict that pitted neighbor against neighbor in a struggle that threatened the future of the young republic.

By the summer of 1786 the new nation was suffering from a postwar depression. Currency was scarce and had little value, taxes were high, and those arcane institutions, debtor's prisons, were overcrowded. In protest, that fall armed mobs in several important Western Massachusetts towns, including Great Barrington, prevented court sessions from being held.

Two former Continental Army officers, Daniel Shays and Luke Day, organized a widespread revolt. Day was captured in an attack on the federal arsenal in Springfield. Shays and about 400 men retreated to Pelham and ultimately to Petersham, where they expected to be able to regroup. They did not expect the government to move quickly in the wintry weather, but Gen. Benjamin Lincoln force-marched his troops through the snow and routed the rebels on February 4, 1787. Even so, a large contingent of rebels remained loose in the Berkshires.

On February 27, 1787, Col. (later Maj. Gen.) John Ashley, son of the prominent John Ashley of Sheffield, cornered some 90 rebels in Sheffield, near the Egremont town line. In the ensuing fight, three rebels were killed, 30 wounded, and most of the rest captured.

Despite the failure of the rebellion, the debtor's prisons that were one of the root causes of the uprising were soon abandoned and a stable system of currency adopted. But for years afterward, sentiment was divided. Some considered the men who participated in Shays' Rebellion heroes; others shared the sentiment on a plaque on the outside wall of the Petersham Historical Society: "Obedience to law is true liberty."

SHAYS' REBELLION MONUMENT

LAST BATTLE OF SHAYS REBELLION WAS HERE FEB. 27. 1787.

Darlene Bordwell

28

Jim McElholm

EGREMONT FREE LIBRARY | The library occupied the front part of the building until 1981, when it took over the entire first floor.

South Egremont

One place you will want to stop in the south village is the **Egremont Free Library** (at One Buttonball Lane). It is open several days a week (check www.egremontfreelibrary.org or phone 413-528-1474 for details). The library was established in 1893 in a building that played a prominent role in the history of a town that has always strived to provide exceptional schooling for its children.

On January 28, 1829, the citizens of Egremont organized a private academy (the equivalent of a high school today) that functioned in this building for over 50 years. When the school closed in 1882, it was sold to the town, which made it available for use as a library.

The archives and history room of the Academy building have a fascinating collection of town memorabilia.

The beautiful **Mount Everett Cemetery** abuts the library. This is one of five historic cemeteries in town.

RED BARN ANTIQUES

David J. McLaughlin

SOUVENIR PLATE

Among the numerous pleasures of Egremont is that it has many well-preserved historic structures that still offer lodging and meals. The **Old Mill** on Route 23 in South Egremont (photo on page 26) is located in a restored 1797 grist mill and blacksmith shop. It offers fine American cuisine in a homey, warm atmosphere.

It is also a joy to find high-quality specialty shops as you wander through the smaller towns of Berkshire County. In South Egremont, at 72 Main Street/Route 23, **Red Barn Antiques** (http://redbarn.antiquejunction.com or 413-528-3230) specializes in antique lighting.

The largest manufacturing business in Egremont was located across from Red Barn Antiques. The Dalzell Axle Co. began in 1845 when David Dalzell of Hudson, New York, purchased a small carriage business and began to specialize in making axles. In 1856 he obtained a patent for a unique wrought-iron case-hardened axle box that greatly expanded the business. The *Gazetteer of Berkshire County* reported that in 1885 the firm employed 60 men, turning out 12,000 sets of axles and 12,000 sets of axle boxes a year.

Catamount Ski Area (www.catamountski.com or 413-528-1262) is located in South Egremont, off Route 23. This facility, which opened in 1939, offers winter adventures on 24 miles of trails over some of the most varied terrain in the Berkshires. The snowfall in most years is adequate, but virtually the entire ski area has snowmaking equipment, just in case.

FALL COLORS >
Paul Rocheleau

NORTH EGREMONT GENERAL STORE

North Egremont

The northern village of Egremont has a charming center with one of those inviting general stores that always surprises with the range of its merchandise.

Just outside the general store, on a small green, is a prominent reminder that **Col. Henry Knox** passed through here in 1776 on his way to help in the liberation of Boston. Earlier that year, Berkshire Militia and Vermont's Green Mountain Boys had captured Fort Ticonderoga from the British, one of the few early successes in this long war.

On December 6, 1775, in the dead of winter, Col. Henry Knox began hauling the cannons captured at Fort Ticonderoga down to Lake George Landing. Then, using 80 teams of horses and oxen, he hauled the artillery to Albany and over the Berkshire Hills—through Egremont, Great Barrington, Monterey, Sandisfield, and Otis, then on to Boston, where he arrived at the end of January. When Knox's rebel artillery appeared on the high ground overlooking the city, Gen. Howe, commander of the British forces, evacuated Boston.

KNOX TRAIL MARKER IN NORTH EGREMONT

Other Excursions

In 1921 a "big-city businessman," Maj. Hugh Smiley, purchased a gentleman's farm in Egremont. He built a deluxe cattle barn there in 1928. In 1935 the barn was turned into a hotel, the Jug End Resort, which lasted about 40 years and included one of the first ski runs in the area, replete with rope tows and T-bars. After the resort closed in the 1980s, the land was allowed to revert to its natural state and is now the **Jug End State Reservation and Wildlife Management Area**. It offers hiking, horseback riding, and cross-country skiing on a particularly scenic 1,158 acres. Jug End Reservation (www.mass.gov/dcr/parks/western/juge.htm or 413-528-0330) is reached via Jug End Road in South Egremont, a little over a half mile from where it crosses Mount Washington Road.

Prospect Lake (50 Prospect Lake Road), known by the Indians as Keewena, is about 4 miles west of the village of North Egremont. This was a major recreational spot in the 1920s and is now ringed with cabins and private homes. However, there is a charming private campground (www.prospectlakepark.com) right along the lake shore, so if you want a family place where you can swim, boat, and fish or simply have a picnic by the water, this is a good bet.

For those who enjoy driving through the countryside, head up **Baldwin Hill**. There are both north–south and east–west roads up to the top of this mountain, which is 997 feet above sea level. This is one of those "less traveled roads" that offer great fall foliage viewing, sans bumper-to-bumper traffic, at the peak of the season.

VIEW AT TOP OF BALDWIN HILL

Paul Rocheleau

COUNTRY STREAM

The early towns of Berkshire County don't have the Gilded Age mansions, art museums, or world-class performing arts venues that you will find in the towns to the north. But you won't find an area more steeped in history and a population more intent on preserving the best of the past. If you seriously want to enjoy the countryside for which Berkshire County is famous, explore Sheffield, Egremont, and Mount Washington. If you want snow, take note that Mount Washington gets about 75 inches a year.

ADDITIONAL RESOURCES

Sheffield: Frontier Town, by Lillian E. Preiss, North Adams, 1976. Must reading for anyone who wants to learn about the history of this area.

Early Life in Sheffield, Berkshire County, Massachusetts: A Biography of its Ordinary People from Early Times to 1850, by James R. Miller, Sheffield Historical Society, 2002. An engaging, well-researched book. The focus on ordinary people provides insights that are often missing in traditional histories.

The Ledges Interpretive Trail Guide. A useful guide to Bartholomew's Cobble. Available online from the Trustees of Reservations.

The Ashleys: A Pioneer Berkshire Family, by Arthur C. Chase, a publication of the Trustees of Reservations. A well-researched 40-page pamphlet.

Mumbet: The Story of Elizabeth Freeman, by Harold W. Felton, N.Y.: Dodd, Mead & Company, 1970. A concise but comprehensive recapitulation of this engaging tale.

If They Close the Door on You, Go in the Window, by Bernard A. Drew, Great Barrington: Attic Press, 2004. Tells the story of slavery in the southern Berkshires during the colonial era. Includes biographies of lesser-known blacks like Jupiter Rogers and Zach Mullen in addition to Elizabeth Freeman.

A History of Mount Washington, Massachusetts, by Evelyn Shearn, self-published, 1976.

"Town Among the Clouds," by Judy Wright, *Berkshire Magazine*, 1974. A touching personal description of Mount Washington.

Egremont, 1756-1976, Great Barrington: The Berkshire Courier, 1976. Written by the town's Bicentennial Committee headed by Committee Chairwoman Gail Hennessey and the Chairman of the History Committee, Mary Louise Fratalone. Includes interesting sketches of early structures and scenes.

34

A TRI-STATE CROSSROADS

Great Barrington, with a Journey to Alford

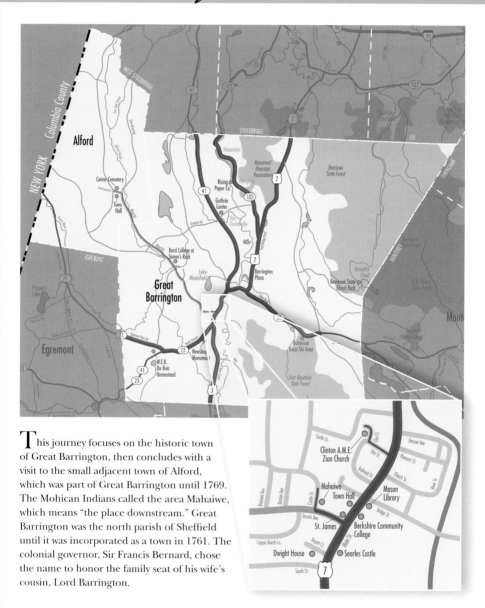

This journey focuses on the historic town of Great Barrington, then concludes with a visit to the small adjacent town of Alford, which was part of Great Barrington until 1769. The Mohican Indians called the area Mahaiwe, which means "the place downstream." Great Barrington was the north parish of Sheffield until it was incorporated as a town in 1761. The colonial governor, Sir Francis Bernard, chose the name to honor the family seat of his wife's cousin, Lord Barrington.

WELCOME TO GREAT BARRINGTON

Welcome to Great Barrington

Route 7, a central Berkshire artery featured in the preceding chapter, cuts through Great Barrington's bustling downtown, where the brick Victorian-era buildings and soaring church steeples tell you that this was an important commercial center in the 19th century. And so it is today. In the southern Berkshires, Great Barrington is the place to go for shopping, dining, movie-going, and reasonable accommodations. The town draws residents and visitors from the entire tri-state region, year round.

With a population of about 7,000—large by Berkshire standards—Great Barrington has the most authentic downtown in the county. This is a place where you can find a restaurant serving a full-course breakfast at 6:00 A.M., buy your groceries at a food coop or an upscale market, dine at one of over 50 restaurants, and have a choice of entertainment: music at sophisticated jazz clubs or hit performances at a restored 1905 theater (appropriately named the Mahaiwe).

NEAR THIS SPOT STOOD THE FIRST COURT HOUSE OF BERKSHIRE COUNTY ERECTED 1764, HERE AUGUST 16, 1774 OCCURRED THE FIRST OPEN RESISTANCE TO BRITISH RULE IN AMERICA

MONUMENT TO FIRST RESISTANCE TO BRITISH RULE

David J. McLaughlin

LOCKE, STOCK & BARREL

Even better, the string of antique shops that began in Sheffield extends into the southern reaches of Great Barrington. There are more gift stores, specialty shops, services, and motels not only in the downtown but to the north along Route 7, which has become an extended commercial area. Route 7 is referred to as Main Street along its southern reaches and as Stockbridge Road to the north of downtown.

Historic Town Center

Great Barrington offers as fascinating a look at the county's past as it does the engaging present. This was the first shire town (county seat) of Berkshire County, from 1761 to 1787. The residents of Great Barrington were the first to openly resist British rule, an event celebrated at a monument on the front lawn of the town hall (see page 37). This monument, erected in 1890, is made of blue dolomite stone hewn from the local Searles-Hopkins quarry.

The cannons that Henry Knox moved from Fort Ticonderoga to Boston traveled through Great Barrington in January 1776, and the British soldiers and mercenaries captured when Burgoyne surrendered in 1777 were billeted here for a time. The most prominent demonstration in the Berkshires during Shays' Rebellion took place in September 1786 at the **Great Barrington courthouse**, where well over 1,000 men stopped the court from opening. A pivotal trial that helped eliminate slavery in Massachusetts took place here in 1781.

PAUL KLEINWALD ART & ANTIQUES

David J. McLaughlin

VICTORY STATUE | The artist who made this statue was Truman Bartlett, who worked in the classical style. This sculpture is said to be based on a figure excavated at Pompeii.

MASON LIBRARY

It is no wonder that this is a downtown loaded with historic buildings. The handsome Georgian-style **town hall** at 334 Main was originally built in 1874–75 to house courtrooms, a library, and town offices.

In addition to the memorial stone in front of the town hall, a bronze **statue of Victory** in the center of the lawn honors those who fought in the U.S. Civil War.

The **Mason Library** (231 Main), an architectural beauty built in 1912–13, is another Georgian Revival-style building.

A number of Gilded Age mansions were built in Great Barrington, including Brookside (now part of the Eisner Camp), the residence of inventor William Stanley; Folly Farm (which now houses the American Institute for Economic Research); and Aston Magna (still a private residence). The most notable structure was Kellogg Terrace, popularly called **Searles Castle**. This medieval-like chateau sits prominently on Route 7 (289 Main Street) behind a wall of blue dolomite stone quarried from land near the 229-acre property. The name Searles refers to the 46-year-old decorator, Edward F. Searles, who married the wealthy older widow of Mark Hopkins and oversaw the building of the "castle."

GREAT BARRINGTON TOWN HALL | The town hall was built according to plans developed by E. L. Robertson.

SEARLES CASTLE | This massive mansion, completed in 1888, measures over 68,000 square feet.

David J. McLaughlin

THE DWIGHT HOUSE | The Dwight House (some signs refer to it as the Bryant House) is on the National Register of Historic Places.

There are more than a score of important buildings and historic sites in this town, some that still sit in splendor on their original sites and others that have survived by being moved. A good example of the latter is the **Dwight House**, a gray saltbox built in 1759, which now houses law offices and has been moved twice. This building, now located at 390 Main, has seen a lot of history. Its original owner, Joseph Dwight, was a prominent soldier in the French & Indian Wars. British General John Burgoyne, who surrendered to the Americans at Saratoga, stayed here for several days in 1777 on his way to Boston. The famous poet and prominent editor of the *New York Evening Post*, William Cullen Bryant, who was town clerk of Great Barrington for a time in the early stages of his career, was married in this building.

An historic property offering accommodations in Great Barrington is the **Wainwright Inn** *(518 S. Main Street). This friendly, Victorian-style B&B first opened in 1766 as a tavern and inn. www. wainwright.com | 413-528-2062*

Great Barrington has a large, energetic Historical Society, founded in 1977, whose comprehensive collection will soon finally have a proper home. In 2007 the Society purchased the historic **Wheeler Homestead** (a former farm south of downtown at 817

Main Street), which dates back to 1776. A visit to this property, which will house a museum and research center, is an important stop for history buffs. To check the ongoing status of renovation and the group's extensive programs, see www.greatbarringtonhistoricalsociety. org. The society offers walking tours of the downtown that are sure to include a stroll along the Housatonic River.

Over the past 20 years the people of Great Barrington have reclaimed much of the scenic Housatonic River frontage. Hundreds and hundreds of volunteers have removed accumulated debris, stabilized and landscaped the riverbank, and created parks and trails through the area. Commercial and private property owners along the half-mile trail have granted permanent public access. The **Housatonic River Walk** was first opened to the public in 1992 and continues to expand. In 2001–02 volunteers extended the trail along the riverbank adjacent to the former Searles Middle School and created a River Garden Park to honor civil rights activist W. E. B. Du Bois adjacent to his birth site in Great Barrington. In 2006 they created the William Stanley Overlook, which contains a handsome native garden and an observation platform with a view of the rubberwear factory where William Stanley developed his alternating-current transformers in 1886. This site celebrates the industrial history of the town and the Berkshire region. For further information see www.gbriverwalk.org.

Signs noting that Great Barrington was the **birthplace of W. E. B. Du Bois** (1868–1963) were erected on Route 41 (at the West Stockbridge line) and Route 23 (at the Monterey line) in 2006. This noted scholar, prolific writer, and African-American activist is arguably the town's most famous son. His boyhood homesite, given National Historic

Landmark status in 1976, lies about 2½ southwest of town, near the junction of Routes 71 and 23. (Unfortunately, the house has been demolished.) Information is available at www.library.umass.edu/spcoll/duboishome/ virtualtour.htm.

Great Barrington has an unusual number of historically significant churches. **St. James Episcopal Church** (353 Main Street), the third church building of a parish organized in 1762, has been a force in the town's life ever since it was built in 1857–58.

ST. JAMES EPISCOPAL CHURCH
This Gothic Revival-style structure is built of blue dolomite from the quarry on nearby East Mountain.

Jim McElholm

Paul Rocheleau

David J. McLaughlin

CLINTON A.M.E. ZION CHURCH | The church was dedicated in 1887.

The Congregational Church (a handsome stone church built in 1860 and restored in 1883), St. Peter's Roman Catholic Church (dedicated in 1911), and the Methodist Church (originally built in 1845) are all imposing structures. Other more modest buildings have played an important role in the diverse religious life of this town. The **Clinton A.M.E. Zion Church**, located at 9 Elm Court, is one of the first African-American churches in the Berkshires and the oldest building in the country (dedicated in 1887) in continual use by an African-American organization.

A short distance past the "Great Bridge" over the Housatonic River, on North Street, is the **Ahavath Sholom (Love of Peace) Synagogue**, chartered in 1926. The building is a former schoolhouse. This is the only synagogue in the Berkshires which is still in its original building.

New religious architecture still characterizes this progressive town.

< ARK AT TWILIGHT - HEVREH OF SOUTH BERKSHIRE | This Reform Jewish Congregation was formed in 1974. Their new, permanent home was dedicated in 1999.

RISING PAPER MILL | The crimson bricks, twin towers, and mansard roof of the Rising Paper Mill make this complex an architectural gem. >

A Prominent Industrial Past

Great Barrington was a significant center of manufacturing in the 19th and early 20th centuries. The Kellogg Mill dressed homespun cloth on the Green River as early as 1748. The Berkshire Woolen Mill near Brown Bridge was one of the locations where the 1968 movie *Pretty Poison*, starring Anthony Perkins and Tuesday Weld, was filmed.

Ample water, good transportation, and energetic business leaders spurred the growth of textile and paper companies. The largest textile company, Monument Mills, operated for over 150 years until it closed in 1956.

Sadly, manufacturing continues to disappear in the region. In 2007 Fox River Paper, which had acquired the Rising Paper Mill in 1988, announced its closing. The mill, founded in 1899 by Bradley D. Rising, made fine-art paper known for its archival qualities. The handsome **Rising Paper Company complex** north of Great Barrington, on Route 183 in Risingdale, represents some of the best Victorian-era industrial architecture left in the Northeast, and there is a vigorous effort to preserve the buildings for another use.

Great Barrington played a prominent role in the early history of power generation. William Stanley (1858–1916) illuminated the Main Street store windows of Great Barrington in

MONUMENT MILLS: REMINDERS OF A MANUFACTURING ERA | The former paper and textile company mills in this region are slowly being converted to other uses. Abandoned machinery and empty former mill sites are still visible.

1886 with the first practical demonstration of an alternating-current system. His company was acquired by General Electric in 1903. GE's Berkshire plants were world leaders in the design, manufacture, and sale of electrical equipment and, somewhat later, plastics.

This town has managed the transition to talent- and service-intensive businesses better than most. Two higher educational institutions—a satellite campus of Berkshire Community College and Bard College at Simon's Rock— are located in Great Barrington, and the town has an extensive tourist infrastructure. Perhaps most exciting of all is its inspiring record in the performing arts.

David J. McLaughlin

The Performing Arts

One of the most illustrious musical heritages in the Berkshires began in 1925 when the renowned violinist Albert Spalding and his wife Mary rented and ultimately purchased property in Great Barrington, where Mr. Spalding built a small acoustically perfect studio. They called the estate **Aston Magna** after the site of an ancient Roman village in the Cotswolds in England. Many of the world-class musicians of that era were his guests, including the pianist and composer Jan Paderewski, the Spanish cellist Pablo Casals, and the famous Finnish composer Jean Sibelius. The property was ultimately acquired by Lee M. Elman in 1971. In 1972 Elman founded the **Aston Magna Festival Orchestra**, dedicated to the performance of 17th- and 18th-century music. It is the oldest summer festival in America devoted to music performed on period instruments. Aston Magna still performs in Great Barrington; see www.astonmagna.org for more information.

Berkshire Bach Society of Great Barrington (413-528-9277) presents professional choral and instrumental concerts of Baroque music year round in various locations, including the Mahaiwe Performing Arts Center in Great Barrington. They also have an active outreach program in area schools. Their extensive Website at www.berkshirebach.org includes their schedule and information on where to obtain tickets.

The society was founded in 1990 by Simon Wainrib and grew out of a lecture series. The first concerts were performed at St. James Church in Great Barrington. There are approximately 120 members. The size of the choral group varies with the repertory and usually includes at least 40 individuals.

For almost two decades, **Close Encounters with Music** of Great Barrington has combined outstanding chamber music with erudite commentary in a series of year-round performances now held in both the Berkshires (at several locations but primarily at the Mahaiwe) and in Scottsdale, Arizona. Artistic Director Yehuda Hanani is noted for adventuresome, top-quality thematic programming. For further information and the program schedule, see www.cewm.org.

The Olga Dunn Dance Company was founded in Great Barrington in 1977. It holds performances at its own studio (321 Main Street, 413-528-9674), the Berkshire Museum in Pittsfield, and other venues in the tri-state area. Perhaps the most important contribution of this dedicated nonprofit, though, has been exposing children to the beauty and magic of dance through its classes, school performances and demonstrations, and other educational efforts.

The larger towns and cities of the Berkshires, particularly Great Barrington, Pittsfield, and Williamstown, have taken the lead in creating or restoring outstanding performance venues.

BERKSHIRE BACH PERFORMING

For decades, **St. James's Episcopal Church**, which has fine acoustics, was where Aston Magna performed each season, and it still does in the winter. Since 2004, when it installed a new Ahlborn-Galanti organ, the church has hosted an acclaimed organ series, **Bach and Beyond**.

Former churches, like the old Trinity Church (in the Van Deusenville section of Great Barrington), have evolved into a more casual performing venue. In 1965, this was the home of Ray and Alice Brock, a place where a young high-school student named Arlo Guthrie sometimes hung out with his friends. Guthrie's arrest for dumping garbage on a hillside in Stockbridge one Thanksgiving Day inspired the talking-blues song featured in his debut album, "Alice's Restaurant Massacree," which immortalized the old church and other sites in the area. Guthrie ultimately bought the church in 1992, and it is now the **Guthrie Center**, a venue for folk music and other concerts.

In 2004, Bard College at Simon's Rock completed the **Daniel Arts Center**, designed by Boston-based Ann Beha, which has become an important new venue.

What has inspired the most confidence in the region's continued ability to attract top-level performers from all over is the recent restoration of the county's two classic theaters, the Colonial Theater in Pittsfield and the famed **Mahaiwe Theatre** in Great Barrington.

Jim McElholm

THE MAHAIWE PERFORMING ARTS CENTER

The Mahaiwe first opened in 1905 as a legitimate theater, later adding vaudeville acts, and in the 1920s was the place that carried the best silent movies and early "talkies." A major renovation, funded in part by Save America's Treasures and the National Trust for Historic Preservation, has restored this acoustically perfect theater, which is now the Mahaiwe Performing Arts Center (413-644-9040; www.mahaiwe.org).

DANIEL ARTS CENTER | The Daniel Arts Center complex, with 53,000 square feet of space, offers a particularly flexible site for music, theater, dance, and the visual arts.

David J. McLaughlin

Daniel Arts
Center

Great Barrington has a vibrant downtown, where you can hear top jazz, folk, rock, and cabaret performers, even in the winter months, at places like Club Helsinki (284 Main Street) and the Celestial Bar at the Castle Street Café (10 Castle Street). Or you can see a movie at the Triplex Cinema on 70 Railroad Street, or dine at one of over 50 eateries, from pizza parlors to upscale gourmet restaurants.

One of the appeals of Great Barrington for many who move there is that you can have the best of both worlds: a real town and a countryside that is only a few minutes away.

No tour of Great Barrington would be complete without covering some of its other attractions, most of which are 15 to 20 minutes' drive from the town center, even in the peak summer traffic.

Monument Mountain

Monument Mountain is a 503-acre reservation accessed off Route 7 in Great Barrington. It has three miles of trails that range from moderate to fairly difficult. Squaw Peak (1,640 feet), the summit, offers panoramic views of the surrounding countryside. It is a spectacular spot during the height of the fall foliage, typically in the first or second week of October. The original acreage was set aside in 1899 and has been added to several times. The Trustees of Reservations manage this property.

MONUMENT MOUNTAIN,
BY ASHER BROWN DURAND

Over the years Monument Mountain has been an inspiration to writers and painters—and anyone who takes the hour-plus required to climb to the peak. The name was popularized in William Cullen Bryant's lyric poem, *Monument Mountain.* The Bryant poem tells the story of a Mohican maiden whose forbidden love for her cousin led her to leap to her death from the mountain's cliffs. A rock cairn marks the spot where she is buried. The best-known painting of this special place was done by Asher Brown Durand (1796–1886), a prominent figure in the Hudson River School of painters.

Monument Mountain
Route 7, Great Barrington
www.thetrustees.org/pages/
325_monumentmountain.cfm

On the east side of Route 7, near the Monument Mountain entrance, **Fountain Pond** is particularly captivating in the fall.

Another outdoor attraction is the town's ski facility, Butternut Basin.

FOUNTAIN POND

BUTTERNUT WELCOME SIGN

"Ski Butternut Today"

Opened in 1963 and greatly expanded over the years, **Butternut Basin** is located at 380 State Road (Route 23), a few miles east of the center of Great Barrington. With 22 trails and 110 ski-able acres just minutes from town, this is a convenient spot for family skiing and snowboarding. The facility also has a well-regarded ski school.

Butternut has become a year-round destination and is now promoted as an event venue. Each year in July, Butternut is the site of the Berkshire Arts Festival, which attracts over 150 artists (www.americancraftmarketing.com/berkshires.htm).

A convenient option for those who like to hike is **Beartown State Forest**, where you can still see plenty of deer and beaver and even the occasional bobcat and black bear that gave the forest its name. This 12,000-acre gem extends over portions of the towns of Great Barrington, Lee, Monterey, and Tyringham. The entrance to Benedict Pond, where there is a beautiful 1.5-mile trail loop, is in Monterey (see page 75).

NEWSBOY STATUE | The stone base of the statue, made of Quincy granite, held a water trough for horses. >

Before we head toward Alford, the last leg of this journey, we will encounter one prominent monument along Route 23, the road between Great Barrington and Egremont. It is a statue located on a grassy triangle at the junction of Silver Street and Maple Avenue in Great Barrington. This is the world's oldest known statue honoring the boys who delivered newspapers. The **Newsboy Statue** was commission by town resident Col. William L. Brown, a newspaper executive. This handsome statue, created by sculptor David Richards of New York, was dedicated in 1895 and beautifully restored to its original condition in 1995.

Along Alford Road

Alford Road offers the most direct route to the next stop on this journey, the decidedly rural town of Alford.

En route, about three miles from the center of Great Barrington, is **Bard College at Simon's Rock** (http://simons-rock.edu), whose pleasant campus houses the Daniel Arts Center (see page 43) and whose library is one of the finest in the southern Berkshires.

This innovative school was founded in 1964 by Elizabeth Blodgett Hall as a women's-only

"early school" that allowed entrance before a student's traditional high-school graduation date. It was acquired by Bard College in 1979 but is still known informally as Simon's Rock (named after a glacial remnant in the woods surrounding the beautiful campus). The college, now coed, still focuses on early students—those who have completed the 10th or 11th grades. It offers a broad range of 43 "concentrations" and grants both Associate of Arts and Bachelor of Arts degrees.

Just past Simon's Rock is the former summer home of James Weldon Johnson (1871–1938), a leading African-American poet, author, educator, and prominent figure in the Harlem Renaissance. It is now a private residence.

Alford is about 2½ miles northwest of Bard College at Simon's Rock. Take Alford Road to Alford Center Road.

< ALFORD CENTER IN 1893 | The children of Alford were taught in the one-room schoolhouse shown in this picture until the 1980s, when the town became part of the Southern Berkshire School District.

ALFORD CENTER TODAY

David J. McLaughlin

ENTRANCE TO BARD COLLEGE AT SIMON'S ROCK

Alford

Alford, the smallest Berkshire town in terms of land area (11.56 square miles), is also one of the least densely populated and least commercial towns in Massachusetts. Alford has no store of any kind, no gas station, no motels or hotels, not even a post office … nothing but a carefully preserved historic center and a fabulous countryside. Alford offers the best chance you have in any Berkshire visit to steal away to another century.

In recent years the population has been growing (but is still under 500), largely with the addition of second homes. However, careful zoning has preserved the unspoiled rural character of the community.

Alford was a quiet farming community in the years after it was settled in 1750, but for a time it became a bustling place with several sawmills, two grist mills, a forge, a furnace for casting hollowware, and a tannery. During the first half of the 19th century there were a dozen operating marble quarries. When David Field published his definitive *History of the County of Berkshire* in 1829, he noted that Alford had one store and a tavern. The population peaked in the 1850s and began to decline after the railroad bypassed the town.

The center of Alford has a marvelous sloping green on which rest the **village school and meeting house**, looking much as they did over a century ago.

The contemporary photograph at the bottom of the page shows Alford Center as it looks today. The school (now used to conduct town business) and the meeting house, built in 1817, are nestled on one side of Alford Road, with the town hall on the other. An outdoor bulletin board contains all you need to know about town events.

David J. McLaughlin

David J. McLaughlin

ALFORD TOWN HALL | These days the town hall is used for town meetings and voting. The Susan Smith Anderson children's library is located on the second floor.

The Alford **town hall**, across from the green, was built in 1855.

The **town library** is named after the Alford native who became the first woman graduate of the University of Massachusetts. Susan Smith Anderson (1900–2001) lived to be 101.

The early town settlers were Congregationalists, but the society languished after the minister was dismissed in 1787 in the tumultuous days of Shays' Rebellion. In 1817 the remaining Congregationalists as well as town Baptists and Methodists joined to build a common house of public worship they called the Union Meeting House.

The **Alford Center Cemetery** is to the left and behind the old school.

David J. McLaughlin

CENTER CEMETERY | There are about 200 graves in the Alford Center Cemetery.

There are still active farms in Alford, and the area is known for its extensive hayfields. A fertile valley extends northward along Alford Brook. Many fields cleared by the early colonists have reforested all over Western Massachusetts, however, and almost two thirds of Alford is now wooded.

This is a marvelous "off the beaten track" area in which to see fall foliage. And **Alford Brook** is one of the best fishing streams in the Berkshires. It feeds into the Green River, which is stocked with trout each year. The highest point in town is **Tom Ball Mountain**, which extends along the northeast edge of Alford, bordering West Stockbridge.

William Cullen Bryant, who loved the woodlands and streams of Alford, would frequently walk the area during the 10 years he lived in Great Barrington. He captured the area's appeal as a place to escape and enjoy nature's beauty in his 1820 poem, *The Green River*, which begins:

When breezes are soft and skies are fair,

I steal an hour from study and care,

And hie me away to the woodland scene,

Where wanders the stream with waters of green . . .

David J. McLaughlin

< FALL FOLIAGE
Jim McElholm

While the abundant shopping, dining, performing arts, and nightlife of Great Barrington are what first draw many visitors to this classic Victorian town, there is also abundant natural beauty minutes away. The 12,000 acres of Beartown State Forest, Monument Mountain along Route 7, and the scenic areas west of the town center and extending into Alford offer a chance to truly enjoy the Berkshire countryside.

ADDITIONAL RESOURCES

Great Barrington Bi-Centennial (1761-1962), John O. La Fontana, Chairman, Great Barrington, 1961.

History of Great Barrington 1676-1882, by Charles J. Taylor, extended to 1922 by George Edwin McLean, Great Barrington: Berkshire Courier, 1928 edition. The first comprehensive history of the town.

PICK YOUR OWN

Great Barrington: Great Town, Great History, by Bernard Drew, 1999. This mammoth work of scholarship is packed with interesting details about this historic town.

A History of Searles Castle in Great Barrington, Massachusetts: "The Great Wigwam," by Lila S. Parrish, Attic Revivals Press: Great Barrington, 1985, 30 pages. An excellent starting point for those who want to know more about this unusual mansion. Be sure to access a copy that includes the supplement *Searles Castle in Maps*, by Bernard A. Drew.

A History of Monument Mills in Housatonic, Massachusetts, by Donna Drew, Attic Revivals Press: Great Barrington, 1984. This 32-page publication has fascinating historic photographs, maps, and drawings, including a wonderful sketch of the village of Housatonic done by I. R. Burleigh in 1890.

Sewing Circles, Dime Suppers and W. E. B. Du Bois: A History of the Clinton A.M.E. Zion Church, by David Levinson, Berkshire Publishing Group: Great Barrington, 2006. Recounts the inspiring 140-year history of this historic church.

Jim McElholm

MADE FOR EXPLORING

New Marlborough, Sandisfield, and Otis

This journey covers an extensive area that has retained its rural character and is sprinkled with ponds and lakes. It contains the largest unrestricted body of water in Massachusetts, the 1,200-acre Otis Reservoir. As the map shows, our journey starts at the beginning of Route 57, on the edge of Monterey, and goes in a southeasterly direction through New Marlborough and Sandisfield. We then head north to Otis along Route 8.

These three towns are in the lower quadrant of Berkshire County and are sparsely settled, although the population expands greatly in the summer months. I will point out several "don't miss" attractions along the way, but it is the countryside itself that is most compelling. You can complete an initial tour of these three towns in a day. I often return to this area to wander the back-country roads and rarely fail to discover some new scenic vista or hidden attraction.

Once Sheffield was an established town (1733), there was pressure to open up the area between Westfield (9 miles from Springfield) and the new territory. At that time there were no roads beyond Westfield, only footpaths.

In 1735 the General Court of the Massachusetts Colony created four new townships in this area. Plantation #2 became New Marlborough and Plantation #3 Sandisfield. The other two plantations were Tyringham (Plantation #1), which evolved into the towns of Tyringham and Monterey, covered in the next journey, and Plantation #4, Becket, covered in Chapter 5.

A trail was hewn through the heavily wooded and rocky terrain. This primitive road, known by various names (Bay Trail, the Great Road, and, after the Revolution, the Knox Trail), passed through these new townships and opened them up to rapid settlement. The road was gradually widened to permit the use of drays and carriages.

Otis, the other town included in this journey, has a more complicated history. It was formed from land that was part of these four plantations. Two early communities, known as the district of Bethlehem and the town of Loudon, were combined into a new, larger town, initially called Loudon but renamed Otis in 1810.

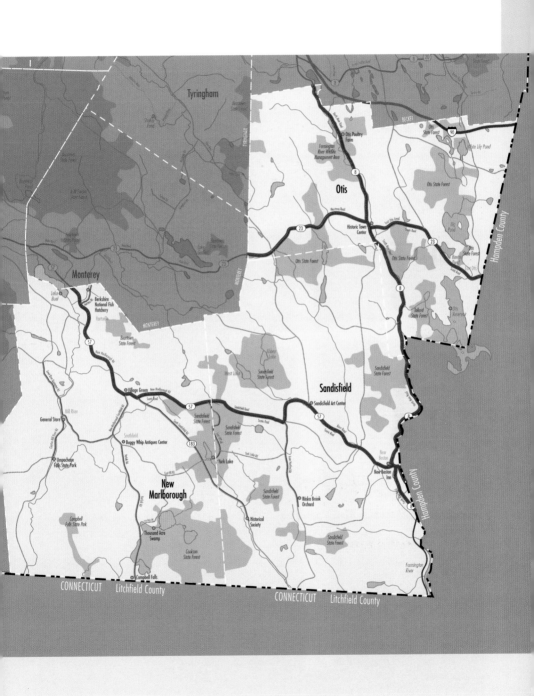

New Marlborough

The original village of Plantation #2 had 63 home lots, two of which were reserved for ministers and one for a school. The first settler, Benjamin Wheeler, moved to the area in 1739. By 1759, less than two decades later, there were enough families for New Marlborough to be incorporated as a town.

Over the years a town center (known as the **Village of New Marlborough**) emerged along a stagecoach route that parallels present-day Route 57. This is one of the most picturesque spots in the Berkshires.

There were ultimately four more villages: Clayton, Hartsville, Mill River, and Southfield.

These villages, particularly Mill River, preserve much of their individual character today and are part of the charm of this unspoiled early town.

The Village Green of New Marlborough

The spacious, unspoiled **New Marlborough common** was the site of the town's first meeting house, built in 1744. The church building that anchors one end of the green is the third church built on the site. It currently houses the **New Marlborough Arts Center**, which stages concerts, art shows, and readings during the tourist season.

NEW MARLBOROUGH GREEN

David J. McLaughlin

Old Inn on the Green, which dates to 1760, was a popular stagecoach stop. This antique-filled gem has one of the best upscale restaurants in the Berkshires. An excursion that combines a concert at the old church and dinner at the Inn, where the tables are lit entirely by candlelight, will be a memorable experience. **The Old Inn on the Green** *has five unique guest rooms upstairs from the restaurant. There are six additional rooms in the Thayer House, just steps from the Old Inn. www.oldinn.com | 413-229-7924*

There are several historic homes in the area, including the **Bigham House** (on Route 57) and the **William House**, on the green.

< MUSIC CONCERT ANNOUNCEMENT | From early summer to fall Music & More in the Meeting House lures knowledgeable insiders to the New Marlborough Green.

Look for the stone monument with an anvil on top, in the center of the green. This marker celebrates the life of **Elihu Burritt** (1810–1879), a linguist, activist for peace, and prolific writer whose journals, books, and personal correspondence are in the Peace Collection at Swarthmore College. Burritt was known as the "learned blacksmith" when he lived in New Marlborough in 1831 and worked at the Harvey Holmes Brass Foundry.

Other Villages of New Marlborough

Take time to explore the rest of New Marlborough. The village of **Southfield**, just south of the green, has a charming store and is a perfect place for lunch. Antique buffs will enjoy the **Buggy Whip Antique Center**, located in a Southfield factory first established in 1792 and currently housing some 95 antique dealers.

MONUMENT TO ELIHU BURRITT | As early as the 1840s, Burritt foresaw the need for a congress of nations and an international court of law.

Southfield was the site of a major tannery and was known for the manufacture of buggy whips and whip cores in the 19th century. The village center contains a Congregational church built in 1794 and a Baptist church that is now a private residence.

< FORMER BAPTIST CHURCH OF SOUTHFIELD Throughout New England you will find churches that have been converted to other uses. In some cases a declining population, fewer churchgoers, or shifts in religious preferences account for the demise of a church, but in other cases churches were retired as two church communities were combined into one.

BUGGY WHIP ANTIQUE CENTER

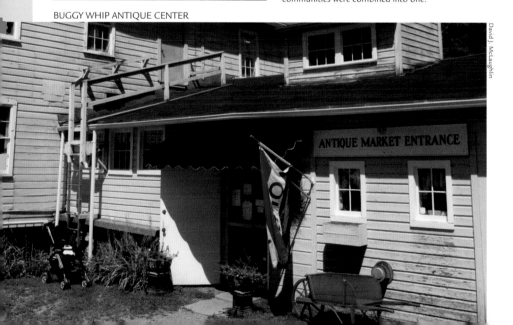

ANTIQUE MARKET ENTRANCE

David J. McLaughlin

BERKSHIRE NATIONAL FISH HATCHERY | The fishery has 10 3,500-gallon fish tanks stocked with Atlantic salmon and both rainbow and brown trout brood stock. It depends heavily on volunteer support.

Mill River officially became a village in 1840, when its first post office opened. Long before then it was an industrial center with a large Irish population. Mill River houses town offices, an active general store, and a handsome public library, which opened in 1923. The Mill River Library is one of 43 free libraries in Massachusetts established with support from Andrew Carnegie.

Hartsville, another village in the northern portion of the town, contains two attractions that it shares with its neighbors. The first is **Lake Buel**, which you pass on Route 57 as you cross the town line into New Marlborough; it is the largest body of water in the area. About two-thirds of this picturesque lake is in Monterey.

Hatchery Road, just off Route 57, will take you to the **Berkshire National Fish Hatchery**, on the edge of Monterey (www.berksfish.org/Aboutus.html). The roads here can be a little confusing. What is called Hatchery Road on the southern end is called River Road at the northern end. The hatchery is well worth a visit on this trip or the next, particularly if you have youngsters with you.

The 148-acre hatchery dates back to 1914, when it was deeded to the federal government by an avid trout fisherman, John Sullivan Scully. Budget cuts forced its closing in 1994, but it was restored and reopened as a center of aquaculture in 1999.

David J. McLaughlin

A VIEW OF LAKE BUEL FROM THE NEW MARLBOROUGH SHORELINE | Lake Buel used to be known as Six Mile Pond (it was six miles from Great Barrington). The lake was renamed to honor a young man, Samuel Buel, who rescued four youngsters in an 1812 boating accident.

The Countryside

The most compelling attraction in New Marlborough is the countryside itself, amply watered by two streams, the Umpachene and the Konkapot. There is a scenic view around just about every turn.

Thousand Acre Swamp (in the southeast quadrant of the town, reached off Hotchkiss Road) contains a 155-acre shallow pond that has some of the best bass fishing in the Berkshires. The area is heavily forested, but the pond is accessible by canoe or shallow draft boat from a concrete boat ramp.

Campbell's Falls, where the Whiting River cascades down an 80-foot drop, is a small scenic area on Campbell Falls Road, at the Connecticut state line. This area is a special treat in the spring when water rushes over the double-pitch waterfall.

ON THE ROAD TO MILL RIVER

York Lake, on the eastern border of New Marlborough in Sandisfield State Forest, is reached off Route 57, past the center of New Marlborough. Turn right on Forest Road. The entrance is about two miles south. You can also reach York Lake by turning left on Forest Road from Route 183. The lake has a 300-foot beach, wonderful picnic areas, and a boat ramp. It is open all year.

Because it is close to major population centers in Connecticut and New York, New Marlborough is an appealing weekend destination.

Gedney Farm *(Route 57 in New Marlborough) offers 16 guest rooms and suites in turn-of-the-century Normandy-style barns built to showcase Percheron stallions and Jersey cattle. www.gedneyfarm.com |
413-229-3131*

< YORK LAKE | York Lake was created by the Civilian Conservation Corps in the 1930s.

Continuing on Route 57 east leads directly to the equally scenic town of Sandisfield, which is bordered to the south by Litchfield County, Connecticut, and to the east and north by Otis, the last destination on this journey.

A FLAG SET AGAINST THE FALL FOLIAGE

David J. McLaughlin

Sandisfield

Sandisfield was an important agricultural and industrial center in the 18th century and a major stopping point on the stage line that extended from Hartford to Albany. The population had soared to 1,857 by 1800, making Sandisfield the fourth largest town in the Berkshires. However, the railroad bypassed the town, and its population steadily declined during the last half of the 19th century. By 1920 there were only 460 residents.

Today Sandisfield is a small rural community of about 800 souls. It is a town that still enjoys some of the best farmland and orchards in the Berkshires, scores of picturesque homes, and great scenic beauty. In area (53 square miles) this is the largest town in the county.

AN OLD BARN ALONG ROUTE 57 | This three-story barn is original and dates back to the early days of Stone Bridge Farm, whose main house was built about 1774. This was once a livestock and vegetable farm.

STEEPLETOP FARM | Another charming house along Route 57.

Along Route 57

Route 57 cuts across the middle of Sandisfield to the town center, known as **New Boston**. This is a lovely stretch of rural road that will take you past historic farms and horse properties.

There are two important historic churches along Route 57. The **Congregational Church**, built in 1879, also known as the Little Brown Church, still contains the original stained-glass windows.

The second, a former church visible off Route 57 and located at 5 Hammertown Road,

is now the **Sandisfield Arts Center** (www. sandisfieldsartscenter.org). This simple classic revival-style building has a fascinating history. It was erected in 1839 as a Baptist Church, but it fell into disuse as the population of Sandisfield declined. Meanwhile, a concerted back-to-the-land movement early in the 20th century attempted to relocate Jewish immigrants from the ghettoes of New York to agricultural communities in the Northeast. Thirty-five families were resettled in Sandisfield. As a result, the church was acquired in 1921 by the Sandisfield village of Montville's growing Jewish community, to serve as a synagogue.

SANDISFIELD ARTS CENTER | Originally a Baptist church, this building became the Sons of Abraham Synagogue for several decades. It was deeded to the town in 1995 to serve as a community center.

New Boston

The commercial center of Sandisfield is in the village of New Boston, at the edge of Berkshire County. To the south is Litchfield County, Connecticut, and to the east, the town of Tolland, part of Hampden County.

The first lodging and tavern in the southeastern Berkshires was established here in 1737. The **New Boston Inn** has, fortunately, survived to this day and is a required stop in any serious exploration of the Berkshires. This remarkable building, which has expanded over the years, was constructed so that the doors close automatically. The walls in the dining room lean out, preventing snow from piling up at the windows. An upstairs ballroom was suspended on chains.

The New Boston Inn serves hearty, reasonably priced meals. Be sure to visit the bar, which is the oldest part of the Inn. If you tarry for a drink, a local may tell you the story of the Sears family. Dr. Edmund Hamilton Sears, who was born in Sandisfield in 1810, wrote the lyrics to the Christmas song "It Came Upon a Midnight Clear." *The* **New Boston Inn** *(101 Main Street in Sandisfield, at junction of Routes 57 and 8) still welcomes lodgers to seven guest rooms. www.newbostoninn.com | 413-258-4477*

New Boston also has a general store, so essential to retaining a sense of community in these smaller towns.

David J. McLaughlin

NEW BOSTON CONGREGATIONAL CHURCH

David J. McLaughlin

NEW BOSTON INN | Daniel Brown, the first settler in Sandisfield, built the New Boston Inn.

David J. McLaughlin

BAR OF THE NEW BOSTON INN | Twenty-two-inch-wide boards were used on the walls and floor of the Inn's bar. Most planks are original.

The Back-Country Roads

Like New Marlborough, Sandisfield invites wandering.

South Sandisfield is a scenic area with an old cemetery and historic homes. The **Sandisfield Historical Society** is headquartered here in a former church, located on Sandy Brook Turnpike.

As you drive around South Sandisfield, keep your eye out for **Riiska Brook Orchards** at 101 New Hartford Road. Sandisfield was heavily forested in the colonial era, with vast numbers of maple trees, which helped the area become the largest producer of maple syrup in New England. Almost all the farms also had apple trees, and the town was a center for cider production in the 19th century. Riiska is a picturesque local orchard that is spectacular in the spring when the trees are in bloom and an apple lover's delight in the fall, when more than 10 varieties of apples are on sale.

David J. McLaughlin

APPLES AT THEIR PEAK

SANDISFIELD HISTORICAL SOCIETY | Getting access to many of the Historical Society buildings in the Berkshires takes advance planning, but it's worth it. You will find members eager to show you artifacts and mementos of each town's early history.

In the early days of my research I found a treasure trove of historic drawings and early photographs in a two-volume book entitled *The Picturesque Berkshires*, published in 1892. Many of these images stuck in my mind as I toured the countryside. I was thrilled to find scenes reminiscent of the Berkshires of a century ago, with a modern twist.

Author's Collection

LITHOGRAPH OF MAN CUTTING WOOD

The **Sandisfield State Forest** has six lakes within its preserves. In the fall, the foliage along the lakes and the west branch of the Farmington River, which parallels the eastern boundary of the town, is spectacular.

The last town on this journey, Otis, is best reached by taking Route 8 north, which leads to the historic center, at the intersection of Routes 8 and 23.

FALL ALONG THE FARMINGTON RIVER

MODERN WOODCUTTING AT RIISKA BROOK

David J. McLaughlin

64

HISTORIC OTIS

Otis

Otis was not a town with which I was familiar prior to researching this book. Occasionally I would see a car with a bumper sticker that read NOTICE OTIS, which piqued my curiosity. I knew that the area is a mecca for boating and swimming enthusiasts, but there is much more to Otis.

One of the first things you "notice" is the picturesque center of the original village, ably captured in a drawing that is on display in the Town Office.

David J. McLaughlin

Town Center

Clustered together in the historic center are several churches (one now a youth center) and the town library.

Another historic house of worship, **St. Paul's Episcopal Church**, is located across the street. It was consecrated in 1832. The pulpit is said to date to 1729 and was moved from the Old North Church in Boston.

The **Otis Cemetery** is spectacularly sited on a steep hill overlooking the town center.

< OTIS CONGREGATIONAL CHURCH | The Otis Congregational Church was organized in 1779. The church itself is spectacular. It was designed by the famous Boston architect Charles Bulfinch and built over four years, 1809–1813.

INTERIOR OF CHURCH

OTIS CEMETERY

David J. McLaughlin

Otis Library and Museum

Otis has had a **library** since 1891, but for years it struggled as a room or two in private homes until the present charming two-story library was completed in 1958 on land contributed by the **Congregational Church**.

David J. McLaughlin

READING ROOM IN LIBRARY | The table and brocaded chairs in the comfortable library reading room are said to have come from New York City and were once owned by Franklin D. Roosevelt.

David J. McLaughlin

CIVIL WAR UNIFORM ON DISPLAY

Otis Reservoir

Otis has always been known for the beauty of its many lakes. It has a substantial number of seasonal homeowners attracted by its small-town charm and ample waterfront.

The **Otis Reservoir** was created from three ponds. It is the largest body of unrestricted water in the state of Massachusetts.

David J. McLaughlin

ACTIVE OTIS RESERVOIR | You'll find just about every form of water activity you can imagine here, with motor boating, sailing, and kayaking particularly popular.

Other Attractions

With so much open land and water, it is not surprising that Otis is a popular spot for camping. Camp Overflow is a family campground with marvelous views of the reservoir. Camp Lenox, along Route 8, is a co-ed summer camp established in 1918. Camp Nawaka, in East Otis, is located on 130 acres of forested land and surrounds a 20-acre private spring-fed pond.

Otis, like New Marlborough and Sandisfield, should be explored. Route 23 West will take you to Monterey. This highway and the roads to the north are quite scenic.

Otis has over a dozen ponds and lakes, all of which offer scenic views and great fall foliage viewing. White Lilly Pond in the northeast corner of Otis is surrounded by **Otis State Forest.**

Be sure not to miss the **Otis Poultry Farm** along Route 8 (the full address is 1570 North Main Road). This farm was established in 1904 and is currently run by the third generation of the founding family. It is a "must visit" destination heralded by quirky, amusing signs.

The Country Store at the Otis Poultry Farm offers fruit pies, homemade breads, and great chicken and turkey pies.

You can see why the town boosters want you to notice Otis!

LAKE IN FALL   Darlene Bordwell

ADDITIONAL RESOURCES

An Informal History of the Town of New Marlborough, Massachusetts, 1739–1975, edited by Claudette M. Callahan, New Marlborough Bicentennial Commission, 1975. This self-published 174-page book is a very readable history. The local library is a good source for this out-of-print classic.

A Pictorial History of New Marlborough: A Visual Reminiscence, 1735–1940, by Jon Swan and John Sisson, New Marlborough Historical Society, 2005, 192 pages. This handsome volume, lavishly illustrated with scores of carefully reproduced black-and-white photographs, is one of the best "updates" of a town history that has been published.

Sandisfield: Biography of a Town, by Anne Hoffman, Sandisfield, 1998, 204 pages. This loving remembrance and well-researched history by a longtime resident of Sandisfield received considerable support from the Sandisfield Arts and Recreation Committee and the Sandisfield Historical Society. Includes 25 oral histories.

A Gift from the Past: Nellie E. Haskell's History of Otis, Massachusetts, edited by Lynn Humason Wood, published in 1974 in Otis. This unique book recreates the records and reminiscences of an early resident of Otis, covering the 1860s through the early 20th century. The material, assembled originally in a diary-like form, is based on the records of the town Congregational Society, notes from the Episcopal Church records, and articles from newspapers.

Our Otis Heritage: A Pictorial History of Otis, Massachusetts, by Barry Hawley, printed in Pittsfield, 1976. This book features more than 250 black-and-white photographs and copies of written material (the latter not too legible) collected by the author. The material is well annotated.

EGGS EATERS

OTIS POULTRY FARM

A SPECIAL BERKSHIRE TREAT

Monterey and Tyringham

Jim McElholm

This journey takes us through Monterey and Tyringham, the two towns that evolved from Housatonic Township #1. Exploring these towns makes for a very simple journey. The biggest challenge in this trip is not the navigation—it's finding enough time to properly explore two of the loveliest towns in the Berkshires, both of which have "must-see" attractions that shouldn't be rushed.

The center of Monterey is about 8 miles east of Great Barrington, easily reached on Route 23. After exploring Monterey, head north on the Tyringham–Monterey road (called Main Road in Tyringham), which connects the two towns. In Tyringham the major attractions lie along and just off this main route.

The southern part of the Township was settled first, beginning in 1739, and for many years was known as South Tyringham. This community rapidly developed its own infrastructure and was incorporated as a separate town named Monterey in 1847. The residents of North Tyringham apparently resented the long trip to the meeting house in the south and supported separation of the township. Politics were also involved. Eloise Myers, in her definitive book *A Hinterland Settlement*, found records "proving that petitions made by men from Hop Brook

(North Tyringham) were often passed over, for the majority vote was from South Tyringham."

Personally I made my first trip through this area an exploratory one, then returned several times to enjoy the scenery during different seasons and to hike Tyringham Cobble and tour the Bidwell House Museum and gardens in a leisurely fashion. When you need a break and want to see the countryside, a drive through the Tyringham Valley is never a mistake.

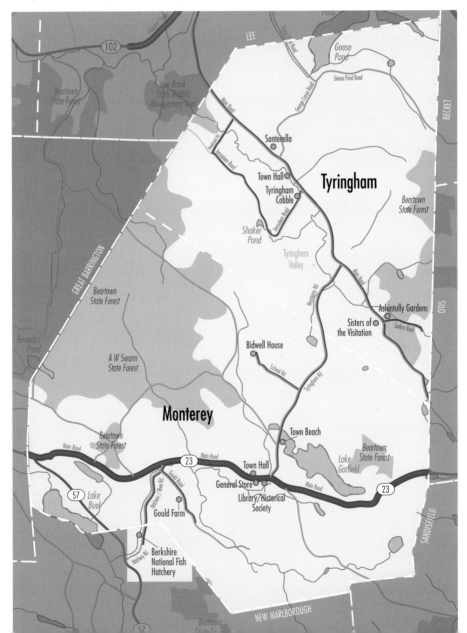

Monterey

Monterey (called the "New England Monterey" in one book) was a major center of cheese making in the 19th century. As this business moved to the Midwest, Monterey emerged as popular resort town. An 1889 guide described the town as "charmingly attractive."

TOWN HALL OF MONTEREY | What is now the town hall was built in 1919 to serve as the Monterey Grange No 291. The building was deeded to the town in 1988. The Monterey Grange was one of the longest-lasting chapters of this fraternal organization.

Town Center

The current center of Monterey, clustered on both sides of Route 23, developed as the population shifted south to be nearer the Konkapot River and the Otis–Great Barrington Road.

The South Tyringham Meeting Society was gathered about 1850 as a Congregational Church. This Greek Revival-style building is little changed today. It is now the **United Church of Christ, Congregational**. Note that the building has a "blind façade"—in other words, no windows and a recessed center entry, both relatively rare features in this style of building.

The **Monterey General Store** (www. montereystore.com), called the Langdon Store after the several generations of Langdons who ran it from 1835–1906, has been a central fixture in the community for two centuries. There has been a store in Monterey since 1780. During the stagecoach era, a mail stage ran between West Otis and Great Barrington and the store was an important stop.

A modern post office and the **town hall** also front on Route 23.

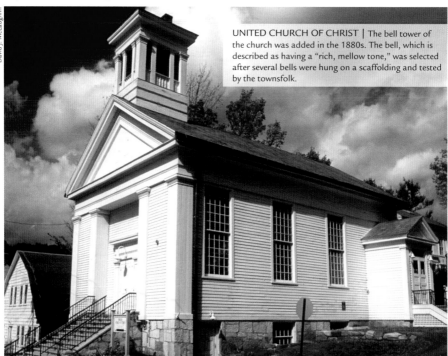

UNITED CHURCH OF CHRIST | The bell tower of the church was added in the 1880s. The bell, which is described as having a "rich, mellow tone," was selected after several bells were hung on a scaffolding and tested by the townsfolk.

The **Monterey Free Library** was formed in 1891. The present building, which contains the town library and the Historical Society, was built in 1930. It is located next to the general store.

TOWN LIBRARY AND KNOX MUSEUM | In the 19th century a sawmill was located on this spot.

ARROWHEAD COLLECTION | One of the displays in the Knox Museum is an impressive collection of Indian arrowheads. The Native American presence in this area was extensive.

An official Knox Trail marker is located in Monterey, just beyond the only remaining original schoolhouse, the **Center School**.

After the revolution, every town with at least 50 families was required to support a school. Monterey had eight school districts. Most of the old one-room schoolhouses became private residences or were torn down as a regional school system was adopted in the 20th century. The Center School is still in use as a kindergarten.

KNOX MARKER AND OLD SCHOOLHOUSE

Bidwell House Museum

The original settlement of Monterey was north of the present town center. A sawmill was erected near the outlet of Twelve Mile Pond (now Lake Garfield), 63 lots were laid out, and a meeting house was built. The first parsonage, a large Georgian saltbox built about 1750, has survived as the **Bidwell House Museum**. The house was built for the town's first minister, Adonijah Bidwell (1716–1774). This authentically restored house, filled with antique furniture, is the only Berkshire County colonial-era house museum that still stands on its original site. The house sits on 196 acres of woodland and gardens. Sotheby's calls this gem "The most perfect example of a New England country home in its feeling, appearance and continuing daily life."

To reach the Bidwell House from the village center, drive north on Tyringham Road, go past Lake Garfield, and turn left on Art School Road, which ends at the museum.

The house ultimately passed from the Bidwell family. It was purchased in 1960 and was meticulously restored over 25 years by Jack Hargis and David Brush, two New Yorkers. The museum was formed in 1990.

Bidwell House Museum
100 Art School Road
Monterey, MA 01245
413-528-6888
www.bidwellhousemuseum.org

BIDWELL HOUSE AND SHED | Successive generations of Bidwells added to the original saltbox. An ell was added to the north of the house in 1790, and the grandson of Adonijah Bidwell added a wing on the east side in 1836.

Jim McElholm

CHILDREN'S BEDROOM | The Bidwell House's textile collection includes this red-star pieced quilt. It is in the Children's Room, which also contains interesting examples of early toys and games.

PIPES ON WALL

The interior of the house is a special treat. The keeping room was the original kitchen and center of activity.

As part of the restoration, Hargis and Brush created terraced perennial gardens and a kitchen garden, which are open to the public and should be part of any tour.

The Bidwell House Museum is open Thursdays through Mondays between 11:00 A.M. and 4:00 P.M. from Memorial Day until October 15. This attraction has a superb Website that provides a history of the house, an online tour, and details on the museum's extensive collections.

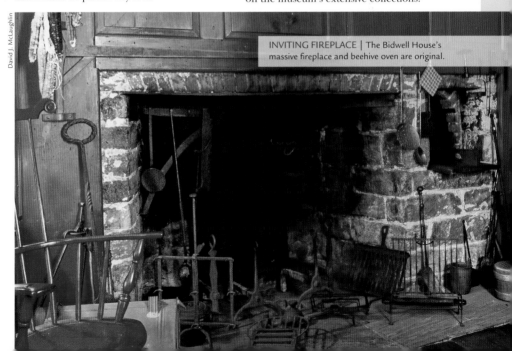

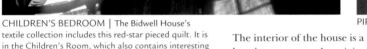

INVITING FIREPLACE | The Bidwell House's massive fireplace and beehive oven are original.

MONTEREY TOWN BEACH

Jim McElholm

Lakes Garfield and Buel

One of my friends who wasn't familiar with Monterey but heard it was a beautiful spot asked where to stay while visiting the area. I told him to make friends with a resident who has a house along one of the town's splendid lakes (**Lake Buel** and **Lake Garfield**).

There are no commercial accommodations in Monterey, and the lovely Lake Garfield town beach is restricted to residents and their guests.

The shoreline is moderately developed with about 75 dwellings, many of which have fabulous views of the water. The Friends of Lake Garfield work diligently to preserve the quality of the water and govern activities on the lake (www.lakegarfield.org).

Lake Buel, described in the preceding chapter, lies at the southwest corner of Monterey. This lake is somewhat smaller (196 acres), deeper, and less controlled than Garfield. There is an unrestricted paved boat ramp.

David J. McLaughlin

David J. McLaughlin

GOULD FARM | The Farm has more than 100 acres of gardens and farmland.

David J. McLaughlin

BERKSHIRE NATIONAL FISH HATCHERY

Other Excursions

Beartown State Forest (www.mass.gov/dcr/parks/western/bear.htm) in Monterey is one of the most enticing parks in the state park system. It is reached from Blue Hill Road, off Route 23. The park contains the pristine 35-acre Benedict Pond, near which the Appalachian Trail passes, as well as an extensive network of trails on over 12,000 acres. In the winter months this is an ideal spot for cross-country skiing.

I recommend the 1.5-mile loop around **Benedict Pond** any time of the year. There is swimming, boating, and fishing here, and the scenery during the peak of the fall foliage season is special.

In 1913 two remarkable people, Will and Agnes Gould, who were part of the Christian social reform movement that flourished early in the 20th century, purchased a farm in Monterey. They had extensive experience rehabilitating society's less advantaged and immediately opened the farm to others seeking a respite or suffering from mental illness. **Gould Farm** evolved into a community offering psychosocial rehabilitation programs "with strong roots in the traditions of social service and fellowship." Gould Farm is a self-contained community located on 600 acres. The farm operates the **Roadside Store and Café** along Route 23, where they sell "farm-raised" goods. If you stop in the morning, be sure to try the pancakes. The complex is located at 100 Gould Road and visitors are welcome. Take Curtis Road (right near the Roadside Store) south and turn left on Gould Road.

If you didn't visit the **Berkshire Fish Hatchery** on your journey through New Marlborough, it is relatively close to Gould Farm, best reached by taking River Road off Route 23.

Monterey has retained its rural character. This is an inviting town to explore by car. Not surprisingly, Monterey has a large second-home community.

< LAKE GARFIELD | Lake Garfield is a 262-acre beauty with an average depth of 16 feet.

David J. McLaughlin

Tyringham

The center of **Tyringham** is a just over 5 miles north of Monterey. The drive into Tyringham Valley takes you through an enticing pastoral landscape. It is no wonder that creative souls like the poet and editor of *Century Magazine*, Richard Watson Gilder (1844–1908), and the sculptor Sir Henry Hudson Kitson, whose storybook studio, Santarella, is one of the town's many wonders, chose to live here.

As you drive toward the center of Tyringham you will see lovely homes along almost every stretch, framed against a spacious and unspoiled valley.

There are several fascinating destinations in Tyringham. A short drive up Jerusalem Road from the town center leads to a Berkshire natural wonder, Tyringham Cobble. Continue on this road, which makes a sharp right turn as you climb into the hills, to enjoy a view of the valley from the heights where a Shaker settlement existed for 64 years. Ashintully Gardens, a unique oasis, is outside the town center on the road to Otis. Santarella, another special attraction, is located about a mile past the town center.

SUNSET FARM | This early farmhouse has been in the same family since 1862. Since 1991 it has been an inviting B&B.

TYRINGHAM VALLEY HOUSE

David J. McLaughlin

Town Center

The stunning Greek Revival-style church in Tyringham was built in 1844. Like many Berkshire towns established in an earlier era when one's denomination mattered, Tyringham had several churches until the Baptists, Methodists, and Congregationalists ultimately agreed to consolidate. The resulting **Union Church** was organized in 1919.

The **Tyringham Cemetery** lies behind the church in an ideal setting that offers great views of the town and the valley.

A few hundred yards down what is usually referred to as Main Road is the **town hall** and library.

The **library**, next to the town hall, was built in 1902. Stones found on Tyringham Cobble were incorporated in the library's fireplace.

Jim McElholm

UNION CHURCH | This church is distinctive in the size of its rich, Ionic fluted columns, the generous front porch, and the square, two-story tower decorated with impressive shell-shaped ornaments. >

TOWN HALL OF TYRINGHAM | The town hall of Tyringham was originally a paper mill, George Garfield's Mill. It was converted to the town hall in 1904.

CEMETERY AND CHURCH >
Jim McElholm

Jim McElholm

80

Along Jerusalem Road

As you turn up Jerusalem Road you will see the only remaining original town **schoolhouse** as well as a pleasant display along the road.

David J. McLaughlin

OLD SCHOOLHOUSE

David J. McLaughlin

ROADSIDE DISPLAY

There are still a few working farms in Tyringham.

The entrance to one of the Berkshire's natural wonders, Tyringham Cobble, is on Jerusalem Road.

David J. McLaughlin

TYRINGHAM FARM

VIEW FROM TYRINGHAM COBBLE

Tyringham Cobble

There are signs and a parking lot for
Tyringham Cobble on the right (north) side of
Jerusalem Road. There is space for sixteen cars.
A display shows the trail network.

This special reserve, open year round, has
a 2-mile loop trail that passes over the twin
knobs of the Cobble and offers spectacular
views of Tyringham Valley. This property is now
managed by the Trustees of Reservations.

Tyringham Cobble has a rich history. The
term *cobble* comes from the German word *koble*,
meaning rocks. It refers to a rounded, exposed
knoll formed of bedrock. The pioneers cleared
the slopes of Cobble Hill in the late 1700s. By
the 1840s the Shaker community of Tyringham
had a 2,000-acre farm that included the
Cobble, on which they grazed sheep and cows.
By 1885 the Shakers had moved away, but the
land continued to be used for grazing and hay.

When development threatened this unique and
scenic area in the form of a proposed ski run,
a group of conservation-minded citizens, who
called themselves "The Cobblers," acquired
the land in the 1930s as tenants in common,
ultimately deeding the property to the Trustees
of Reservations as a gift in 1963.

ENTRANCE AND PARKING AREA | There is parking
space for 16 cars just off Jerusalem Road. A display
shows the trail network.

SHAKER SEEDS DISPLAY | This display is from the Shaker Museum in Old Chatham, New York, which is covered in Chapter 10.

ALONG JERUSALEM ROAD

The Shaker Community of Jerusalem

Jerusalem Road climbs above the valley floor as you drive beyond Tyringham Cobble. The road veers sharply to the right less than a mile out of town. It was here that the Shaker settlement of **Jerusalem** was centered, along the southwestern headwall of Tyringham Valley. The early members united their farms and other property in 1792 to form a Church Society. There were three clusters of buildings about ½ mile apart on Jerusalem Road. The Shakers built a magnificent stone dam here in 1832, creating Shaker Pond.

This Shaker village was renowned for its seeds, and the complex included the largest Shaker seed house in the country.

The Shaker settlement began to fall apart toward the middle of the 19th century. Twenty-three young adults left abruptly in 1858. The surviving Shakers soon moved to Hancock Shaker Village, Mount Lebanon, and other Shaker communities. The land and buildings were ultimately sold. Only a few original houses survive, all in private hands. Ninety-nine Shakers lie buried in the cemetery here.

There are no signs identifying the former Shaker houses and none are open to the public. Please respect the privacy of those who now live along Jerusalem Road. Do make the drive along this road, however. A drive along Jerusalem Road will give you a sense of the scale and beauty of **Tyringham Valley**.

Depending on the weather, you can take the steep Breakneck Road, so named for a gruesome carriage accident a century ago, down the hillside and across the bottom of the valley and back onto Main Road. When you return to Main Road you will want to double back and head south. About two miles from the town center, the left fork of Tyringham Road (which leads to West Otis and connects with Route 23) will take you to Mont Deux Coeurs and Ashintully Gardens.

Mont Deux Coeurs

A cloistered community of nuns, the Sisters of the Visitation of Tyringham, live in a monastic complex called **Mont Deux Coeurs** (www.vistyr. org) just off Tyringham Road.

The complex doors are open from 6:00 A.M. to 6:00 P.M. You may glimpse the sisters at prayer through the latticed divider in the L-shaped chapel if you come for a service. The rose window in the chapel was made by the monastery's part-time neighbor, Viggo Rambusch, of the well-known Rambusch Studio of New York. The sisters sell handmade vestments and other items displayed in the shop next to the chapel.

This self-contained community is part of a contemplative order founded in Annecy, France, in 1610.

Ashintully Gardens, our next destination, is to the east of the monastery, just down Sodem Road.

MONT DEUX COEURS MONASTERY, BUILT IN 1995 | This self-contained community is part of a contemplative order founded in Annecy, France, in 1610.

Jim McElholm

Ashintully Gardens

One of the most picturesque spots in the Berkshires, **Ashintully Gardens** has a fascinating history.

Early in the 20th century, Robb de Peyster Tytus (1876–1913), a Yale graduate who became an Egyptologist and politician, assembled an estate of some 1,000 acres in Tyringham and Otis. Between 1910 and 1912 he and his wife, Grace Seeley Henop Tytus, built a Palladian-style mansion known as the Marble Palace. In their marvelous book *Houses of the Berkshires 1870–1930*, Richard S. Jackson Jr. and Cornelia Brooke Gilder show nine stunning photographs of this residence and explain that the stucco walls, made with sand imported from Nantucket, shimmered in the light and were mistaken for marble. Tytus named the estate Ashintully, which in Gaelic means "on the brow of the hill."

After Robb Tytus died prematurely of tuberculosis, his widow married John McLennan. Their only child, John Stewart McLennan, acquired the estate in 1937. Sadly, the Marble Palace burned to the ground in 1952, but by then McLennan had settled into the farmhouse below the big house. An accomplished composer of contemporary music, McLennan renovated a barn on the property as a music studio and furnished it

with items that had survived from the ill-fated family mansion. Over the course of 30 years he created a magnificent terraced garden around the farmhouse.

A picturesque stream passes through the garden. Footpaths, bridges, and stone stairs connect various garden "rooms." Rare ornamental trees and shrubs are planted throughout. A half-mile trail leads to the ruins of the Marble Palace. This is one Berkshire attraction you don't want to miss.

Ashintully Gardens are open to the public Wednesday and Saturday afternoons, 1:00–5:00 P.M., between June and October. The 594-acre McLennan Reservation (which includes sections of the land assembled by Robb de Peyster Tytus) adjoins Ashintully Gardens. This is another property of the Trustees of Reservations.

STAIRWAY TO HEAVEN >
Paul Rocheleau

Ashintully Gardens
Sodem and Main Roads
Tyringham, MA
413-298-3239
www.thetrustees.org/
pages/251_ashintully_gardens.cfm

VIEW OF ASHINTULLY

Jim McElholm

86

Do head back north to view Santarella, the former studio and residence of Henry Kitson, located about a mile past the town center on the right side of Main Road. You will pass George Cannon Road just before you reach Santarella. This precipitous road (open seasonally) leads to the second major cluster of homes in Tyringham, mostly summer residences located around picturesque Goose Pond.

This area is another wonderful spot in which to wander the back-country roads. The wishing-well photograph shown on the next page was taken along Goose Pond Road.

Santarella

Sir Henry Hudson Kitson (1865–1947) was an English-born sculptor who lived most of his life in the United States. Sometime after 1909, after separating from his wife, Kitson began a relationship with Marie Hobran (whom he subsequently married, but only after his wife's death). Marie's parents owned property in Tyringham, where Kitson transformed a barn into a storybook-like studio, **Santarella**, also known as the Gingerbread House.

For over 40 years after Kitson's death, Santarella functioned as the Tyringham Art Galleries. The present owners, who are restoring the property, now make Santarella available for special events. Overnight accommodations are available in the colonial-style house and in the studio. Tours are possible and well worth the effort but have to be scheduled, with a small donation required.

The construction of Santarella nearly bankrupted Kitson. Creating the rolling roof reminiscent of the English countryside took a team of three workers 12 years to complete. Kitson had originally planned a thatched roof. When the rye that he persuaded local farmers to grow turned bad, he decided to use different-colored asphalt shingles, each of them hand cut, to create the wave-like effect. The roof weighs 80 tons!

Santarella
75 Main Road
Tyringham, MA 01264
413-243-2819
www.santarella.us

SANTARELLA

Paul Rocheleau

OLD WISHING WELL

ROYAL POND AT MONTEREY–SANDISFIELD
TOWN LINE

Complete this journey by continuing north on Main Road/Tyringham–Monterey Road, which connects with Route 102 in Lee. You will be quite near the main Berkshire connection to the Mass Pike (Interstate 90), Exit 2.

Although Tyringham is a scant 4 miles away from Lee, you will have spent time in a surprisingly quiet, unspoiled corner of the Berkshires. If you are like most visitors, you will surely return to the Tyringham Valley and the "Lake District" of Monterey.

ADDITIONAL RESOURCES

New England's Monterey: Stories of the Town, Its Church, by Julius Miner and Margery Mansfield. This interesting 70-page monograph was sponsored by the Monterey Congregational Church. Even the casual visitor will enjoy the original stories contained in this volume.

Monterey: A Local History 1847–1997, Peter Murkett, ed., Town of Monterey, 1997. This sesquicentennial history, well illustrated with nicely reproduced vintage photographs, received considerable town support, and it shows.

A Hinterland Settlement: Tyringham, Massachusetts, and Bordering Towns, by Eloise Myers, Pittsfield, 1966. This information-packed 95-page book tells the history of Tyringham through the early decades of the 20th century, when "summer-landed proprietors" began to arrive in great numbers.

Tyringham Old and New, Old Home Week Souvenir.

Views of the Valley: Tyringham 1739–1989, by Cornelia Brooke Gilder, Tyringham, 1989. This marvelous, well-annotated collection of black-and-white images was assembled by a longtime resident and historian, aided by Hop Brook Community Club.

A TOUR AROUND

Becket and Washington

The towns of Becket and Washington contribute their own special flavors to the mélange that is the Berkshire region. Becket has many excellent attributes, though they are often overshadowed by its primary attraction, **Jacob's Pillow Dance Festival**, the pioneering modern dance organization in Becket's southwest quadrant. Washington is a wonderful little town that still retains its rural charm.

Because the location of Jacob's Pillow is off Route 20, you can attend a performance

without ever seeing most of the town, which lies along the north–south leg of Route 8. Hopefully this chapter will give you a sense of Becket that will inspire you to enjoy more of what the town has to offer beyond dance.

This journey covers many of Becket's attractions in a circular tour that has several side excursions and then continues north on Route 8 to explore Washington and immerse you in its rural spirit.

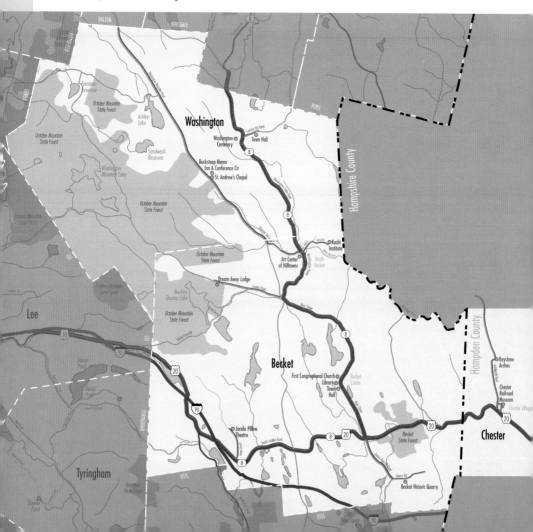

MONUMENT TO THE CAR

David J. McLaughlin

Becket

Becket was founded in 1751 when a sawmill was built on Walker Brook, in the eastern part of town. In the early years the area's abundant timber made forest-related products the town's primary business. Becket was incorporated in 1765 and named by the royal governor, Sir Francis Bernard. It is thought that he selected this name because his family's country estates were in Beckett, England.

Until the middle of the 19th century the population was concentrated in the Old Center in the middle of the township. It shifted north about five and a half miles to Becket Village (or what is also referred to as North Becket) when a depot of the Western Railroad was built there.

For a complete tour of Becket, begin by driving east along Route 20 from the gateway town of Lee. This is one of the earliest mountain roads in Massachusetts. In the days of the horse, the main stagecoach line between Boston and Albany traversed the backbone of the Hoosac Range in Becket. Switchbacks had to be created for the stagecoaches to make it up the steep slope. Viewed from a distance, this stretch of road looked like a ladder. The early residents,

who knew their Bible, were reminded of the story in Genesis 28 where Jacob "dreamed, and behold a ladder set up on the earth, and the top of it reached to heaven." So, they called the road **Jacob's Ladder Trail**.

Legend has it that Johnny Appleseed hiked to the summit of the Trail around 1801, during one of his trips back east. Jacob's Ladder Trail was designated a National Scenic Byway in 1992 by Scenic America (whose motto is, "Change is inevitable. Ugliness is not").

The state expanded and improved the route in the early 1900s, bypassing the steepest part of the trail. Route 20 was still a challenge for the early cars (the summit is 2,300 feet above tidewater), but the road was such an improvement that auto club members from all over the Northeast celebrated the opening of the "modern" highway in 1910 by creating a rock cairn near the summit. The monument was moved to its present location and the stones cemented together in 1940.

Keep your eye out for this large rock pile on the north side of the road, known as the **Monument to the Car**.

Jacob's Pillow Dance Festival

The first and longest-running dance festival in the United States had its beginnings in 1931 when a pioneering male dancer, Ted (Edwin Myers) Shawn (1891–1972), purchased the historic Carter farm, which dated back to 1790. The Carter homestead was called "the Pillow." Some say it was named after the Trail, others for a fluffy-looking boulder on an adjacent farm.

SIGN TO JACOB'S PILLOW

As Shawn and his friends cleared the land, the largest barn on the property was converted to a dance studio. It became the home base of the legendary dance group, Ted Shawn and His Men Dancers. The group's first public performance was held in the renovated barn in 1933.

Shawn and his troupe toured all over the country for seven years, always performing part of the time in Becket and gradually improving the facilities at the Pillow. The studio was the site of several acclaimed performances in the transition years 1940–41, but Shawn could no longer personally finance the operation and the property was put up for sale. In October 1941 a Jacob's Pillow Dance Festival Committee was formed to purchase the property and build a proper theater.

Despite all the artistic successes of these early years, it took time for Jacob's Pillow to achieve a solid financial footing (unlike many competing organizations, it was not generously endowed). However, for over 70 years it has been considered one of the premier dance venues in the world, and each year it attracts groups from all over to perform at one of its three performance venues: the Ted Shawn Theater, the Doris Duke Studio Theater, and the Inside/Out Stage.

JACOB'S PILLOW DANCE COMPLEX

Jacob's Pillow is surrounded by woodlands. There are paths to stroll and gardens to view, including a lovely Tea Garden.

Jacob's Pillow is open from mid-June to the end of August. It reaches out to the overall Berkshire community with education programs, scheduled "Day at the Pillow" visits for groups, and a free Community Day performance in July.

A few miles further along Route 20, where Route 8 veers directly north, you will have easy access to another major attraction, the **Becket Land Trust Historic Quarry**, described by industrial archeologists as "the best-preserved quarry in the Northeast." Turn right onto Bonny Rigg Hill Road at the intersection. Follow this road up the hill and turn left on Quarry Road, where signs will direct you to the entrance and parking lot.

Marta Fodor

TEA GARDEN

Stephanie Motta

ARMITAGE GONE!

Jacob's Pillow Dance Festival
358 George Carter Road
Becket, MA 01223
413-243-9919
www.jacobspillow.org/festival/at-a-glance.asp

Jim McElholm

VIEW FROM TOP OF QUARRY

H. David Stein

Becket Land Trust Historic Quarry and Forest

The former Hudson-Chester Quarry, which dates to the 1850s, was a granite quarry whose stone was shipped by railroad to nearby Chester, Mass., and Hudson, New York, for polishing. Gravestones and monuments were the primary end products. The quarry closed abruptly in 1960. In 2000, when there was an effort to reopen the quarry to excavation, concerned citizens helped the Becket Land Trust, founded in 1991, acquire the 300-acre property.

There are detailed maps at a kiosk in the parking lot, laying out a self-guided walk through the historic quarry and showing the trails through the adjacent Forest Preserve. The maps can also be downloaded from the organization's Website (www.becketlandtrust.org/quarry/index.htm).

Volunteers spent over a decade clearing the area, saving what rusting equipment they could, reconstructing a unique 55-foot guy derrick, and creating discovery paths through the site. This is a splendid area for walking. The terrain is not particularly difficult.

David J. McLaughlin

SIGN FOR QUARRY | The quarry and adjacent forest opened to the public in 2005.

David J. McLaughlin

COUPLE WALKING DOGS

David J. McLaughlin

DOOR OF ABANDONED TRUCK

The objects you can see on the walk include quarry equipment (bullwheels, drills, winches, and the like), rusted trucks, and an electric generator shed, along with huge grout piles—jagged rock that was the waste product of the quarrying process. The objects have had over 40 years to rust.

For many visitors, the reconstructed quarry derrick, which stands 55 feet tall and has a 50-foot boom, is the highlight of the trip.

The Becket Quarry is a tranquil spot. It's a bit off the beaten track, but it is worth every effort to include a visit on your itinerary. It is a perfect spot to picnic, enjoy a stroll at any time (particularly in the fall), and wonder about the many men who quarried granite here for over a century.

Becket Land Trust Quarry
Museum and Offices
12 Brooker Hill Road
Becket, MA 01223
413-623-2100
Historic Quarry and Forest
Quarry Road
www.becketlandtrust.org/quarry/index.htm

H. David Stein

RESTORED GUY DERRICK

Courtesy Becket Land Trust

HISTORIC IMAGE OF QUARRY IN OPERATION

David J. McLaughlin

BECKET TOWN HALL

Courtesy Becket Historical Society

BALLOU BASKET WORKERS

Along Route 8

Our journey of discovery to the many attractions of Becket continues along Route 8 North to the **Becket Town Hall**. The Becket Historical Commission has its headquarters here, in the back of the building. They have a fascinating collection of memorabilia and historic photographs that capture the town's early history. Becket was a vibrant center of basket weaving in the late 19th century. The M. E. Ballou Basket Company was the only firm east of Michigan that commercially manufactured pounded-ash baskets.

The first churches in Becket were located in Becket Center. The **First Congregational Church** of Becket was organized in 1798 and was the nation's first self-supporting Congregational society at a time when most religious groups sought state support. This handsome church, the town's third meeting house, was built in 1850.

BECKET FIRST CONGREGATIONAL CHURCH
This historic church stands in splendid isolation just off Route 8.

Darlene Bordwell

The only bell in the Berkshires made by Paul Revere still hangs in the belfry of the First Congregational Church. It was brought from Boston by horse and wagon in 1812. Unfortunately, this precious Revere bell was damaged during one vigorous ringing and had to be recast. During the remolding (done in Troy, New York), a number of silver dollars were dropped into the molten metal and are said to have much to do with the mellow tone of the bell.

The cemetery just behind the church contains gravestones of many of the early settlers. Looking at the early gravestones is like reading a history book.

Route 8 continues to the North Village of Becket.

PAUL REVERE BELL | Only 30 Revere bells are known to still be in existence.

GRAVESTONE OF JAMES HARRIS, REVOLUTIONARY SOLDIER

North Becket Village

There are several historic structures in **North Becket**, nicely located on a small green.

The Baptists were the first to move from the original town center, in 1814. Their church, a new structure built in 1859, merged with the Congregational Church of North Becket in 1926 and is now the **Federated Church of Becket**.

The headquarters and evolving museum of the **Becket Land Trust** is located here.

The former North Congregational Church is now the town library, and the former school is now an art center.

BECKET LAND TRUST HOUSED AT MULLEN HOUSE EDUCATIONAL CENTER | The museum has a great collection of historic images.

ARTS CENTER SIGN

The **Becket Arts Center of the Hilltowns** (serving Becket, Chester, Hinsdale, Middlefield, Otis, Peru, and Washington) was founded in 1970 and is a dynamic community asset. This nonprofit organization holds workshops and stages exhibits in the facility's galleries. Since 1978 the organization has been housed in the former town school, a handsome Greek Revival-style building.

FEDERATED CHURCH OF BECKET

David J. McLaughlin

BECKET ARTS CENTER | Seminary Hall, which the art center leases from the town of Becket for one dollar per year, was built in 1855.

Enjoying the Outdoors

Becket is a favorite spot for those who love the outdoors. In addition to hiking or mountain biking, there are three special attractions.

The Westfield River, along the town's northern borders, offers great fishing. Dams constructed to power the town's mills have been removed from the river and from Yokum Brook. There is a concerted effort to restore the river so that it will again be a spawning ground for Atlantic salmon and Eastern brook trout.

The Berkshire Fishing Club is located on Palmer Brook Lake, a serene 125-acre beauty nestled amid 850 acres of heavily forest land.

This private club will accept a trial membership that allows a small party to fish for a day. The catch-and-release fishing does not require a license. Contact them at www.Berkshirefishing. com or 413-243-5761.

Buckley Dunton Lake is an interesting spot. This "lake" was created in the 1800s when industrialists dammed Yokum Brook to provide power for downstream mills. The resulting 161-acre reservoir is a great spot to view mountain laurel in late June. However, the shoreline is heavily wooded, and the lake is best enjoyed with a flat-bottom boat or canoe. (There is no boat ramp, but you can launch from a landing near the dam.)

DREAM AWAY LODGE | A former actor, producer, and director, Daniel Osman, bought and restored the lodge in 1997.

DOG ON FRONT PORCH

Other Excursions

Dream Away Lodge is a place with a naughty past and alluring present … and a lot of history in between. This may be the most difficult attraction to find in the Berkshires. It is located on a 43-acre private parcel in the middle of October Mountain State Forest. The address is 1342 County Road, Becket (phone: 413-623-8725).

This legendary spot is rumored to have been a brothel at one time and was definitely a speakeasy during Prohibition. During the years when the lodge was owned by Mama Frasca, it housed an Italian restaurant known for its hearty food and a Wednesday-night hootenanny she pioneered in the 1940s. The lure of the lodge was enhanced when Bob Dylan picked this location to celebrate his legendary 1975 tour of the Northeast. On the recommendation of his friend Arlo Guthrie, Dylan held a revue party at Dream Away Lodge. The guests included Guthrie, Joan Baez, Allen Ginsberg, and Ramblin' Jack Elliott.

The slope of the front porch of the lodge careens downward at a 30-degree angle, an innovation of Mama Frasca to minimize the accumulation of rain or snow. You can usually find the Dream Away Dog on the front porch.

The lodge now offers family-style dining and live music. Call ahead for details.

Be sure to get specific directions and carry a cell phone with you if you get lost. The present owner continues the tradition of Mama Frasca, who was known to proclaim: "If you can't find it, you can't come."

POUR YOUR OWN COFFEE | The lodge is filled with artifacts and memorabilia, most of it collected by Mama Frasca.

Becket is a perfect jumping-off place for railroad buffs. There are huge, magnificently crafted stone **railroad arches** in and around Becket, built between 1833 and 1841. They were constructed without mortar or steel reinforcements. The Western Railroad (later the Boston and Maine) crossed the west branch of the Westfield River here on bridges supported by these arches. Five of the original 10 arches remain.

The center of the area's railroad history is in nearby **Chester** (easily reached by taking Route 20 East). Chester has an impressive **railroad museum** in the town's former rail depot.

CHESTER MUSEUM

The museum, which is open weekends from July–October, is located at 10 Prospect Street. (For further information call 413-354-7878 or check their Website at http://chesterrailwaystation.org). They can also arrange a guided tour of the bridges.

The five remaining keystone arch bridges comprise the **Middlefield-Becket Stone Arch Railroad Bridge District**, listed on the National Register of Historic Places. There is a detailed map of the bridges' locations and a proposed 2.5-mile **Keystone Arch Bridges Trail** posted on a large display on Middlefield Road, just outside the town of Chester.

The trail provides great scenic views of a huge gorge on the Westfield River. If you're lucky you will see a kayak shooting under the bridge.

It should be obvious that there is a lot to do and see in Becket!

ENTRANCE TO TRAIL

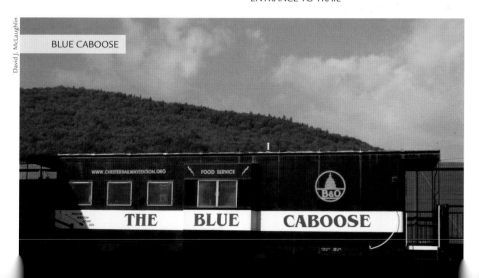

BLUE CABOOSE

WWW.CHESTERRAILWAYSTATION.ORG   FOOD SERVICE   B&O

THE   BLUE   CABOOSE

Washington

The town of **Washington** is just north of Becket, reached via Route 8, which cuts northward from Becket to Hinsdale. Over one third of the housing in Washington has been built since the 1980s, when this became a popular bedroom community for people who work in Pittsfield and Dalton, towns which are easily reached via Washington Mountain Road. Washington is heavily forested and well watered. The headwaters of the east branch of the Housatonic River are located here.

The town had a rocky start, however. The first proprietors learned that the land sold to them by one Robert Watson of Sheffield was a real estate scam. The Indians had never been paid for the land. By the time early investors discovered this, Watson was insolvent and "in gaol." The proprietors had to repurchase the land. After settlement finally began in 1761, the proprietors quickly changed the name of the township from Watsontown to Greenock. In 1762, in the final resolution of conflicting claims to the land, the General Court of Massachusetts confirmed the ownership of 60

proprietors, renaming the town Hartwood. The town name was finally settled for good in 1777 when the settlement was incorporated as the town of Washington, safely named after the commander of the Continental Army, who became the first President of the United States.

Visitors make the trek to Washington for its scenic beauty and unspoiled outdoors. Those in the know are attracted by historic **Bucksteep Manor** and the beautiful stone chapel sited along Washington Mountain Road, at the entrance to the former estate built by wealthy New York attorney George F. Crane in 1897 as a replica of an English estate he admired. The Crane family used Bucksteep as a vacation and summer home.

In 1899, the Cranes built **St. Andrew's Chapel** as a memorial to their parents.

ST. ANDREW'S CHAPEL | During the years when the chapel was owned by the Cranes, Episcopal church services were held when the family was in residence. >
Jim McElholm

BUCKSTEEP MANOR

Jim McElholm

MEMORIAL BENCH | In a tranquil spot near the church is a memorial bench honoring Virginia A. Sacco and Gary Love, who lost their lives in 1993 in an airplane accident in Alaska.

The Crane estate was deeded to the Episcopal Church in 1927. With the exception of St. Andrew's Chapel, the property passed into private hands. **Bucksteep Manor** *(885 Washington Mountain Road) is currently a family inn (22 rooms), conference center, and event venue. www.bucksteepmanor.com | 413-623-5535* 🏨INN

The town of Washington now owns St. Andrew's Chapel, which it acquired in 1977. The chapel is available for nondenominational services. Bucksteep Manor is a particularly popular venue for weddings, with services held in the chapel or on the grounds. It would be hard to find a more secluded and romantic place to be married than this architecturally stunning church.

Over the years there have been concerts held at the chapel and in the beautiful carriage barn of Bucksteep Manor. One hopes that some new version of the Stone Chapel Concerts of years past will emerge. The talent is certainly nearby, as Washington is home to many musicians, including Arlo Guthrie and his extended family. *Berkshire Living* magazine did an extensive article on one of those residents, James Taylor, in the August 2007 issue.

October Mountain

The largest state forest in Massachusetts, 16,500-acre **October Mountain**, occupies over half of Washington and spills into three surrounding towns (Lenox, Becket, and Lee). The campgrounds are on 256 Woodland Road in Lee, but there is access to October Mountain from all four towns. The largest body of water, **Washington Mountain Lake**, is in Washington.

The name October Mountain is attributed to Herman Melville, who could see the hills from his home in Pittsfield and loved the view in the fall.

October Mountain was the location of a 1,000-acre private game preserve developed by financier William C. Whitney (1841–1904) and opened on April 1, 1903. The park, across from Woods Pond, was stocked with buffalo, moose, elk, deer, and an aviary of pheasants, grouse, and quail. Whitney imported the animals into New York and brought them by train to the Berkshires. He ultimately owned over 11,000 acres here.

The state of Massachusetts acquired the Whitney land from his estate in 1915 and opened it to the public the same year.

Whitney's wild animals are long gone, of course. If you want to see buffalo you have to visit the **Eastover Resort and Conference Center** in Lenox.

BUFFALO AT EASTOVER | The founder of Eastover, George Bisacca, began to assemble a small herd in 1963, acquiring the animals at auction in Oklahoma. The resort continues this tradition.

Henry Dondi

< FALL FOLIAGE
Jim McElholm

Washington is an appealing small town whose
residents are justly proud of the fact that it still
has a town hall, a school, and a church and has
preserved much of the original town common.
A visit to Washington will reward anyone who
enjoys the outdoors, historic structures, and
friendly people.

ADDITIONAL RESOURCES

*A Bicentennial History of Becket, Berkshire County,
Massachusetts,* by Cathaline Alford Archer and Mitchell
J. Mulholland, Pittsfield, 1965. Full of important facts,
but it is a little hard to read and the early photographs
aren't well reproduced.

A Certain Place: The Jacob's Pillow Story, by Norton
Owen, 2002. A concise but comprehensive story of the
founding and development of Jacob's Pillow Dance.
60 pages. On sale at the Jacob's Pillow online store.

Courtesy Jacob's Pillow Dance

MARK MORRIS DANCING AT "THE PILLOW"

David J. McLaughlin

GATEWAYS TO THE BERKSHIRES

Lee and West Stockbridge

When you seek driving instructions to most major Berkshire attractions, they are likely to start with "Take the Massachusetts Turnpike west to Exit 2 (Lee)."

The "Mass Pike" is the 138-mile stretch of Interstate 90 extending from Boston to the New York State border; I-90 continues west all the way to Seattle. The turnpike opened on May 15, 1957, with a "half" connection (Exit 1) in West Stockbridge. You can get off the turnpike if you are going westbound and leave the Berkshires if you are willing to stay within the state and go east. Some think this was retribution for the many years it took to settle on the boundary between the two states, which wasn't resolved until 1787, but there were practical and local political considerations. In any event, a full interstate link to the Berkshires (Exit 2) was located just south of the Lee downtown, with good state highway

connections to the region's major towns. As a result of this convenient access, the town's central location, its inviting downtown, and vigorous promotion, Lee has become the major gateway to the Berkshires and an important tourist destination as well.

This chapter focuses on Lee and the smaller gateway town of West Stockbridge, both of which trace their roots to the Upper Housatonic Township authorized by the Great and General Court of the Province of Massachusetts in June 1722. By 1724 the township had been surveyed and the Indians had relinquished their rights for the consideration of "460 in money, three barrels of cider and 30 quarts of rum." West Stockbridge was incorporated in 1774. Lee (whose territory was augmented by other grants) was incorporated in 1777.

MASS PIKE

David J. McLaughlin

Lee

The center of **Lee** is about a mile north of Exit 2, easily reached via Route 20. The towering steeple of the **First Congregational Church** marks the historic center of Lee, which was named after Gen. Charles Lee, second in command to George Washington in the Continental Army.

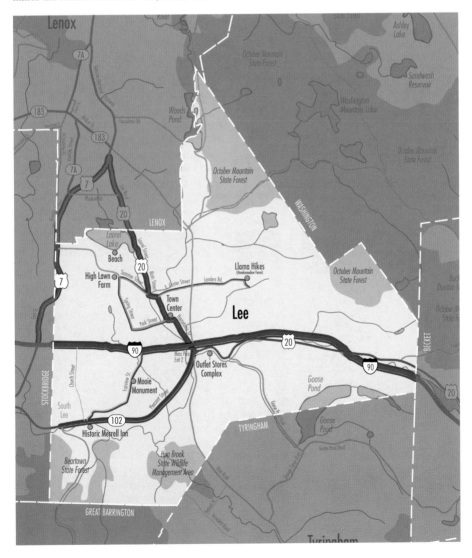

David J. McLaughlin

The well-sited Congregational Church of Lee was first organized on May 25, 1780. The current 1857 Romanesque-style church has a clock system built by Turret and Marine Clock Co. of Boston and a Seth Thomas clock movement to drive the dials that strike the bell.

Lee is one of the few towns that has fully documented and illustrated its sequence of early meeting houses. You will find depictions of the first and second Congregational Church buildings in the church lobby.

If at all possible, try to see the church interior, which was decorated by two German artists and, according to the Lee Historical Society, "is one of the finest examples of a technique called *trompe-l'oeil*." This technique, translated from the French as "trick of the eye," involves the use of extremely realistic imagery that creates the illusion that objects appearing in two-dimensional paintings actually exist in a three-dimensional space.

< VILLAGE INFORMATION BOOTH | The Lee Information Center, at 3 Park Place, is open between 10 A.M. and 4 P.M. Monday through Saturday from May to early January and from Wednesday through Saturday during the rest of the year.

Downtown Lee

The area in front of the church is the village green, which has been laid out to provide convenient visitor parking. The **information center** (413-243-0852), staffed with the most energetic and knowledgeable volunteers you will find in any Berkshire town, is a good place to start.

FIRST CHURCH
Built in 1780 —

SECOND CHURCH
Built in 1800

ARTIST RENDITIONS OF FIRST AND SECOND CHURCHES

< FIRST CONGREGATIONAL CHURCH
This church was built in 1857, the third church on the site. The 171-foot steeple is the largest wooden framed steeple in the United States.
David J. McLaughlin

David J. McLaughlin

INTERIOR OF CHURCH

There are important monuments to places and people who played a role in the town's history in what the residents call **the Park**. The Daughters of the American Revolution marked the location of the first campsite of the Housatonic Indians with a plaque in the southwest corner of the Park. Another plaque, in the southeast corner, shows the location of the first meeting house. The most intriguing and artistically significant monument, though, is a two-sided marble **fountain** created in 1899 by the famous sculptor Daniel Chester French (see page 137 on Chesterwood).

The back of this fountain (where water flows through the carving of a fish) functioned as a horse watering trough when the fountain was first installed at the intersection of Railroad and Main streets. The fountain was originally designed to include dog watering bowls, but they have been broken off.

The fountain honors a late 19th-century community leader, a woman who helped raise funds for the fountain but died before its completion. Amelia Jeannette Kilbon was a forceful advocate of Prohibition and a founding member of the Loyal Temperance Union of Lee.

David J. McLaughlin

FOUNTAIN | The front of the fountain depicts Chief Konkapot, the Mohican sachem who sold the English the land that is now the core of the towns of Stockbridge, West Stockbridge, and Lee.

David J. McLaughlin

MEMORIAL HALL OF LEE | Memorial Hall was dedicated on May 30, 1874.

To the left of the church is **Memorial Hall**, where the town offices and police station are located. It originally also housed the town library and post office. This impressive building was erected to honor the 41 sons of Lee who died in the Civil War. Some of these men were members of the all-black 54th Massachusetts Infantry, which suffered heavy casualties in a frontal assault on Fort Wagner, South Carolina, in July 1863. The story of the 54th was the focus of the 1989 movie *Glory*.

Lee's Main Street (Route 20) is listed in the National Register of Historic Places. Just across from Memorial Hall is the **Morgan House**, a Federal-style residence built in 1817 and converted to an inn where traveling theater groups often stayed. Guests have included President Ulysses S. Grant and playwright George Bernard Shaw.

Lee's "Lower" Main St. is also listed in the National Register.

Jim McElholm

THE MORGAN HOUSE | In the 1970s Maria Cole, the widow of Nat King Cole, owned the Morgan House.

PARK BUILDING | If you examine the front of this building you will find an original skylight built into the sidewalk to let light into the front of the basement.

As you stroll down Main you will see a number of marble buildings. From the last half of the 19th century through the early 1900s, Lee marble, famous for its durable qualities, became known throughout the country. It was used to build the Customs House in lower Manhattan and St. Patrick's Cathedral and Grant's Tomb in New York City. Thousands of the headstones at Arlington National Cemetery are made from Lee marble.

Buildings made of Lee marble abound in Lee: St. George's Episcopal Church (1865, with its pitched gable roof), Lee Library (1907), and the **Park Building** (1914) are among the most notable.

The stunning Beaux Arts-style building at 100 Main is the **Lee Library**, built on the site where the first town meeting was held in 1777.

LEE LIBRARY

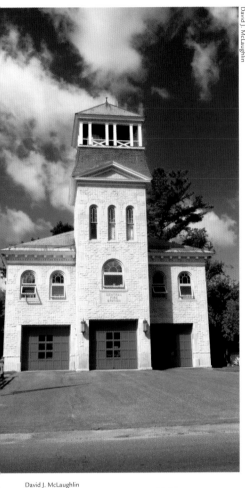

David J. McLaughlin

< CENTRAL FIRE STATION | The bell in the tower was purchased by the citizens of Lee for an earlier (1866) firehouse.

The Lee Library Association (413-243-0385) is one of the major Berkshire County Libraries, well worth visiting. For information check out their nicely organized Website: www.leelibrary.org.

The Lee Fire Department, which bought its first fire engine, the "Water Witch," in 1856, is a central town institution, playing a prominent role in the parades and festivals for which the town is noted, in addition to its firefighting duties. The handsome **Central Fire Station** (179 Main) was built in 1912—of Lee marble, of course.

The town's Historical Society has an information-packed Website: http://leehistoricsociety.homestead.com. The Society organizes lectures on the town's history. The Lee Historical Commission offers walking tours of downtown and a guided tour of the Congregational Church. Another (commercial) Website loaded with information on Lee is www.townoflee.com.

A quiet, upscale B&B about a mile from the Lee downtown is the **Devonfield Inn** *(85 Stockbridge Road). This gracious English-style manor house offers six rooms, three suites, and a separate guest house and is set on 32 acres. www.devonfield.com | 413-243-3298*

FUTURE FIREFIGHTERS ON PARADE

OUR Future Lee Firefighter

David J. McLaughlin

< LAUREL LAKE | There is a splendid view of the lake from the north side, where Bramble Lane skirts a portion of the shore.

As you drive north out of town, take note that **Troop B** of the Massachusetts State Police is located just off Route 20 at 215 Laurel. The Massachusetts State Police were founded in 1865. There are now barracks in Lee and Cheshire.

Laurel Lake is a 170-acre town pond that offers great fishing and swimming. To reach Lee's town beach, turn left on Lake Road, just before the Lenox town line.

High Lawn Farm has been operated by the Wilde family for the past 100 years. The history of this unique complex is fascinating. In 1909, near the end of the Gilded Age, Lila Vanderbilt Sloan Field and William Bradhurst Osgood Field built a magnificent Georgian house in Lee. The estate had a model-farm complex designed by Burnett & Hopkins of New York. The best description of the complex is in the definitive *Houses of the Berkshires* by Richard S. Jackson Jr. and Cornelia Brooke Gilder (p. 84):

To the North of the Town Center

There is so much to see and do in the center of Lee that it is easy to forget that the town's 20 square miles contain other attractions. Interesting excursions to the north include Laurel Lake, High Lawn Farm (one of the few operating dairies left in the Berkshires), and Hawkmeadow Farm B&B, which offers llama hikes.

"Two picturesque cottages with sweeping roofs and jerkinhead gables frame the entrance … reinforced concrete farm buildings, a cow barn, bullpens, a calf barn, and a dairy are ranged around a courtyard … the architectural centerpiece of the farm is a grand Bavarian water tower, equipped with a clock and bell, by which the life of the farm was regulated."

AERIAL VIEW OF HIGH LAWN FARM | The land on which the Gilded Age mansion and model farm were built was already called High Lawn, and the Fields retained this name.

High Lawn was a hobby farm until 1936, when Marjorie Field, daughter of the founders, and her husband, Col. H. George Wilde, transformed it into a professional dairy. The Wildes are proud of their Jersey herd and their state-of-the-art equipment and quality products. They welcome visitors, and tours can be scheduled.

High Lawn Farm extends over 1,300 acres. You can see small herds of these pampered bovines as you drive around north Lee and south Lenox.

A bed and breakfast located in the northeast quadrant of Lee, **Hawkmeadow Farm**, offers

Berkshire Mountain llama hikes, a favorite with kids. They are located at 322 Lander Road (413-243-2224).

October Mountain State Forest covers much of the northern edge of Lee. The primary camping area for this 16,500-acre state forest (the largest in Massachusetts) is at 356 Woodland Road in Lee. Information is available at www.mass.gov/dcr/parks/western/octm.htm.

High Lawn Farm
535 Summer Street
Lee, MA 01238
413-243-0672
www.highlawnfarm.com

David J. McLaughlin

David J. McLaughlin

Exploring to the South of Downtown

South of downtown, near the I-90 interchange, is the Berkshire's largest complex of outlet stores, hardly a Berkshire-specific attraction but a magnet for some visitors.

Prime Outlets of Lee (www.primeoutlets.com), wisely placed outside the historic downtown, is sited on a hillside overlooking I-90.

South Lee, along Route 102 near the border of Stockbridge, was once a thriving village.

The **Historic Merrell Inn** *(1565 Pleasant Street) is a brick stagecoach that has welcomed guests to its 11 rooms for almost two centuries. Be sure to see the unique "birdcage" bar. www.merrell-inn.com 413-243-1794*

ON THE PORCH OF THE MERRELL TAVERN
The Inn was built in 1794. It was included in the Historic American Buildings Survey done in the 1930s, when detailed architectural drawings were made.

Those who enjoy reminders of a time long past should visit the **Mooie Monument** in South Lee. This is a marble monument dedicated to a cow, Colantha Mooie, who held the world record for lifetime milk production during her years on earth (1919–1937). She produced 205,928 pounds of milk in those 18 years.

To visit the Mooie Monument, take Fairview Street North, off Route 102, just past Davis. The monument is on the right. In the early 20th century this was the location of Highfield Farm.

David J. McLaughlin

BIRDCAGE BAR

David J. McLaughlin

MOOIE MONUMENT

David J. McLaughlin

As you drive around this town you will be reminded that Lee was once the center of the paper industry in the Berkshires. Samuel Church began to make paper here in 1806 and within 50 years there were 25 paper mills in Lee and a network of supporting companies producing lime and paper-making machinery, constantly improving the paper-making processes. During the golden years of Berkshire paper making in the late 1860s, the Smith Paper Co. of Lee was the largest paper producer in the world. In a painful decades-long transition, however, Lee continues to lose paper plants.

Festivals and Special Events

The people of Lee are very community minded and promote the town about as effectively as any other community in the Berkshires. During the summer season there is hardly a weekend that doesn't offer a parade, an art show, or some other special treat. Founders Weekend, typically held the last weekend of September, is a special three-day event. The parade along Main Street draws marching bands and fire departments from all over, as well as just about every kind of community group you can imagine.

David J. McLaughlin

David J. McLaughlin

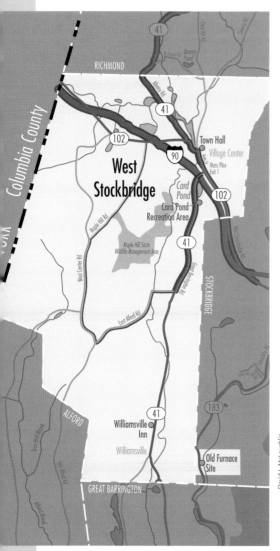

West Stockbridge

During the tumultuous years of the French & Indian Wars there was no permanent settlement in the lands west of **Stockbridge**, an area which the English referred to as Queensboro. A disputed section of the border with New York State, called Gore, was settled in 1758. Queensboro itself was settled in 1766.

This picturesque fertile valley, amply supplied by water from the Williams River, quickly attracted other settlers, and a vital, self-contained agricultural community soon emerged. When the town was incorporated in 1774 by combining West Stockbridge and Gore, there were 40 families residing here.

The first meeting house in town, a simple structure with no windows (and no heating), was built in the West Center of town and shared initially by Congregationalists and Baptists. (The historic West Center Church was struck by lighting and destroyed in 1956. A chapel of fieldstone marks the site.) By the 1830s the population had shifted to what is now the center village. **Congregational Society of West Stockbridge** was organized in 1833.

CONGREGATIONAL CHURCH OF WEST STOCKBRIDGE | This church, built in 1882, is the second structure on this site. The original church burned in 1881.

WEST STOCKBRIDGE VILLAGE LOOKING NORTHWEST, C.1839, JOHN WARNER BARBER

While West Stockbridge was a good place for farming, which thrived here in the 18th century, it was what was under the soil that shaped the destiny of the community. Large quantities of marble, iron, and lime were discovered. Between 1790 and 1830 there were 30 quarries in West Stockbridge. As many as five marble mills finished the cut marble, which was then carried by teams of horses to the Hudson River for shipment south. Lime kilns sprang up to use the refuse stone. Iron ore was also plentiful, largely picked up from the ground and forged into tools in cottage industries until an open-pit mine was dug beginning in 1826. The ore was carted to nearby Richmond for processing. Charcoal was needed to fuel the smelting furnaces, and there were "charcoal pits on every mountainside around the town … where trees were cut, stacked and burned to make charcoal" and "the denuded hills were a smokey [sic] sight," according to Edna Bailey Garnett in her definitive history of the town.

With its extensive industry and proximity to the state of New York, West Stockbridge became the first railroad terminus in Berkshire County.

The Hudson and Berkshire Railroad line (built between 1836 and 1838) ran 34 miles, from Hudson, New York, to West Stockbridge, facilitating the shipment of marble and iron ore.

David J. McLaughlin

ONLY REMAINING EXTRACTIVE BUSINESS IN WEST STOCKBRIDGE

Courtesy West Stockbridge Historical Society

RAILROAD COMPLEX AT STATE LINE, 1932

120

The industrious Shakers of Tyringham operated a grist mill in West Stockbridge between 1821 and 1851 at a site along the river, near the center of town.

The industrialization of West Stockbridge peaked in the early 1900s, and the population declined. Gradually the scars on the landscape disappeared, and from the last half of the 20th century to today the town has become a thriving residential community whose scenic countryside and easy access attracts many families and, in recent times, more and more second-home buyers.

West Stockbridge has a charming and very active center that contains two general stores, several locally popular restaurants, a centrally located inn, and plenty of enticing shops laid out in a compact square block. The Williams River snakes through town.

This is a fun town through which to stroll, shop, and have lunch. **Charles H. Baldwin & Son**, located on the banks of the Williams River, dates to 1888. The pure vanilla extract for which it is renowned has been made in the same facility (a former carriage shop) since 1912.

RESTORED SHAKER MILL | This was a grist mill "raised by the brothers of Tyringham" in 1821. It was sold in 1851.

THE CARD LAKE INN ON MAIN STREET | The Card Lake Inn contains a spacious tavern and well-regarded restaurant.

HOTCHKISS MOBILES GALLERY

Several contemporary galleries give the village an "artistic air."

Since 2004 West Stockbridge has held an annual zucchini festival, typically on the second Saturday in August. It draws visitors from all over. They also celebrate the "Grand Opening of Summer" on Memorial Day with a parade and gallery tours.

West Stockbridge maintains a tourist information booth during the season. The Website www.weststockbridgetown.com lists all the town establishments and offers suggestions on things to see and do in the area.

TOWN HALL WITH ZUCCHINI FESTIVAL SIGN

SAWYER'S MARBLE HOUSE

One of the most handsome 19th-century **marble houses**, built in early the 1800s, still stands intact on the edge of the village center.

Many of the homes built during the years when West Stockbridge was an active industrial center have been restored in recent years.

Just south of town, the **Card Pond Recreational Area** has a playground and beach. This is one of the nicer spots to swim in the southern Berkshires, and free parking is available.

< THE AMASA SPENCER HOUSE | Amasa Spencer, who moved to West Stockbridge from East Haddam, Connecticut, in 1791, was a joiner and probably built the original structure, expanded c. 1810 by his son, who became the village postmaster. Spencer ultimately joined the Mormon Church and moved to Utah.

David J. McLaughlin

CARD POND RECREATIONAL AREA

It is easy to see why West Stockbridge has become such a popular second-home and telecommuting community. Hamilton Child got it right in his 1885 *Gazetteer of Berkshire County* when he described "the beautiful valley of Williams River ... winding gracefully through the town ... between Stockbridge mountain on its eastern border and Tom Ball mountain [on the southern edge]."

Williamsville Inn *(280 Great Barrington Road, West Stockbridge) offers 10 guest rooms in the main house, four other rooms in an historic barn, and two cottages. The "Taste of Germany" restaurant is well regarded. This historic facility, which dates to 1797, was converted to an inn in 1951 and recently fully updated. www.williamsvilleinn.com |* 413-274-6118

Paul Rocheleau

HOUSE AND BARN, WEST STOCKBRIDGE

< WEST STOCKBRIDGE IN FALL
David J. McLaughlin

The citizens of Lee and West Stockbridge are justly proud of their history, architectural heritage, community spirit, and coherent downtowns. Lee is so central to the county that it would be difficult to avoid driving through the town center, but it deserves a special stop or two during any visit to the Berkshires. West Stockbridge is easy to reach from the Mass Pike, Route 102 from Stockbridge, or Route 41 from Richmond. If you enjoy shopping in a compact, charming village, make time for a visit here.

READINGS AND RESOURCES

West Stockbridge, Massachusetts, 1774–1974: The History of an Indian Settlement, Queensboro or Qua-Pau-Kuk, by Edna Bailey Garnett, The Berkshire Courier, 1976. A bit dated but the only full book on West Stockbridge.

Lee: The Centennial Celebration and the Centennial History of the Town of Lee, Mass., by Rev. C. M. Hyde and Alexander Hyde, Springfield, MA: Clark W. Bryan Co., 1878. The definitive history of the early days of Lee.

See All the People: Life in Lee, by Florence Consolati, 1978. Very informative. Has the best cover of any of the 100-plus town histories that have been published.

LEE FOUNDERS DAY PARADE

David J. McLaughlin

"THE BEST OF NEW ENGLAND"

Stockbridge

Stockbridge, chartered in 1737 and incorporated in 1739, is one of the oldest settlements in the Berkshires. This town's unique legacy as a mission station, its history of cultural leadership, inviting layout, and large number of top-tier attractions—apparent on the map—make Stockbridge special. Of course, any area so blessed with things to see and do presents a special challenge to the modern traveler who is pressed for time. This chapter proposes a series of bite-sized excursions that begins on the Main Street made famous by Norman Rockwell and then extends to other clusters of attractions—some world famous, others lesser known, all deserving attention.

David J. McLaughlin >

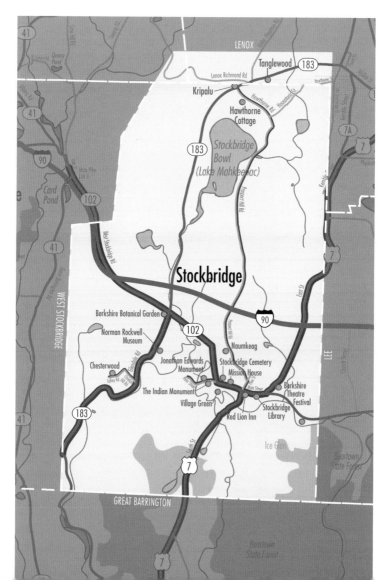

JONATHAN EDWARDS MONUMENT | This rose granite monument honors Jonathan Edwards (1703–1758), the noted scholar and second missionary to the Stockbridge Indians. It sits on a traffic island across from the town green. Stockbridge was established as an Indian Town, and the Native Americans who settled there (primarily Mohicans) came to be called Stockbridge Indians.

MAIN STREET AT CHRISTMAS, BY NORMAN ROCKWELL

The Village Center

In 1967, America's favorite illustrator, Norman Rockwell, after 10 years of research and painting, completed one of his best-known works, *Main Street at Christmas,* which was featured in *McCall's Magazine's* holiday issue that year. This captivating painting of the Stockbridge Village Center during the holiday season, and Rockwell's other illustrations of the town and its residents, has made Stockbridge America's hometown in the minds of millions. Each year, on the first weekend in December, the residents recreate the scene depicted in the painting, complete with vintage automobiles.

A stroll along **Main Street** at any time of the year is a special experience. *At the town crossroads, the intersection of Main and South streets (Route 7), is the famed* **Red Lion Inn***, which has welcomed travelers for over two centuries. The Red Lion now offers 108 rooms located in the Inn itself (rebuilt in 1897) and at several adjacent downtown Stockbridge buildings, including the town's former firehouse. www.redlioninn.com |* 413-298-5545

Even if you aren't lucky enough to stay at the Inn and watch the goings-on from a comfortable chair on the long front porch, do stop to have a meal in the spacious dining room or at Widow Bingham's Tavern (casual dining), or enjoy the live entertainment at The

THE RED LION | The Red Lion, which began as a general store in the 1770s, soon evolved into a tavern and inn. The present main building replaced a smaller structure that burned to the ground in 1896. The sign for this historic establishment has always featured a red lion.

STAGECOACH SIGN | In the 1820s, stagecoach travel expanded, connecting the Berkshires to Boston, Hartford, and Albany. Though the railroad ultimately replaced the stagecoach for most long-distance travel, use of stagecoaches continued throughout the 19th century for local travel until they were ultimately replaced by the car.

CAT AND DOG FOUNTAIN

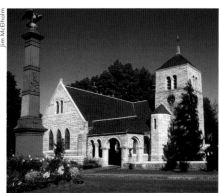

SOLDIER'S MONUMENT AND ST. PAUL'S CHURCH

Lion's Den. The Inn is filled with fascinating memorabilia, including a sign that was posted when this was an important stagecoach stop.

Just outside the Inn, along Route 7, is the **Cat and Dog Fountain**, erected in 1862, a Stockbridge landmark.

Directly across Main Street is **St. Paul's Episcopal Church**. Make a special effort to see the inside of this historic church, which contains a chancel window by LaFarge, a nave window by Tiffany, and a baptistery designed by Louis St. Gaudens (brother of sculptor Augustus). The town's tribute to those who died in the Civil War, the Soldier's Monument, is on Pine Street, across from the Episcopal Church.

As you stroll along Main Street, heading east, you will see many of the buildings featured in Rockwell's drawings, including the original town offices and vintage shops. A small visitor's information booth, staffed by knowledgeable locals during the season, is a useful source of information and directions. Be sure to explore the mews, a cul-de-sac of enticing shops. Notice the sign on the outside wall of the central market, marking the spot of the original Alice's Restaurant featured in Arlo Guthrie's 1967 talking blues song, "Alice's Restaurant Massacree."

The charming shops of Stockbridge continue down Elm Street. At the corner of Main Street and Elm is another Stockbridge landmark, the Watering Trough, erected in 1881.

THE WATERING TROUGH | This working fountain contains two homilies: "Utility is preferable to grandeur" and "Merciful Man is Kind to His Beast."

Be sure to visit the **Stockbridge Library Association** at 46 Main.

In addition to a fine collection of reading material, the library has an inviting reading room and impressive original art. The History Room, staffed by a knowledgeable research librarian, is filled with fascinating artifacts and town memorabilia.

THE MOHICAN ETOWAUKAUM, BY JOHN VERELST | In 1710 the Mohican tribal leader Etowaukaum, along with several Mohawk sachems, traveled to London, where they were feted by the English. During their stay John Verelst painted each sachem in full-length dress, accompanied by symbolic accoutrements (in the case of Etowaukaum, a ball club).

READING ROOM AT STOCKBRIDGE LIBRARY | The Stockbridge Library dates to 1864. In those days proceeds from a dog tax were the primary source of support.

Courtesy Stockbridge Library Association

AN ORIGINAL BALL CLUB IN HISTORY
ROOM OF STOCKBRIDGE LIBRARY

David J. McLaughlin

THE AUSTEN RIGGS CENTER | Originally established
as the Stockbridge Institute for the Treatment of
Psychoneurosis when Dr. Austen Fox Riggs moved to
Stockbridge in 1907, the organization became the
Austen Riggs Foundation in 1919.

Going West Along Main

As you walk west along Main, away from the
village center, you will see beautiful mansions
erected during the opulent Gilded Age, when
one third of the land in Stockbridge was
occupied by these "cottages." The **Merwin
House** at 14 Main Street, also known as
Tranquility, is a 19th-century house that is open
to the public. This impressive brick structure,
built in the 1820s as a summer home, is filled
with European and American furniture and
decorative arts. If you visit, be sure to stroll
through the gardens and down the lawn to the
Housatonic River. See www.historicnewengland.
org or Phone I (413) 298-4703) for information.

Another prominent set of structures right
along Main is the **Austen Riggs Center**, known
for its pioneering work in psychotherapy. The
complex includes an early 1890s inn, a medical
office building, and the Elms, now residential
housing. Timothy Edwards, the son of Jonathan
Edwards, built the Elms as his home in 1772.

The Mission House

At the corner of Main and Sergeant streets is
the **Mission House** that was built in 1739 by the
Reverend John Sergeant, the first missionary to
the Mohican Indians. During the mission era
this house was located on Eden Hill and had a
commanding view of the town. It was relocated
to the present site and fully restored between
1926 and 1927.

This historic structure, now owned and
managed by The Trustees of Reservations
(www.thetrustees.org), has magnificent gardens
and is enclosed by a tidewater cypress fence.

EXTERIOR VIEW OF THE MISSION HOUSE | The Colonial Revival Garden of the Mission House was designed
between 1928 and 1929 by the noted landscape architect Fletcher Steele. The garden features larkspur, coleus, and
balsam as well as hollyhocks, which were Steele's signature plants.

Amanda Merullo

The ornate carved doorway of the Mission House, built by a carpenter from the Connecticut River Valley, was added in 1769 by Abigail Williams Sergeant, the widow of John Sergeant, who died in 1749. Sergeant descendants remained in possession of the house until 1867.

A replica of an old cobbler shop serves as the entrance to the property. A grape arbor in the Well Courtyard (behind the house) leads to a small Native American museum that tells the story of the Mohicans. The interior is tastefully furnished with period furniture, some of it belonging to the Sergeants.

The Mission House, first opened to the public in 1930, today invites visitors from Memorial Day Weekend through Columbus Day.

The Mission House
19 Main Street
Stockbridge, MA 01262
413-298-3239
www.thetrustees.org

INTERIOR OF THE MISSION HOUSE | Mabel Choate, the daughter of the man who built Naumkeag, funded the purchase, relocation, and restoration of the Mission House and the creation of its magnificent gardens. The interior paint colors are based on notes made by Mabel when she purchased the property.

Stockbridge Cemetery

Stockbridge Cemetery, entered right off Main Street, is one of the most picturesque and well-maintained final resting places in the Berkshires. This was not always the case, however. In 1853, dismayed by the shoddy appearance of the cemetery, Mary Hopkins established the Laurel Hill Association, the oldest village improvement society in America. The group's first project was to improve the appearance of the cemetery by fencing it in and planting the spruce trees that still grace the entrance road.

Anyone interested in understanding the history of Stockbridge and appreciating its many illustrious citizens should visit this tranquil oasis, which also offers great views of the surrounding countryside.

Thirty-eight soldiers who served in the Revolutionary War are buried here, along with such notables as Cyrus West Field, who laid the first transatlantic cable, and Norman Rockwell, who is buried between his second and third wives, Mary and Molly.

The most famous part of the cemetery is the so-called **Sedgwick Pie**, a section that contains the graves of the members of the prominent Sedgwick family, including the writer Catharine Maria Sedgwick (1789–1867). The gravestones are laid out in concentric circles.

THE SEDGWICK PIE | The former slave Elizabeth "Mumbet" Freeman (c. 1742–1829) is buried here next to Catharine's father Theodore, who was the lawyer who successfully pleaded her case. For a discussion of Mumbet, see page 19 in the section, "The Col. John Ashley House."

The Village Green and Indian Monument

Just beyond the cemetery, on the other side of Main, is the 19th-century **Village Green**, which contains the striking Congregational Church, war memorials, and the **Children's Chime Tower**, dedicated in 1878.

A short distance farther to the west (if you are driving, go straight a couple hundred yards; don't turn right on Route 102) is the **Indian burial ground monument**. This memorial was hewn from stone quarried from the nearby Ice Glen.

The many other attractions of Stockbridge are best reached by car. The town's two premier museums, the Norman Rockwell Museum and the Chesterwood Estate and Museum, are about a mile and half from the center of town, along Route 183. Naumkeag, the stunning Gilded Age mansion, is north of town, as is the National Shrine of the Divine Mercy on Eden Hill. The Berkshire Theater Festival venues are just east and north of town.

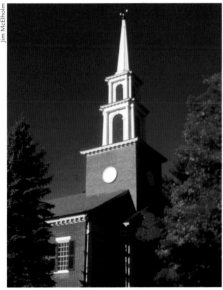

CONGREGATIONAL CHURCH | The Congregational Church was first organized in 1734 by John Sergeant. This current church was erected in 1824.

CHILDREN'S CHIME TOWER | In accordance with the wishes of its donor, the Chime Tower is rung at 5:30 every evening between "apple blossom time and the first frost on the pumpkin"—that is, between June 1st and Labor Day.

< INDIAN MONUMENT | This monument to the "Friends of Our Fathers" was erected on this site in 1878. The majority of the Stockbridge Indians left Massachusetts to settle on Oneida lands between 1885 and 1887, eventually settling in Wisconsin.

BERKSHIRE BOTANICAL GARDEN | The Berkshire Botanical Garden was founded in 1934. Its display gardens are among the oldest in the United States.

HARVEST FESTIVAL

GIRL TOUCHING SUNFLOWER | Youth programs organized by the Garden attract busloads of children from all over the region and nurture youngsters' interest in nature.

Berkshire Botanical Garden

Traveling west from the town center, take a diagonal right on Route 102 (Church Street) after the cemetery, passing the Jonathan Edwards monument, until you reach the intersection of Route 183. The **Berkshire Botanical Garden**, located at this crossroads, is well worth a stop. This not-for-profit, 15-acre complex is a lively center for horticulture, educational programs, and community events. The collections include over 3,000 species and varieties and emphasize plants that thrive in the Berkshires.

Berkshire Botanical Garden holds a plant sale each May and a flower show in early August. Its premier program is the Fall Harvest Festival, held on the first weekend in October.

Berkshire Botanical Garden
Routes 102 and 183
Stockbridge, MA 01262
413-298-3926
www.berkshirebotanical.org

Norman Rockwell Museum

About a mile south on Route 183 is the **Norman Rockwell Museum**, set on 36 rolling acres overlooking the Housatonic River. The museum contains the world's largest collection of Rockwell's original paintings and drawings. Highlights include the 322 *Saturday Evening Post* covers Rockwell drew over 47 years, his inspirational 1943 Four Freedoms drawings, and other popular illustrations.

ROCKWELL PAINTING ROCKWELL

THE NORMAN ROCKWELL MUSEUM
The first Norman Rockwell Museum was located in the Old Corner House in Stockbridge. The stunning contemporary building that now houses the collection was designed by Robert A. M. Stern.

The museum grounds contain the museum; Rockwell's Stockbridge studio (see following page for a photograph), which was moved to this site; and a Gilded Age mansion named Linwood, whose land was acquired for the museum.

The studio contains Rockwell's art materials and equipment, his personal art library, hundreds of prints, decorative objects, personal mementos, and artwork sent him by admirers.

THE LINWOOD HOUSE | Charles and Susan Sedgwick Butler built Linwood in 1859.

The Norman Rockwell Museum is an expanding center of the art of illustration. It stages captivating exhibits of contemporary and past masters. This makes each visit a fresh experience.

The Museum is open daily throughout the year, except for Thanksgiving, Christmas, and New Year's Day. The hours are from 10:00 A.M. to 5:00 P.M. on weekends and during the months of May–October and from 10:00 A.M. to 4:00 P.M. Monday through Friday from November to April.

Norman Rockwell Museum
9 Glendale Road (Route 183)
Stockbridge, MA 01262
413-298-4100
www.nrm.org

COCK IN BLOOM, BY PATRICIA BLAIR RYAN

ROCKWELL'S STUDIO >
Jim McElholm

Chesterwood

As you continue south on Route 183, look for signs directing you to another star in the constellation of Stockbridge attractions. **Chesterwood**, the 120-acre estate and museum of the famous American sculptor Daniel Chester French, is located on Williamsville Road, just of Route 183.

Daniel Chester French (1850–1931), like many creative people before him and since, was drawn to the Berkshires, where he bought and transformed a farm in the Glendale section of Stockbridge. French spent 34 summers at the place he came to call Chesterwood.

Chesterwood features one of the largest collections of fine art devoted to a single American artist—over 500 pieces of sculpture, including molds, life casts, and studies. A favorite of visitors is the models French made for his most famous statue, the *Seated Lincoln*, the centerpiece of the Lincoln Memorial.

Incidentally, keep alert for other work by French as you tour the Berkshires. One of my favorites is the splendid horse fountain he designed, now resting on the village green of the town of Lee.

The Chesterwood estate also includes a barn gallery, a gift shop, walking trails, and picnic grounds. This is one of the choice spots in the Berkshires, somewhat less crowded than other venues. The museum is open daily from May to October, from 10:00 A.M. to 5:00 P.M.

THE STUDIO | French's studio was designed by Henry Bacon, the architect who designed the Lincoln Memorial.

MODEL OF *SEATED LINCOLN* | The actual *Seated Lincoln* statue is 19 feet tall and weights 175 tons. The statue was carved out of 28 blocks of white Georgia marble and took four years to complete.

CHESTERWOOD, FRENCH'S SUMMER HOME
The Colonial Revival-style residence of Daniel Chester French.

Chesterwood Estate and Museum
4 Williamsville Road
Stockbridge, MA 01262
413-298-3579
www.chesterwood.org

Naumkeag

In 1885–86, at the height of the Gilded Age, Joseph Hodges Choate, a prominent New York attorney and subsequently American ambassador to England (1899–1905), built a country house in Stockbridge. He named it **Naumkeag**. This was the original Native American name for Salem, Massachusetts, where Choate was born. Naumkeag is located on Prospect Hill Road, a little over a half a mile from the center of Stockbridge. Take Pine Street north, then bear left on Prospect Hill.

David J. McLaughlin

NAUMKEAG | This 44-room shingle-style "cottage" was designed by McKim, Mead & White.

Paul Rocheleau

The house is filled with original furniture, artwork, and ceramics collected from all over the world by Choate and his artist wife Caroline Dutcher Choate. Be sure to take a tour of the interior and enjoy the quality and integrity of the mansion's furnishings and art.

Naumkeag is famous for its eight acres of gardens, surrounded by 40 acres of woodland, meadows, and pasture. The splendid gardens are the result of a collaboration between Joseph Choate's daughter Mabel, who inherited the estate, and the landscape architect Fletcher Steele, who worked together for 30 years to create a series of terraced gardens and garden rooms.

< ENTRYWAY AT NAUMKEAG

THE AFTERNOON GARDEN AT NAUMKEAG
Steele was noted for creating a "garden room."

THE ROSE GARDEN AND BACK OF NAUMKEAG

The **Blue Steps** are one of the most noteworthy exterior features of Naumkeag. They consist of a series of blue fountain pools flanked by flights of stairs and overhung by birch trees. They allowed Mabel to descend to lower levels of the grounds serenely and safely.

One of my favorite spots in this magical landscape is the **Chinese Garden**, created after Mabel traveled to Asia in 1935 and returned with an extensive collection of Korean, Chinese, and Japanese statuary, vases, and other ornaments. (A photograph of the Chinese Pavilion in this garden, by Paul Rocheleau, appears on the following page.)

Upon her death in 1958 Ms. Choate bequeathed her estate to the Trustees of Reservations, along with an endowment for the upkeep of the house and gardens. Naumkeag is open between May and October. This Gilded Age beauty should not be missed.

THE BLUE STEPS | The Blue Steps were completed in 1938, at the height of the Art Deco movement.

Naumkeag
5 Prospect Hill Road
Stockbridge, MA 01262
413-298-3239
www.thetrustees.org

< PAVILLION IN CHINESE GARDEN
Paul Rocheleau

Berkshire Theatre Festival

There are two outstanding performing arts organizations associated with Stockbridge: Tanglewood and the Berkshire Theatre Festival. Though most of the Tanglewood property lies in Stockbridge, the official address and main entrance are in Lenox, and thus we will cover this world-class attraction in the next chapter.

The **Berkshire Theatre Festival** is an exclusive Stockbridge creation. The origin of what is one of the finest regional theaters in the country dates back to 1888, when a marvelous structure designed by the famous Gilded Age architect Stanford White was built on Main Street, where the Mission House is now located. Known as the Stockbridge Casino, it became the center of the town's social and cultural life. When times changed in the 20th century and the Casino was in danger of being torn down, it too was rescued by Mabel Choate. The building was relocated to the bottom of Yale Hill Road, at the east end of Main Street. A stage and seating for 415 were added. The renamed Berkshire Playhouse began a stellar run in 1928 that continues to this day, attracting some of the best playwrights and actors of each successive generation to the Berkshires.

In 1970 an additional venue for emerging actors, directors, and playwrights was created a short distance away. The Unicorn Theatre and

a 9.5-acre compound called the Lavan Center (which operates as a residence for summer apprentices and interns) have enabled the organization to expand its educational mission.

The Berkshire Theatre Festival offers performances on two stages from May to December. Attending one of these performances is often the highlight of a trip to the region.

David J. McLaughlin

UNICORN THEATRE COMPLEX

Berkshire Theatre Festival
6 Main Street (Main Theater)
Stockbridge, Ma 01262
413-298-5536
www.berkshiretheatre.org

Courtesy Berkshire Theater Festival

BERKSHIRE THEATRE FESTIVAL MAIN STAGE
The former Stockbridge Casino is the now the main stage for the performing arts organization known, since 1967, as the Berkshire Theatre Festival.

Kevin Sprague

LOVE! VALOUR! COMPASSION! (2007)
This Summer 2007 performance on the BTF main stage featured Romain Frugé, James Lloyd Reynolds, Matthew Wilkas, Stephen DeRosa, and Ricky Fromeyer.

Other Excursions

There is much to enjoy in the Stockbridge countryside.

Ice Glen is a favorite hiking spot only a few blocks south of Main Street. You reach it by turning left off Route 7 onto Park Street, then crossing a footbridge over the Housatonic River. There are three trails. The Mary Flynn Trail, which is handicapped accessible, is a paved walkway along the river. To reach the other trails you cross the railroad tracks. The left fork takes you to Laura's Tower, which offers a three-state view. The right fork leads to Ice Glen itself. This spot contains glacial boulders that have magical ice formations much of the year (in some years as late as early July).

The Stockbridge Bowl (Lake Mahkeenac) is a mile-wide lake about four miles north of Main Street. The Bowl offers boating, fishing, and swimming in the summer months and is known for its spectacular autumn vistas. The Great Josh Billings RunAground race (a mid-September 27-mile triathlon), which starts in Great Barrington, includes a canoe or kayak sprint around the Stockbridge Bowl and concludes with a run around the lake. You can reach the Stockbridge Bowl by driving north on Prospect Hill Road, passing several Gilded Age mansions that are still in private hands. My favorite view of the Stockbridge Bowl during the peak of the fall foliage season is from Olivias Overlook along Lenox Mountain Road.

David J. McLaughlin

THE COUNTRYSIDE NORTH OF THE TOWN CENTER | This image shows the Naumkeag barn in the foreground. The house in the background is a private residence.

Kevin Sprague

STOCKBRIDGE BOWL

Berkshire County was a literary center beginning in the first half of the 19th century. Catharine Maria Sedgwick (1789–1867), considered one of the founders of American literature, was born in Stockbridge. Her reputation and hospitality—and the beauty of the Berkshires—attracted many of the literary giants to the area, including Nathaniel Hawthorne, who had a cottage in Stockbridge, near the Stockbridge Bowl, from 1850–51. It was here that he wrote *The House of the Seven Gables.* Herman Melville, whose house, Arrowhead, is in Pittsfield, was a frequent visitor.

Jim McElholm

THE LITTLE RED HOUSE OF NATHANIEL HAWTHORNE | In 1891 Hawthorne's cottage was destroyed by fire. An exact replica was built by the Federated Music Clubs of America in 1948. It is open for tours in the summer.

Norman Rockwell once called Stockbridge "the best of America, the best of New England." No visit to the Berkshires would be complete without a stop in this charming town, which many make the center of their visit.

ADDITIONAL RESOURCES

Stockbridge, Past and Present, or Records of An Old Mission Station, by Miss Electra F. Jones, Samuel Bowles & Company: Springfield, 1854 (reprinted by Higginson Book Company). This classic reference is now available as a reprint.

Stockbridge 1739–1939, A Chronicle, by Sarah Cabot Sedgwick and Christina Sedgwick Marquand, Berkshire Courier: Great Barrington, 1939. Written by two descendants of the illustrious Sedgwick family, this is a very readable account of this important town.

"Stockbridge: A New England Village," by W.H. Eggleston, in *Harper's Magazine,* November 1871, pp. 3–16.

The Laurel Hill Association, 1853–1953, by Margaret French Cresson, Eagle Printing and Binding Company: Pittsfield. Every village improvement group in the country should read about the history of this pioneering association.

"CURRIER & IVES LOVELY"

Lenox is thrice blessed. It is sited beautifully on a plateau between Lenox Mountain and October Mountain in what Hamilton Child described as an area of "reposeful beauty … free from blemish." The town's long tenure as the Berkshire County seat (1784–1868) led to the creation of architecturally distinctive public buildings and an elegant downtown. Lenox's popularity during the Gilded Age preserved much of the pastoral landscape, when half the land was occupied by grounds of the "cottages" built by wealthy summer visitors. Most of these mansions have survived and continue to grace the landscape.

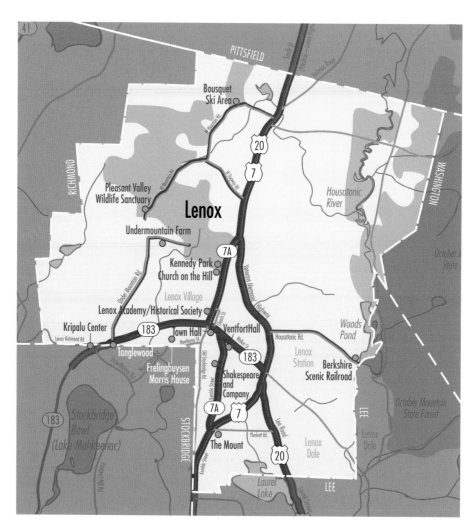

AERIAL VIEW OF LENOX

Lenox has also been fortunate in its friends and benefactors. No one did more for the reputation of the Berkshires in the 19th century than the English actress Frances Ann (Fanny) Kemble, who always stayed at the Curtis Hotel in Lenox and ultimately purchased property in town. America's most famous author at the beginning of the 20th century, Edith Wharton, gave the Berkshires and Lenox a special cachet when she built a summer home, The Mount, here in 1902. The Berkshires' future as America's Premier Cultural Resort was assured when the Tappan family, who had hosted private musical concerts at their country estate in Lenox for over 80 years, gave their estate, Tanglewood, to the Boston Symphony orchestra as its permanent summer home.

For these reasons and more, a trip to Lenox is sure to be rewarding.

LENOX IN 1840, BY J. W. BARBER, ENGRAVED BY S. E. BROWN

David J. McLaughlin

LENOX LIBRARY | This handsome building was designed by Isaac Damon. Lenox Library is a National Historic Register building.

Historic Lenox and Its Compelling Center

Most visitors to Lenox are drawn initially to the downtown. The **Curtis Hotel** where Fanny Kemble stayed still stands. It's still charming, though it now houses private apartments with stores on the ground floor.

The stately former court house at 18 Main Street, constructed in 1815–1816, is a Greek

Revival building with soaring ionic columns and a graceful cupola. In 1871 Mrs. Adeline Schermerhorn, a wealthy summer resident, purchased the building and donated it to the town for use as a public library.

The Lenox Library Association, incorporated in 1856, moved into the space in 1874. This is one of the major libraries in the county. It has an extensive collection of Gilded Age material, inviting reading space, and many paintings, drawings, and treasured town artifacts donated by residents over the years. There is also an outdoor reading park. The library's collection of historical artifacts includes the sled featured in Edith Wharton's novella *Ethan Frome*. Lenox Library also has one of the largest collections of classical music recordings and scores in the country.

The Lenox Library at 18 Main Street is open between 10:00 A.M. and 5:00 P.M. Tuesdays through Saturdays (until 8:00 P.M. on Thursdays). For information, see http://lenoxlib.org/ or phone 413-637-0197.

David J. McLaughlin

LIBRARY INTERIOR

The overall charm of the downtown is enhanced by its many public buildings, monuments, and a graceful park.

Lilac Park is a one-and-a-half acre gem that serves as the town's village green. Located in the middle of Lenox's Historic District, the park contains 19 inviting benches and offers a tranquil setting for reading and lounging. The park is also the site of several craft fairs throughout the season. The land for the park was given to the town in 1908 by the Servin family and initially planted with lilacs. It was extensively restored and the design updated in the 1950s and again in 1991. The Lenox Garden Club helps maintain the park.

The park contains two historic structures: the former **Lenox Academy** building and the **Congregational Chapel**. In 1803 a private boys' preparatory school, the Berkshire Academy (soon renamed Lenox Academy), opened. Later uses included the town's public high school and the private coeducational elementary Trinity School. The Lenox Historical Society now occupies this space.

LILAC PARK | The memorial cannon honors George J. Bisacca, founder of the Eastover Resort in Lenox. The American Heritage Room at the resort contains one of the largest private collections of Civil War memorabilia in the country.

LENOX ACADEMY | This Federal-style building was built in 1803.

Jim McElholm

CHURCH ON THE HILL

Be sure to visit the **Historical Society Museum**, which has an extensive collection of well-preserved town memorabilia nicely displayed in the expansive interior of the Lenox Academy building.

The **Chapel of the Church on the Hill** (55 Main) was built in 1877 for the convenience of parishioners who wanted a "right in-town" place to worship that was more easily heated. Sunday services are regularly held at both the chapel and the famous Church on the Hill, both now United Church of Christ facilities.

The **Church on the Hill**, high above the town at 169 Main, dominates the Lenox landscape. This well-proportioned church is perfectly sited, enclosed on two sides with a sloping cemetery that contains gravestones of many of the town's notables.

David J. McLaughlin

MONUMENT HONORING GEN. JOHN PATERSON
This obelisk was erected in 1892.

David J. McLaughlin

PILL BOXES USED BY HAGYARD'S DRUGS

Paul Rocheleau

ETUDE (2007), BY ANDREW DEVRIES | DeVries Fine Art International, Ltd.is located at 62 Church Street.

The remains of Maj. Gen. John Paterson (1744–1808) lie in the Church on the Hill cemetery. As a young lawyer Paterson represented Lenox in the first and second Provincial Congresses in 1774–75. As war threatened he raised a regiment that was one of the first in the field after the Battle of Lexington. He served with distinction throughout the entire Revolutionary War, fighting in virtually all the major battles.

Paterson and Maj. Azariah Egleston of Lenox, who also served throughout the war, are honored with a commanding black polished granite obelisk in the center of town. Two hundred thirty-three men from Lenox served in the Revolutionary War, one of the largest contingents in all Berkshire County.

Lenox has excellent boutiques, art galleries, a great bookstore, and several upscale restaurants in the inviting downtown, concentrated on Church, Housatonic, and Walker streets and a portion of Main (see map).

The Lenox **Town Hall** (6 Walker Street), designed by Pittsfield architect George C. Harding and built in 1901, is a commanding structure that adds to the historic appearance of the downtown.

In **Triangle Park**, at the junction of Main and Cliffwood streets, stands a charming granite fountain, originally a horse watering trough with a special lower trough for dogs. It was erected in 1884 and is inscribed: "He prayeth well, who loveth well, both man and bird and beast."

David J. McLaughlin

FOUNTAIN | This fountain was designed by Harriet Hosmer in honor of her friend Emma Stebbins, a sculptor and painter.

The reenactment of the Gilded Age "Tub Parade," marking the end of summer, makes the entire downtown a special fall destination.

Gilded Age Mansions

Lenox is the place to rediscover the Gilded Age. Two former "cottages" are now museums, and upscale accommodations are now offered in several of the most elegant mansions. Many Gilded Age houses that have been put to other uses are preserved on the grounds of major cultural venues.

A good place to start is **Ventfort Hall Mansion and Gilded Age Museum** at 104 Walker Street. This was the summer cottage of Sarah Morgan, sister of financier/banker John Pierpont (J. P.) Morgan.

This unique structure was almost lost to posterity in 1996 when there were plans to tear it down and replace it with a nursing home. A group of preservationists purchased the building and 12-acre property in 1997 and began a decade-long effort, which is still continuing, to restore Ventfort Hall to its former glory.

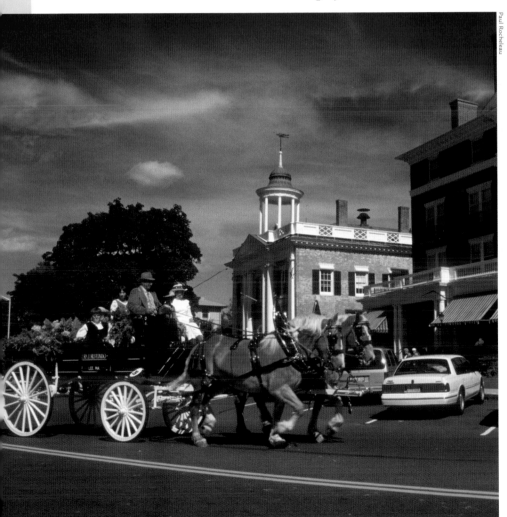

Paul Rocheleau

TUB PARADE CARRIAGE | This event is sponsored by the Lenox Chamber of Commerce and the Colonial Carriage and Driving Society. Many of the "tubs" are antique carriages pulled by ponies, horses, and draft horses.

VENTFORT HALL | Ventfort Hall, a Jacobean Revival-style structure, was designed by Boston architect Arthur Rotch and completed in 1893.

The elegant exterior brickwork and roof and much of the interior—ornate paneling and the grand staircase—already have been restored. Be sure to look at the gabled carriage house on the property.

In 1998 the orphanage scenes for the movie *The Cider House Rules* (Miramax Films) were shot here.

Ventfort Hall not only offers a fascinating look at one of the more elegant Gilded Age mansions, but the museum's exhibits and displays tell the story of life in the Gilded Age in the Berkshires. This is a wonderful aid in creating a context for subsequent explorations.

Ventfort Hall is open daily from 10:00 A.M. to 3:00 P.M. During the peak season (Memorial Day to October 31) daily guided tours start on the hour, between 10:00 A.M. and 2:00

Ventfort Hall Mansion and Gilded Age Museum
104 Walker Street
Lenox, MA 01240
413-637-3206
www.gildedage.org

P.M. During the balance of the year there are guided tours at the same times on Saturdays and Sundays and self-guided tours on weekdays. The museum is closed on New Year's Day, Easter, Thanksgiving, and Christmas.

INTERIOR OF VENTFORT HALL

DISPLAY FROM 2007 *"LES PETITES DAMES"* EXHIBIT AT VENTFORT HALL

THE MOUNT

The Mount

You are in for a special treat at **The Mount**, the summer home of the novelist Edith Wharton, who personally designed and decorated the mansion, which was built in 1902. In creating The Mount, she followed the principles set forth in her 1897 book, *The Decoration of Houses*.

This extensive property has been carefully restored in phases over the last two and a half decades, at considerable expense. Renovations have been funded by the nonprofit Edith Wharton Restoration, Inc. (founded in 1980), grants from Save America's Treasures and the National Trust for Historic Restoration, generous corporate and individual donors, and support from the general public. As of this writing, the house's exterior has been restored, and the downstairs rooms in the mansion are finished. In 2005 The Mount acquired the 2,600-volume Edith Wharton library for $2.6 million from a Yorkshire bookseller.

Edith Wharton was an avid gardener and an expert on European landscape design. Three acres of formal gardens surround The Mount, laid out as a series of "rooms" that integrate effectively with the house and the natural landscape. Over $3 million has been invested in the preservation and restoration of the gardens, which are a highlight of any visit to this magical place.

EDITH WHARTON LIBRARY

The Mount: Edith Wharton's Estate and Gardens
2 Plunkett Street
(Route 7 and Plunkett Street)
Lenox, MA 01240
413-551-5111
www.edithwharton.org

The meticulous and ambitious restoration of this stellar property has stretched its resources. In 2008 the institution defaulted on its bank loan and faced foreclosure. A special fundraising effort was initiated to "save" The Mount. We can only hope that successful fundraising and prudent management will enable all of us to continue to enjoy this most special of estates.

The Mount is typically open between May and October, but you should check out the status, hours, and program before any visit.

Quite a few Lenox Gilded Age "cottages" have been transformed into accommodations that enable visitors to expand their experience of the Gilded Age "in style." We recommend two upscale converted mansions for a special experience.

Blantyre *(16 Blantyre Road) was built in 1902 to replicate a Scottish manor house. It was has been beautifully restored by the Fitzpatrick family (who have owned the Red Lion Inn since 1968). This top-* *tier attraction has eight expertly decorated rooms in the main house and four private cottages as well as an award-winning dining room offering New French Cuisine. www.blantyre.com | 413-637-3556*

Another Lenox jewel is **Wheatleigh** *(Hawthorne Road), a Gilded Age Italianate villa built in 1893 by Henry H. Cook, a financier and real estate tycoon. It was purchased and creatively restored by Susan and Linfield Simon. There are 19 guest rooms. Breakfast is limited to guests, but lunch and dinner (French cuisine) are available to the public. This gracious property offers a total experience of sophisticated luxury. You enter the estate on a winding drive through grounds designed by Frederick Law Olmsted, pull into a spacious courtyard graced by an ornate fountain, and enter a great hall whose décor and hand-carved terra-cotta fireplace preserve the original craftsmanship. Cook imported materials and artisans from Italy for the original construction. Wheatleigh was brilliantly updated in 2001 to become what* Travel & Leisure *describes as "the most modern, luxurious, tightly run country hotel in the United States." www.wheatleigh.com | 413-637-0610*

GARDENS AT MOUNT >
Kevin Sprague

BLANTYRE

Kevin Sprague

Other Gilded Age Facilities

A recent addition to upscale accommodation choices in Lenox is **Stonover Farm** *(169 Undermountain Road), tastefully created from a Gilded Age cottage that served as the Stonover estate farmhouse. This luxury B&B offers three suites in the main house, a separate cottage, and a converted 1850 schoolhouse, all set on 10 scenic acres. It's a unique blend of country inn and boutique city hotel.*
www.stonover.com | 413- 637-9100

Many are drawn to the Berkshires to rejuvenate their lives and improve their physical fitness and health. Where they stay can be central to that goal. Three large complexes (two resorts and a yoga center) offer these experiences with a Berkshires flavor that includes traces of the Gilded Age. Canyon Ranch in the Berkshires, a world-class destination spa; the Cranwell Resort, Spa and Golf Club; and the Kripalu Center for Yoga and Health each have the distinction of being located on historic properties, which have been integrated into the overall layout and design.

Canyon Ranch. *Between 1896 and 1898 two wealthy socialites, Giraud and Jean Van Nest Foster, built one of the grandest Gilded Age estates,* **Bellefontaine**. *The mansion was designed by Carrere & Hastings (who went on to design the New York Public Library in 1911). The estate was sold by the Fosters' son in 1946 and for a time was a Jesuit monastery. Near the edge of the property, there are gravestones from the years when there was a monastery (and later an Immaculate Heart of Mary seminary) on the site. The interior of Bellefontaine was destroyed by fire in the winter of 1949. When the former estate was purchased in 1987 by Canyon Ranch, the mansion was restored and expanded to serve as the property's architectural focal point. The former mansion now contains the resort's elegant dining room, the original library, and a two-story solarium that has guest lounges and conference rooms.*
www.canyonranch.com | 413-637-4400

Cranwell Resort. *Another Lenox resort with a rich and unique history is located on a hillside above Route 20, offering breathtaking views of the countryside. The Cranwell Resort, Spa and Golf Club is where the avid golfer might elect to stay. The first 18-hole professional golf course in the Berkshires*

GOLFING AT CRANWELL

was built here in 1926, and it remains one of the few championship golf courses in the region. Before the course was built, the Berkshire Hunt Club operated here for a few years in the early 1900s.

The centerpiece of the current four-star resort is the castellated ochre brick mansion, **Wyndhurst**, *designed by architects Peabody & Stearns and built in 1894 for the Sloane family. The Cranwell Resort also embraces an adjoining estate with another Peabody & Stearns designed shingled mansion built a decade earlier and known originally as* **Coldbrook**. *From 1939 until 1975 the Wyndhurst and Coldbrook properties formed the campus of a Jesuit boys preparatory school named Cranwell. Today the 380 acres of the Cranwell School create an elegant setting for this well-regarded 114-room resort.*
www.cranwell.com | 413-637-1364

The unique property that is the **Kripalu Center for Yoga and Health** also has a colorful history. In 1894 the then largest house in the United

Many of the Gilded Age mansions of Lenox are still in private hands, but others have been converted for other uses. For example, the **Lenox Club**, a private membership club, dates back to 1864 and features as its clubhouse **Windyside**, the 1875 estate and home of Richard Cranch Greenleaf and Adeline Stone Greenleaf. If you can wangle an invitation for the Thursday evening buffet dinner, you will be attending an affair that has been held without interruption since 1914.

Kripalu Center
Intersection of West Street (Route 183)
and Richmond Mountain Road
Stockbridge, MA 01262
1-866-200-5203 (toll free)
413-448-3152
www.kripalu.org

States was built on a hillside overlooking the Stockbridge Bowl. **Shadow Brook** was built by Anson Phelps Stokes and Helen Louisa Phelps Stokes of New York City. The house was ultimately acquired by Andrew Carnegie, who died there in 1919. The Jesuits subsequently acquired the property for a seminary. Several priests and seminarians died in 1956 when the vast stone and half-timbered mansion burned to the ground. The Jesuits built the present brick institutional structure on a nearby site with stunning lake views.

In 1983 the former seminary was purchased to serve as a spiritual and yoga retreat center. It operates as a nonprofit entity, a spiritual and volunteer organization modeled after the Hindu yoga ashram. Kripalu's entrance is located just before the intersection of Route 183 (West Street) and Richmond Mountain Road, right at the border of Stockbridge and Lenox. Almost all Kripalu's 126 acres are in Stockbridge.

KRIPALU CENTER

Cesar Silva

ON THE LAWN AT TANGLEWOOD

Lenox and the Performing Arts

"Music in the Berkshires" is so pervasive a phrase and so extensive a reality that it comes as no surprise that **Tanglewood** alone draws over 300,000 visitors a year to the preeminent summer music festival of the Northeast.

One of the most famous and influential music venues of the 20th century, however, was just down the road from Tanglewood, where jazz and folk artists performed at the **Music Inn**, opened by Philip and Stephanie Barber in 1950 and owned and operated by David Rothstein from 1970–1979. The Inn began as a summer resort where artists participated in roundtables and gave impromptu performances, but by 1955 the Barbers had created a 1,000-seat auditorium, the **Berkshire Music Barn**.

During the "jazz era" leading artists of the period (Louis Armstrong, Count Basie, Duke Ellington, Sarah Vaughan, and Ella Fitzgerald, to name a few) played, innovated, and recorded at the first venue of its kind. The School of Jazz (1957–1960) attracted students from all over the world. The Folk and Rock era (1970–1979) featured artists like Arlo Guthrie, Joan Baez, Pete Seeger, Van Morrison, Bruce Springsteen, and Bob Marley.

Sadly, the Music Inn closed in 1979. In 1984 the property was sold and converted into White Plains Condominiums. Ironically the innovative jazz that the Music Inn pioneered has now flowered again in the Tanglewood and Williamstown Jazz Festivals.

Tanglewood

Tanglewood occupies the grounds of two Gilded Age estates. The 500 acres of land lie predominantly in Stockbridge, but the main gate (and mailing address) is in Lenox.

What would become one of Massachusetts' most prominent cultural institutions began in 1934 when an associate conductor of the New York Philharmonic Orchestra, Henry Hadley, had the idea of staging a summer music festival in the Berkshires. His original idea was to hold several events where professional musicians would perform excerpts from popular classical music. In 1935 the first series of concerts of what was then called the Berkshire Music Festival were held at the Hanna Horse Farm in Stockbridge and again in 1936 at the fairgrounds in Great Barrington. The orchestra consisted of 65 professional musicians recruited from the ranks of the New York Philharmonic.

Hadley's principal financial backer, Gertrude Robinson-Smith, pushed to expand the event so that it could feature a full symphony orchestra and include complete musical works. In 1937 she persuaded Serge Koussevitzky (1874–1951), the legendary longtime conductor of the Boston Symphony Orchestra (BSO), to give three performances, which took place in August of that year. The crowd of over 15,000 exceeded all expectations. That fall, the Tappan family donated their summer estate as a permanent home for the orchestra … and the country's first summer music festival became an annual event.

Tanglewood
297 West Street (on Route 183)
Lenox, MA 01240
413-637-5165 (tickets and information)
www.bso.org

COPLAND-INSPIRED PERFORMANCE AT TANGLEWOOD

Paul Rocheleau

Paul Rocheleau

SCENE AT OZAWA HALL

Both the facilities and range of musical performances have expanded dramatically over the years.

In 1938 a "music pavilion" was designed by Finnish American architect Eero Saarinen, but the cost proved prohibitive in those Depression years, so a simple functional shed designed by a local engineer, Joseph Franz, in collaboration with Saarinen, was built. The **Koussevitzky Memorial Shed**, which seats 5,200, proved to be an acoustical masterpiece. The audience spills over onto the adjacent lawn, where up to 10,000 additional music lovers can listen to music under the stars. Acquisition of the Highwood estate in 1986 expanded the acreage, and in 1994 Ozawa Hall, a smaller and more intimate building designed for chamber music, was added. The facility is named for

Seiji Ozawa (b. 1935), who was appointed BSO musical director in 1973.

The cumulative impact of Tanglewood on music excellence stems in part from the creation of the **Tanglewood Music Center** for advanced musicians, added in 1940. The Center now counts as alumni some 20 percent of members of America's major orchestras.

The offerings at Tanglewood have continued to expand from classical music symphonies to chamber music, opera, jazz, and contemporary music. One of the most popular programs is **Tanglewood on Parade**, which features both the BSO and the Boston Pops orchestras, which play together in a program that culminates in Tchaikovsky's *1812 Overture* followed by fireworks.

Shakespeare & Company

Nineteen seventy-eight turned out to be an important year in the Berkshires' advance to "America's summer cultural resort" when Tina Packer founded **Shakespeare & Company** in Lenox. Initially this company, which performs "as the Elizabethans did," purchased The Mount, Edith Wharton's turn-of-the-century estate, and then went on to become tenants for more than 20 years while performing Shakespeare, Wharton adaptations, and new works.

In April 2000 Shakespeare & Company acquired another magnificent site (30 acres) on which it currently has three theatres and continues to develop its campus that will eventually include a recreation of the original Tudor-era Rose Playhouse surrounded by an Elizabethan village. This is the flagship project in the evolution of Shakespeare & Company from a fine regional company to an international center for Shakespearean performance and studies. Meticulously researched by the Company, the Rose Theatre Trust, and the Museum of London and aided by the discovery of the footprint of the original 17th-century Rose beneath a London building site in 1989, the initial plans are complete. The current focus is on fundraising, which will be led by Tina Packer and several other key players, including actor Dustin Hoffman, Honorary Chair of the Rose Playhouse project, and a committee of other influential artists,

scholars, and business leaders, aided by a $1 million seed grant organized by Massachusetts Senators Edward M. Kennedy and John F. Kerry and Congressman John Olver.

Created by David Bakalar and donated to Shakespeare & Company in 2001

THE PREGNANT CUBE

Shakespeare & Company
70 Kemble Street
Lenox, MA 01240
413-637-1199
413-637-3353 (Box Office)
www.shakespeare.org

RECONSTRUCTIVE VIEW OF THE ROSE
PLAYHOUSE AND SURROUNDING VILLAGE

By William Dudley, incorporating material by Jon Greenfield and C. Walter Hodges

162

FOUNDERS' THEATRE

The Founders' Theatre, completed in 2000, is a brilliant renovation of a gymnasium-turned-cabaret space, redesigned to be a space within a space offering multiple seating configurations. This building includes an inviting lobby bar, gift shop, and rehearsal spaces.

The Elayne P. Bernstein Theatre, which opens in 2008, has added a flexible theater with seating capacity of 150–180.

The quality of the productions at Shakespeare & Company—not only the classic Shakespeare but new plays of social and political significance—is enough to put this venue high on any itinerary. However, the beauty and harmony of the site and the exciting expansion now under way make Shakespeare & Company an essential Berkshire experience.

Shakespeare & Company combines tours with seasonal performances at three stages in Lenox (the Founders' Theatre, the Rose Footprint Theatre, and the Elayne P. Bernstein Theatre). The group's comprehensive, well-designed Website provides details: www.shakespeare.org.

THE MERRY WIVES OF WINDSOR

Frelinghuysen Morris House and Studio

There is a gem of a house museum on Hawthorne Street in Lenox that the art critic of the *New York Times* characterized as a place where "nature takes a backseat to culture and abstraction." **The Frelinghuysen Morris House and Studio** has an extensive collection of American and European Cubist art as well as the paintings, frescoes, and sculptures of two of the early members of the American Abstract Artists group, founded in 1936.

George Morris built a studio on his family's estate in Lenox in 1930. After his 1934 marriage to Suzy Frelinghuysen, the couple built a Bauhaus-inspired modernist home linked with the studio. They used this as their summer home for 50 years.

The house and studio complex is set on 46 acres. It opened as a museum in 1998.

The Frelinghuysen Morris House and Studio is open in July and August on Thursdays through Sundays, between 10:00 A.M. and 4:00 P.M. There are hourly guided tours (the last tour is at 3:00 P.M.). During the month of September through Columbus Day (2nd Monday in October) the house museum is open the same hours on Thursdays, Fridays, and Saturdays. To reach the museum, take Hawthorne Road off Route 183 (just south of the main entrance to Tanglewood) for 0.7 miles, then turn left on Hawthorne Street. The entrance is 0.4 miles on the left. It is a pleasant 10-minute walk through the woods to the house.

STAIRCASE IN FRELINGHUYSEN MORRIS HOUSE

Frelinghuysen Morris House and Studio
92 Hawthorne Street
Lenox, MA 01240
413-637-0166
www.frelinghuysen.org/fmf/

HOUSE AND STUDIO

INTERIOR OF STUDIO

Berkshire Scenic Railroad

In 1850 the Stockbridge and Pittsfield Railroad (leased to the Housatonic Railroad) began train service from the village of Van Deusenville, in Great Barrington, through Stockbridge, Lee, and Lenox and on to Pittsfield. In the early years train service was slow. It took five hours to get from Bridgeport, Connecticut, to Lenox because there were 22 stops along the way. By the 1880s, though, as "cottagers" and their large retinues flocked to the Berkshires, service had improved. You could reach Lenox from Grand Central Station in New York City in five hours on the New York, New Haven, and Hartford Railroad (which had absorbed the Housatonic Railroad in 1892). In the peak years of the Gilded Age over a dozen trains a day plied this route. Some of the wealthy travelers had their own private railroad cars. They rented custom-made baggage cars to transport their carriages and horses.

In this era Lenox had two train stations. When the 50-year-old wooden station burned in 1902, a new, more commodious station was built (it opened in 1903). This station served the community for some 50 years until it was abandoned. In 1986 the building was donated to the **Berkshire Scenic Railroad**, whose volunteers have restored the station to its former glory for its new role as a museum.

The Berkshire Scenic Railroad offers a narrated train ride along the Housatonic River between Lenox and Stockbridge twice a day in season. This 20-mile round trip, along with a visit to the museum and a "Gateway to the Gilded

GATEWAY MUSEUM AT BERKSHIRE SCENIC RAILROAD

Age" exhibit set in a refurbished coach, is an essential stop in any Gilded Age tour. Visitors with children in tow will find that they have a keener interest in railroad stock than mansion architecture. Incidentally, the current train service, which began in 2002, is the second such venture. Between 1984 and 1989 the Berkshire Scenic Railroad operated an excursion train on weekends between Lee and Great Barrington.

The Berkshire Scenic Railroad runs twice a day (at 10:00 A.M. and 1:30 P.M.).

Culture and architecture are primary attractions in Lenox; however, the surrounding countryside also warrants exploration.

Berkshire Scenic Railway Museum
Willow Creek Road
Lenox, MA 01240
413-637-2210
www.berkshirescenicrailroad.org

TRAIN LEAVING LENOX STATION

KENNEDY PARK   Kevin Sprague

Pleasant Valley Wildlife Sanctuary

The **Pleasant Valley Wildlife Sanctuary** in Lenox is, as you would expect of an Audubon facility, an important center for birding. But it is much more. The 7 miles of trails that weave through the sanctuary's 1,314 acres cover a diverse terrain of wetlands, meadows, ponds, and hardwood forests that extend up the eastern slope of Lenox Mountain. Beavers are plentiful, and their lodges are scattered on dammed sections of Yokun Brook. Salamanders migrate in the spring along West Mountain Road. You can rent canoes to use on the Housatonic River (about 10–15 minutes away).

This is a fabulous area to view fall foliage when the sugar maples are at their fiery best. Mountain laurel is abundant and spectacular in late June, particularly around sunny Pike's Pond. The facility has knowledgeable naturalists available who can help you appreciate this special sanctuary.

A popular community event staged in mid-October is the Enchanted Forest, a Halloween-themed evening that combines games and crafts with doses of education to help children learn more about conservation. You can walk along luminaria-lit paths in the twilight to learn how beavers, frogs, bears, and other Berkshire critters feel about their environment.

The trails of the wildlife sanctuary are open from dawn to dusk throughout the year on the days when the nature center is open. The nature center is open Tuesdays through Fridays from 9:00 A.M. to 5:00 P.M., with shorter hours on Saturdays, Sundays, and "in season" Mondays (10:00 A.M. to 4:00 P.M.). The entrance is 1.6 miles from Route 7. Don't miss this magical spot where nature makes the music.

Adjacent to the wildlife sanctuary, **Kennedy Park** is a 500+ acre Lenox Town Preserve with miles of trails and scenic overlooks. This is a multiuse area that attracts hikers, mountain bikers, and dog lovers throughout the year and cross-country skiers in the winter. Horseback riding is also permitted on the trails.

Kennedy Park is located on the grounds of the former Aspinwall Hotel (built in 1902, burned in 1931). It is named for long-time Lenox resident John D. Kennedy, who lived at Stonover Farm and helped create the park in 1973.

Pleasant Valley Wildlife Sanctuary
472 West Mountain Road
Lenox, MA 01240
413-637-0320
berkshires@massaudubon.org

Horseback Riding

Lenox has two equestrian facilities, both of which offer opportunities to ride through the beautiful Berkshire countryside. The **Aspinwall Adult Equestrian Center** at 29 Main Street (Route 7A) offers scenic trail rides of varying lengths, including overnight rides as part of **Berkshire Horseback Adventures** (413-637-9090).

Undermountain Farm and Riding Stable provides boarding and licensed instruction in hunt, seat, and dressage. They also offer guided trail rides and run a riding day camp for youngsters during the summer months. The complex is located along one of the more scenic back roads of Lenox, at 400 Undermountain Road (413-637-3365).

ASPINWALL EQUESTRIAN CENTER

UNDERMOUNTAIN FARM | Henri Braem, New York's
Danish Consul, built this farm complex around 1885 for
his Jersey herd.

Successive generations of full- and part-time
residents and visitors from every era have
considered Lenox a special Berkshire treat.
With an unusually high share of top-tier
attractions, some of the best restaurants and
shops in the county, an inviting downtown, and
a majority of the Berkshires' four- and five-star
inns and resorts, this is an upscale destination.
Even so, those without deep pockets will find
plenty to do and see.

ADDITIONAL RESOURCES

Lenox: Massachusetts Shire Town, by David H. Wood,
published by the town in 1969, 219 pages.
This book was commissioned by the Lenox
Bicentennial Committee.

Lenox and the Berkshire Highlands, by R. DeWitt Mallary,
New York: G. P. Putnam's Sons, 1902.

History of Lenox and Richmond, by Charles Palmer,
Pittsfield, MA: Press of the Sun Printing, 1904.
An early history that is still used as a reference.

Hawthorne's Lenox, by Cornelia Brook Gilder and Julia
Conklin Peters, The History Press, 2008. Packed with
information and interesting anecdotes.

The Lenox Chamber of Commerce has an
information-packed Website that can aid further
planning at *www.lenox.org.*

BERKSHIRE COUNTY SEAT

The City of Pittsfield

Pittsfield, the first Berkshire city and still its largest, has been the seat of county government for over 140 years. It is the undisputed industrial and manufacturing center of this region, though it lost much of its luster as a cultural center and important tourist destination in the middle years of the 20th century. Today it is heartening to see broad signs of a renaissance that should put Pittsfield back on every visitor's itinerary.

Any visit to Pittsfield should start with a tour of historic **Park Square**. For years modern Route 7 has wended its way (rather busily) through what was considered for much of the 19th century one of the most elegant, architecturally distinctive town centers in New England.

A stately elm anchored the square until it was struck several times by lightning in 1841 and was finally taken down in 1864. Most of the magnificent churches and public buildings that were built in the 1800s are located in this area.

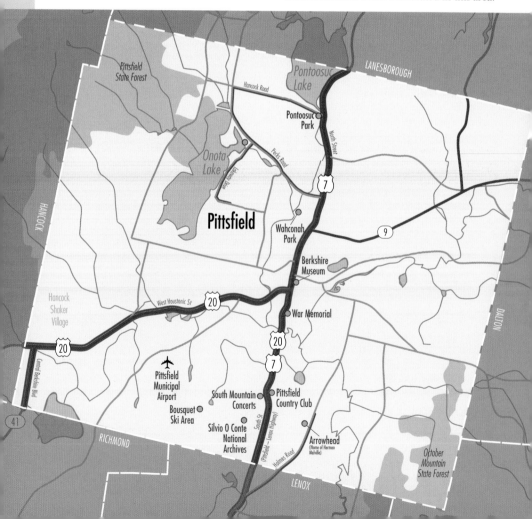

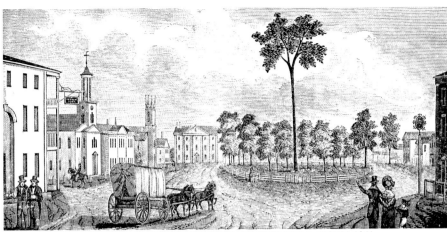

CENTRAL PITTSFIELD IN 1840, *DRAWN BY J.W. BARBER, ENGRAVED BY S.E. BROWN, 1841*

Exploring Park Square

Instead of attempting to see anything as you navigate Route 7, pull over, park, and explore the square on foot. This will become easier after completion of the five-year **Pittsfield Streetscape Project**, which begins in 2008. This will ultimately eliminate the current circular flow of vehicles around Park Square for northbound traffic, add special sidewalks, plantings, and period lighting, and improve park access.

At the front of the park is a handsome Civil War monument, designed by Irish-American sculptor Launt Thompson. It shows a bronze Union color sergeant perched on top of a granite shaft.

CIVIL WAR STATUE | Pittsfield's Civil War Monument, erected in 1872, contains the names of 147 residents who served in the War of the Rebellion. Twenty-nine of them died in that bloody conflict.

Jim McElholm

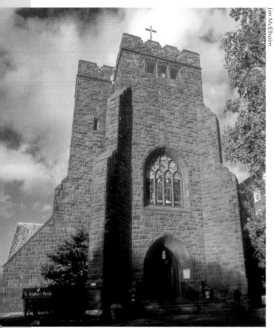

Pittsfield grew rapidly, particularly in the second half of the 19th century, when it was the center of wool manufacturing and then, in 1868, named the county seat. The population increased from 5,872 in 1850 to 21,766 in 1900. It 1891, after prolonged debate, Pittsfield residents voted to become a city, the first in the Berkshires.

The city's churches led the way in creating memorable structures. **St. Stephen's Episcopal Church** was built on Park Place in 1832. The Congregationalists built a handsome new stone church in 1853 at 27 East Street (now the **First Church of Christ, Congregational**). **St. Joseph's Roman Catholic Church** on North Street was consecrated in 1866. The Methodists built an elegant brick church (**First United Methodists**) at 55 Fenn Street, dedicated in 1874.

ST. STEPHEN'S EPISCOPAL CHURCH | St. Stephen's was rebuilt on the north side of Park Square in 1890.

As you tour Pittsfield you will see that the public sites are clean and attractive. This is the result of active beautification efforts by such organizations as the Friends of Pittsfield, Pittsfield Beautiful, the Pittsfield Tree Watch, and various city task forces and departments.

The old **Pittsfield Town Hall**, also built in 1832, still stands at 25 East Street. It was acquired and restored by Pittsfield-based Berkshire Bank in 1970.

The **Berkshire County Holocaust Memorial Monument** is located on the southwest corner of the square, on the lawn of the courthouse.

OLD TOWN HALL

Berkshire Athenaeum

Undoubtedly the most impressive structure fronting Park Square is the **Athenaeum**, built in 1874–75 and given a broad charter. The *Berkshire County Gazetteer* reported that the Athenaeum's role was to "aid in promoting education, culture and refinement, and diffusing knowledge by means of a library, reading-rooms, lectures, museums, and cabinets of art, and of historical and natural curiosities." Pittsfield was thus the first town in the Berkshires to have a museum, and within three decades would create a separate structure to house its growing collection.

This building served as the town library until 1975, when library collections outgrew the space. The Athenaeum was converted to serve as the Berkshire County Registry of Deeds and now also includes courtrooms.

The building was constructed of blue stone from Great Barrington, pillars of red Missouri granite, and cornices made of red freestone quarried in Longmeadow, Massachusetts. It is a superb example of what is known as the "rich Gothic" style of architecture.

David J. McLaughlin

ENTRANCE TO THE ATHENAEUM | The Athenaeum was designed by William Appleton Potter, a New York architect. The building was a gift to the city from its native son, Thomas Allen (1813–1882), a railroad magnate and Congressman.

The Pittsfield Library (still referred to as the Berkshire Athenaeum) is just east of Park Square, on Wendell Avenue. It is a major county library with superb genealogical resources, an extensive local history collection, and a special Herman Melville Room, which first opened in 1953 and houses the largest collection of Melville family memorabilia in the world.

Berkshire Athenaeum
Pittsfield's Public Library
1 Wendell Ave.
Pittsfield, MA 01201
413-499-9480
www.pittsfieldlibrary.org

THE ATHENAEUM, *LIBRARY OF CONGRESS*

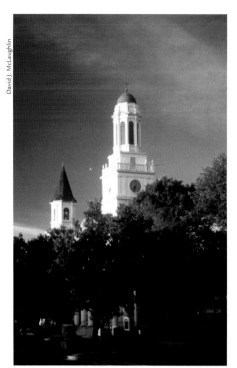

David J. McLaughlin

CHURCH SPIRES ALONG SOUTH STREET

To the south of the square, where Route 7 is also called South Street, are two attractions that by themselves should lure any Berkshire visitor to Pittsfield: the Berkshire Museum and the restored Colonial Theatre.

As you look down South Street from the square you will see more spires reaching to the skies. The South Congregational Church, organized in 1850, is located at 110 South Street; the First Baptist Church is at 88 South Street.

Just across Route 7 at 111 South is a 21st-century success story, the restored **Colonial Theatre**, built in 1903.

Just about every name performer of the early 20th century played the Colonial. Touring productions included Ethel and John Barrymore. Sarah Bernhardt appeared here several times, and so did Douglas Fairbanks. The famed Irish tenor John McCormack sang at the Colonial. The Ziegfeld Follies appeared here in 1928.

David J. McLaughlin

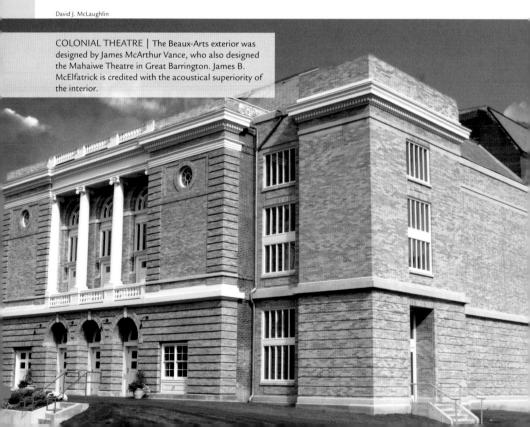

COLONIAL THEATRE | The Beaux-Arts exterior was designed by James McArthur Vance, who also designed the Mahaiwe Theatre in Great Barrington. James B. McElfatrick is credited with the acoustical superiority of the interior.

SOUNDING BOARD

This jewel of a playhouse had near-perfect acoustics. A sounding board painted with a mural representing music and art hung over the main audience area. The original color scheme was quite Victorian.

The Colonial fell on hard times during the Depression. For a while (1937–49), it survived as a movie theater, but it was then closed. The theater was saved from demolition by George Miller, who purchased the Colonial in 1952, boarding up (and thus preserving) most of the original theater while using the front of the building for his paint and art supply business.

The Colonial was fully restored in 2006 and is now again an inviting performance venue. Perhaps more than any other single event, the rebirth of the Colonial has revitalized Pittsfield's downtown.

Every visitor to the Berkshires should check the theater's extensive website and "do the Colonial." While you are at it, have dinner in the city, where there are a number of restaurants.

Thaddeus Clapp House, *at 74 Wendell Avenue, is located in the historic district of Pittsfield, offering easy access to downtown restaurants, museums, and theaters. This 1871 residence was converted to an* *upscale B&B in 2002, with eight suites, each named for an historic figure associated with Pittsfield. www. clapphouse.com | 413-499-6840*

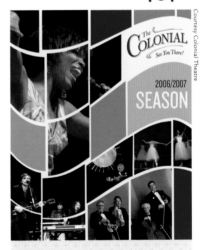

www.thecolonialtheatre.org
TICKET OFFICE (413) 997-4444

COLONIAL POSTER

Colonial Theatre
111 South St.
Pittsfield, MA 01201
413-997-4444
www.thecolonialtheatre.org

Berkshire Museum

A few steps farther down South Street is the **Berkshire Museum**, one of the most interesting museums in Berkshire County. It was opened the same year as the Colonial, in 1903, as the Museum of Natural History and Art, when it became apparent that there simply wasn't enough space in the Athenaeum to fulfill that institution's ambitious charter.

David J. McLaughlin

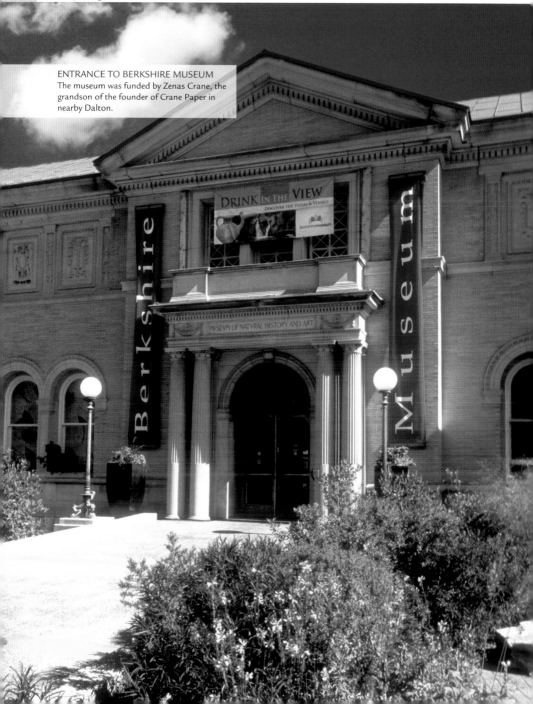

ENTRANCE TO BERKSHIRE MUSEUM
The museum was funded by Zenas Crane, the grandson of the founder of Crane Paper in nearby Dalton.

The museum has been careful to update its facilities and expand the range of its offerings over the last century. In 1935 the museum converted its original central courtyard to a theater and built galleries on the second floor. It was then able to better display its extensive collections, which range from art of the ancient world to an impressive collection of Hudson River School paintings and ever-changing natural science displays. At the lower level of the museum, an aquarium features both local and exotic species. One of the most original collections is an interactive exhibit that showcases original wooden "push and pull" toys created by Alexander Calder in 1927.

The tradition of innovation at the Berkshire Museum continues with the new Feigenbaum Hall of Innovation, which opened in 2008. This latest gallery features interactive exhibits of local innovators, from science and business to arts and culture.

ART OF THE ANCIENT WORLD

Say hello to Wally as you enter the museum.

The Berkshire Museum is open Mondays–Saturdays, 10 A.M. to 5 P.M., and on Sundays from 12 to 5 P.M. It is closed most major holidays.

Berkshire Museum
39 South St., Pittsfield
413-443-7171
www.berkshiremuseum.org

WALLY | Wally, a life-sized model of a stegosaurus, was installed outside the museum in 1997. It is a version of a dinosaur created for the Sinclair Dinoland Pavilion of the 1964–65 World's Fair, sculpted by Louis Paul Jonas.

MUSEUM GALLERY

SOUTH MOUNTAIN CONCERT HALL

South of City Center

One of my favorite sculptures in this region is the **Soldiers and Sailors Monument** at Colt Road and Veterans Way in Pittsfield. To reach the monument, which honors the city's veterans from all wars, you turn east on Broad Street (as if you were going to Knesset Israel), then make two right-hand turns. The monument, erected in 1929, features life-sized statues of men from all branches of the service who served their county and country in World War I.

The "War to End All Wars" has special significance to Pittsfield. One of its sons won the Congressional Medal of Honor as commander of the "Lost Battalion" during that war. Lt. Col. Charles W. Whittlesey (1844–1921) grew up in Pittsfield and graduated from nearby Williams College. His battalion was cut off during the battle of Argonne Forest in October 1918. By the time they were rescued, only 194 of the original 550 men were alive and uninjured.

Route 7 south of Pittsfield has changed a lot in the 20th century. Berkshire Life Insurance Company moved its headquarters here from downtown to get "out in the country"; farther south an array of shops, motels, and restaurants lines Route 7, including the very convenient Guido's Fresh Marketplace at 1010 South Street.

However, there are two important historic sites here. **The Country Club of Pittsfield** is located at 639 South Street, across from Berkshire Life. The main part of the clubhouse is an historic structure built in 1785 by Henry Van Schaack of Kinderhook, New York.

Another place of considerable importance in the history of the Berkshires is also here, hidden away on South Mountain. In 1918, decades before Tanglewood, a remarkable woman, Elizabeth Sprague Coolidge, built a concert hall on South Mountain and pioneered a series of chamber music concerts that continue to this day. The hall, built in a colonial style from timber salvaged from an old textile mill, has impeccable acoustics. You won't have a more pleasant Sunday afternoon in the fall than attending one of the **South Mountain Concerts** performances, which feature both string quartets and individual performers.

The entrance up the mountain is on Routes 7 and 20, just about 2 miles south of Park Square, on the west side of the highway. A sign reads "South Mountain Western Region." There is a wooden panel at the bottom with white lettering that reads "South Mountain Concerts."

David J. McLaughlin >

South Mountain Concerts
Routes 7 and 20, Pittsfield
413-442-2106
www.southmountainconcerts.org/concerts.html

SOLDIERS AND SAILORS MONUMENT | The statue was created by an American sculptor Henry August Lukeman (1871–1935). Lukeman studied under both Daniel Chester French, of Chesterwood fame, and Launt Thompson, who created the Civil War monument on Pittsfield's square.

Herman Melville's Arrowhead

The most famous destination in south Pittsfield is, of course, **Arrowhead**, the home of Herman Melville from 1850–1863. You reach the historic home by turning east off Route 7 onto Holmes Road (at the traffic signal). Arrowhead is 1.5 miles down this road, on the left side.

The Berkshire Historical Society acquired Arrowhead in 1975 and has been diligently restoring this historic property. Its appearance now more closely resembles the way it looked in Melville's day, with an authentic 1850s front door, a piazza (porch) Melville added on the north side of the house, a cedar shake roof, and the same paint coloring.

Herman Melville (1819–1891) was only 13 when he first visited his uncle, Major Thomas Melville of Pittsfield, and fell in love with the Berkshires. At the time Thomas Melville owned the mansion that is now the core of the Country Club of Pittsfield. Melville visited his uncle regularly, and in 1850 he and his family spent all summer at his uncle's farm, during which time he became friends with Nathaniel Hawthorne and Oliver Wendell Holmes, both of whom had homes in the Berkshires. He impulsively decided to buy an old farmhouse that had been built in 1780 and move to the solitude of the Berkshires where he could farm, raise a family (three of his children were born there), and write.

Arrowhead contains Melville artifacts and family heirlooms as well as furnishings appropriate to the time period.

CHINA DISPLAY IN DINING ROOM

HOME OF HERMAN MELVILLE

THE MELVILLE STUDY | The highlight of any visit is the study, now fully restored, where Herman Melville wrote *Moby Dick*.

Jim McElholm

MELVILLE BARN

The barn at the back of the property now contains a gift shop. Melville was serious about farming and cultivated several vegetable gardens on the property.

Herman Melville's Arrowhead is open daily (except Thursday) from Memorial Day weekend to Columbus Day, from 10:30 A.M. to 4:00 P.M. Hourly tours start at 11:00 A.M., with the last tour at 3:00 P.M. Tours of Arrowhead are available in the off-season by appointment only.

The **Berkshire Historical Society** (www. berkshirehistory.org) is headquartered at Arrowhead, where the Margaret H. Hall Local History Library and Archives has a collection of over 4,500 local history artifacts.

Research assistants are typically available on Tuesday mornings. It is advisable to call in advance, particularly if you want to have access to the library and archives.

Herman Melville's Arrowhead
780 Holmes Road
Pittsfield, MA 01201
413-442-1793
www.mobydick.org

Courtesy Berkshire Historical Society

VINTAGE CLOTHING FROM THE
HISTORICAL SOCIETY COLLECTION

_180

The Lakes of Pittsfield

Pittsfield has two of the prettiest lakes in Berkshire County. The 617-acre **Onota Lake** lies completely within the city boundaries. It was originally 486 acres but was enlarged in 1864 to serve as a town reservoir. A hill on the southwestern shore was fortified during the French & Indian Wars. This is now a popular boating, swimming, and fishing spot. The average depth is 22 feet. Portions of the lake, particularly the coves, can be weedy because of the excessive growth of aquatic plants, an infestation that is being combated by the city and the Lake Onota Preservation Association.

There is a boat ramp on the southeast shore of Onota Lake and a well-sited fishing pier that offers a chance for average fisherpersons to land one of a very diverse array of fish. (Some 20 species have been caught here, including trophy-size brown trout.) Onota Lake is home to the Berkshire Rowing and Sculling Society, founded in 1995 (www.berkshiresculling.com).

Pontoosuc Lake, which Pittsfield shares with Lanesborough, is a 480-acre pond that also has convenient public access, ample stocks of fish, and a scenic park on the south shore, which offers great views of the lake. According to my Berkshire friends, this is a very popular spot

Henry Dondi

for ice fishing, where the goal is to catch tiger muskies, regularly stocked in the lake since 1980. The Pontoosuc Lake Country Club is nearby and has an 18-hole golf course open to the public.

If you don't have time to fully explore these lakes, do pull off Route 7 into the ample parking lot along Pontoosuc Lake and admire the view, which is particularly enticing in the fall.

SAILING ON ONOTA LAKE

FALL FOLIAGE REFLECTIONS

Other Outdoor Attractions

There are several places in Pittsfield that will appeal to outdoor enthusiasts: Canoe Meadows Wildlife Sanctuary, Pittsfield State Forest, and the Bousquet Ski Area. Planning is also underway to extend the Ashuwillticook Rail Trail, whose terminus is now located just north of the city (see page 249 in Chapter 13 for the trail's history).

The **Canoe Meadows Wildlife Sanctuary** is a 264-acre Massachusetts Audubon Society property that borders the Housatonic River and offers three miles of nature trails. There is an observation area over a beaver wetland from which you can watch these industrious creatures. Canoe Meadows is open Tuesdays–Sundays from 7:00 A.M. to dusk. You reach the entrance by taking Holmes Road 2.7 miles past Arrowhead. Additional information is available at the Canoe Meadows Website (www.massaudubon.org/Nature_Connection/Sanctuaries/Canoe_Meadows/index.php).

Programs are available at Audubon's larger Pleasant Valley Wildlife Sanctuary in Lenox.

Pittsfield State Forest, noted for its stunning azalea display at the summit in mid-June, extends over some 10,000 acres of Pittsfield, Lanesborough, and Hancock. There are 30 miles of trails, including one three-quarter-mile paved stretch (Tranquility Trail) that offers wheelchair access. The Cascade Street (west of Onota Lake) entrance in Pittsfield is on the left-hand side of the road. Pittsfield State Forest includes two special attractions. Berry Pond (in Hancock) is the highest natural body of water in Massachusetts, at 2,150 feet. When conditions are right the top of Berry Mountain is one of the best places in the Berkshires to watch the sun set. There are 13 rustic campsites. Balance Rock, in Balance Rock State Park, within the forest, features a 165-ton limestone bolder miraculously poised upon bedrock. We will visit that park in Chapter 11.

The **Bousquet Ski Area** is a fun family ski resort established in 1935. It offers 21 trails evenly divided by skill level, with one 5,280 foot trail. The vertical drop is 750 feet. Bousquet is popular among families because of its convenient location, excellent snow, and well-regarded training school. In summer it offers aquatic entertainment.

Other Notable Places

Pittsfield has a special place in the heart of baseball enthusiasts. In 1892 George W. Burbank created the country's first baseball stadium, **Wahconah Park**, in downtown Pittsfield. Lou Gehrig made his professional baseball debut at this park in 1924, playing for the Hartford Senators (he hit a home run into the Housatonic River). Satchel Paige, Ted Williams, and a host of other baseball notables played here. In 2005 the park became the home stadium of the Pittsfield Dukes. An information-packed Website is available at www. wahconahpark.com. Pittsfield was also the site of the first intercollegiate baseball game in the United States, in 1859. Williams College played Amherst College in a 26-inning marathon. Amherst won.

THOMAS COLT HOUSE

Jim McElholm

There is evidence that baseball was played in Pittsfield well before it was "invented" by Abner Doubleday in Cooperstown, New York, in 1839. In 2004 an historian uncovered a 1791 Pittsfield town bylaw prohibiting anyone from playing "baseball" within 80 yards of the town's meeting house. The so-called Broken Window Bylaw is the earliest known reference to "baseball" in North America.

One of the country's leading preparatory schools for women is located in Pittsfield. **Miss Hall's School** (492 Holmes Road) was founded in 1898 by Mira Hinsdale Hall. The main campus of **Berkshire Community College** is also in Pittsfield, at 1350 West Street (phone: 413-499-4660).

Of course the city itself has any number of historic properties. The **Thomas Colt House** (42 Wendell Avenue) is a stately mansion that is now owned by the Women's Club of the Berkshires (413-447-7641), an active community organization and center. One of the best ways to enjoy some of the residential architecture and elegant gardens of Pittsfield is to take the Garden Tours organized each July (www.pittsfieldgardentour.org).

Another Pittsfield institution that will interest anyone doing genealogy research is the **Silvio O. Conte National Archives and Records Administration** complex located on 10 Conte Drive (413-236-3600). This regional center (one of 13) was established in 1994 to facilitate access to microfilm copies of federal records of high research value. It is named for Pittsfield native and 16-term Congressman Silvio O. Conte. While vital records (birth, marriage, death) are best found at the Pittsfield Library, the Conte National Archives is the place to come for federal records ranging from immigrant passenger lists to records of military service. It is reached via Dan Fox Drive, off Routes 7-20, two miles south of Park Square.

The **Hebert Arboretum** is a relatively new arboretum, created in 1999. The Arboretum (located at Springside Park, at 874 North Street) displays a diverse collection of trees and other plants in formal landscapes and in a natural setting.

The Performing Arts

In addition to South Mountain Concerts and an expanding number of performing arts venues (including the Koussevitzky Arts Center at Berkshire Community College as well as the Colonial Theatre), several important arts groups are headquartered in Pittsfield.

The **Albany Berkshire Ballet** was organized in 1960 in Pittsfield as the Cantarella School of Dance, renamed the Berkshire Ballet Company in 1975. It evolved into a full-time professional ballet company. In 1989 the ballet expanded again and established offices in both Pittsfield and Albany as the Albany Berkshire Ballet. Under the leadership of founder and artistic director Madeline Cantarella Culpo, the company performs classical and contemporary dance. In the Berkshires they have performed at the Koussevitzky Arts Center, Jacob's Pillow, and the Clark Art Institute. For information on this impressive regional dance company, visit their website at www.berkshireballet.org.

Another Pittsfield performing art institution is the **Berkshire Lyric Theatre**, which presents choral repertoire each year from September to June, typically in Berkshire churches such as Trinity Church in Lenox and the Congregational Church in Stockbridge. The Berkshire Lyric Theatre was founded in 1963 by Robert P. Blafield. A Children's Chorus performs and practices at the Berkshire

Courtesy Berkshire Opera Company

ANDREW GANGESTAD IN *MADAMA BUTTERFLY*

Athenaeum. For further information, visit www.berkshirelyrictheatre.org (413-448-0258).

The **Berkshire Opera Company** was founded in 1985 by Rex Hearn to bring professional, fully staged opera to the Berkshires. It is the only professional opera company performing in Massachusetts during the summer months. In 1999 BOC launched a Resident Artist program, an intensive training program for young singers and pianists. The organization's commitment is to become the "premier vocal music storyteller in the United States." Since 2003 the Berkshire Opera Company has been based in Pittsfield (297 North Street). Over the years BOC has performed at many venues in the Berkshires. The 2008 program will be held at the Mahaiwe Performing Arts Center in Great Barrington and the Colonial Theatre in Pittsfield. For further information, visit www.berkshireopera.org (413-443-9279).

Kevin Sprague

< ALBANY BERKSHIRE BALLET PERFORMANCE OF *NUTCRACKER*

The **Town Players** (413-443-9279), one of the oldest community theaters in the country, performs at the Koussevitzky Arts Center of Berkshire Community College from October through May.

Since 1995 the **Barrington Stage Company** (30 Union Street) has produced award-winning plays and musicals, focusing on new productions of undiscovered works. Their world-premiere performance of The *25th Annual Putnam County Spelling Bee* in 2004 was a huge success. The show went on to Broadway, where it captured two Tony Awards and three Drama Desk Awards. After performing at the Consolati Performing Arts Center in Sheffield for 11 years, the group acquired and renovated an old vaudeville hall in Pittsfield in 2005–2006 and now has a permanent home. The Barrington Stage Company also runs Kids Act, a training program for 10- to 17-year-olds. For further information and tickets, call 413-499-5446 or visit www.barringtonstageco.org.

CITY SILHOUETTE

Jim McElholm

COLONIAL THEATRE

The economy in Pittsfield has been in transition for decades. The population peaked in the late 1960s and has gradually declined from 58,000 to under 45,000. However, this city, with its proud legacy and innovative people, is revitalizing its downtown, restoring historic venues such as the Colonial Theatre, and launching new events, while magnet attractions like the Berkshire Museum, Arrowhead, and Hancock Shaker Village (covered in the next chapter) get better each year.

ADDITIONAL RESOURCES

The History of Pittsfield, Massachusetts, by J. E. A. Smith, Lee and Shepard: Boston. Published in two volumes. Volume One, published in 1869, covers the years 1734–1800. Volume Two, published in 1876, covers the years 1800–1876. Modern reprints are available. The definitive early history of this historic town.

The History of Pittsfield, Massachusetts, from the Year 1876 to the Year 1916, by Edward Boltwood, Eagle Printing and Binding: Pittsfield, 1916, 387 pages. Covers 40 years of growth and change, during which Pittsfield became the first Berkshire County city.

The History of Pittsfield, Massachusetts, 1916–1955, by George F. Willison, Pittsfield: Sun Printing Corporation, 1957. Updates the town history during a time of significant economic growth and expansion.

Pittsfield, Massachusetts (Images of America Series), by Susan Eisley, Arcadia Publishing, 2001. An interesting pictorial history; well researched.

Pontoosuc Lake: The Railways Ride to It, by J. E. A. Smith, William Nugent Publishers, 1890. An enjoyable recounting of what it was like to take the trolley to Pontoosuc Lake more than 100 years ago.

Pittsfield: Gem City in the Gilded Age, by Carole Owens, History Press, 2007. Covers the central role of Pittsfield during the Gilded Age years 1865–1917. Generously illustrated with vintage and contemporary photographs.

The Heart of the Berkshires: Pittsfield ... Where Legends Begin, by Phyllis Kerle, 2006. A concise, 115-page contemporary retelling of the history of the city.

A UNIQUE JOURNEY
The Shaker Experience

The Berkshire region was the spiritual and organizational center of an unusual religious movement called the Shakers. This special chapter tells the story of the Shaker communities in Tyringham (active from 1792–1874); at **Mount Lebanon** (1787–1947), just across the border in Columbia County, New York; and at **Hancock Shaker Village** (1790–1960). This chapter describes a journey in time more than in space. It is more a story of why rather than where.

The Arrival of the Shakers

On August 6, 1774, a "straight and well proportioned in form … majestic looking woman" from Manchester, England, disembarked at the port of New York, accompanied by a reluctant husband, her brother, and seven followers, all of them members of a religious sect known as the United Society of Believers in Christ's Second

Appearing. Within two years Mother Ann Lee (1736–1784), whose charisma and strength of character made her a natural leader, moved to upper New York State with a core group of Believers (not including Abraham Stanley, her husband, who disappeared from history). They settled into a communal way of life in Niskayuna, in the township of Watervliet, near Albany, where they built log cabins in the wilderness, grew crops, and worshipped. Word of this new religion spread and by 1780 there were converts and many more prospects. Interest was particularly strong in New Lebanon, some 40 miles southeast of Niskayuna, and in the Berkshire region of Massachusetts.

The sect became known as the Shaking Quakers, later shortened to **Shakers**, because of the violent shaking, singing, shouting, dancing, and prophesying they manifested during their religious services.

SHAKERS DANCING | This N. Currier lithograph, published and widely circulated in 1870, is based on a "drawing from life" by Anthony Imber, c. 1830.

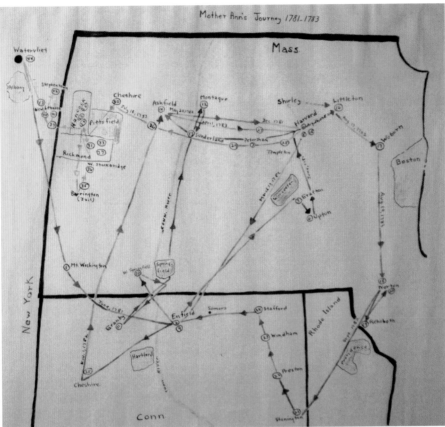

MAP OF MOTHER ANN'S JOURNEYS | During this trip Mother Ann stayed for a month in the Hancock area. During her stay she and her followers were beaten and harassed by local mobs.

Shaker Museum and Library

The Shakers believed in racial and gender equality, celibacy, and pacifism (not a popular belief in 1776, at the beginning of the Revolutionary War). They were committed to establishing "heaven on earth." They challenged prevailing ideas about worship, marriage, and family.

Improbably, over the next 50 years the Shakers became one of the most successful (and ultimately the longest-lived) utopian religious communities in the nation. Although the total Shaker population never exceeded 6,000, the movement had a profound impact that persists to this day—not only because of the Shakers' splendid architecture, crafts, and furniture design, but in the compelling testimony of the simple but remarkably industrious lives of its members.

Development of the Shaker Communities

Encouraged by the growing interest in the Shaker way of life, Mother Ann and a number of the society's elders began an extensive missionary journey through New York, Massachusetts, and Connecticut in 1781, visiting their followers and spreading the word. In their wake, small bands of Believers began to meet and hold services in their homes. By 1786 several families in Hancock had consolidated their possessions and started construction of a meeting house. (By 1795 this practice would be formalized with a written covenant requiring the holding of goods in common.)

Mother Ann died in 1784 at age of 48, but a succession of strong leaders, particularly Joseph Meacham (1742–1796) and Lucy Wright (1760–1821), refined the guiding principles of the society and systematized its organization. The seat of spiritual authority moved to New Lebanon. Ultimately, 19 independent and highly productive communities extended from Indiana to Maine and as far south as Kentucky.

The early Shaker settlements were agrarian communities with large herds of cattle. To facilitate their dairy operations, the communities built remarkable barns whose distinctive design still evokes admiration. The famous "round barn" in Hancock, built in 1826, has survived. The ruins of the four-story barn at Mount Lebanon still dominate the landscape in the former North Family section of Mount Lebanon.

The Shakers were very industrious. They were among the first in the area to harness water power for grist mills and sawmills and for carding and fulling mills. They extracted iron ore and fashioned the hardware seen on their distinctive buildings. They ran broom shops and an extensive seed business. They made much of their own furniture, not only chairs, tables, and beds but washstands, sewing boxes, and even clocks.

The Shakers were also quite inventive. The ladder-back chair the Shakers of Mount Lebanon designed received a medal at the 1876 Philadelphia Centennial Exhibition for combining "strength, sprightliness, and modest beauty." The Shakers obtained a U.S. patent for a ball-and-socket chair-tilter—the precursor for that found in many types of chairs today.

Artist Unknown

HANCOCK SHAKER VILLAGE, 1860 | This drawing is labeled "East View of Brick House, Church Family." It was exhibited in 2000–2001 at a Hancock Shaker Village special exhibition, "Seen and Received: The Shakers' Private Art."

Historic American Buildings Survey

ROUND BARN AT HANCOCK SHAKER VILLAGE, C. 1935

STONE BARN AT MOUNT LEBANON

Library of Congress

Their architecture, furniture, and decorative arts had clean lines and brilliantly manifested the traditional Shaker values of simplicity, utility, and fine craftsmanship. Shaker became a compelling brand name. Shaker chairs were sold through department stores such as Marshall Field & Co., and dozens of products were available in widely distributed catalogs.

As the railroads began to bring more and more travelers to the Berkshires in the last half of the 19th century, visiting the Shaker Village at Hancock became one of the main attractions on a trip along the Western Railroad. The Shakers, whose ranks contained more than a few astute businesspeople, did a thriving business at their Hancock store. Particularly popular items included rocking chairs (made at Mount Lebanon), rugs, brooms, dolls, and capes.

Ironically, the number of Shakers steadily declined in these years.

The celibate Shaker communities grew in the late 1700s and early 1800s by attracting new Believers. Their continuity also benefited from their practice of accepting orphans and abandoned children into their communities, many of whom embraced the Shaker religion and form of life as adults. The movement

SHAKER TOOTHACHE PELLETS

David J. McLaughlin

SHAKER APPLE SAUCE

peaked in the 1840s. At Hancock there was still a sizable population of 217 Shakers living in six families in 1846. However, a growing number of "seceders," the advent of the U.S. Civil War, the state assumption of responsibility for orphans, and less effective leadership resulted, according to John Ott, in "an almost continual decline" over the next century from this 1846 high-water mark. A major blow to the Shaker presence in the Berkshires came in 1874 when the Shaker settlement in Tyringham closed.

David J. McLaughlin

< SHAKER STORE SIGN | This sign is from the Shaker Museum and Library collection.

Courtesy of National Register of Historic Places

CHURCH FAMILY COMPLEX AT JERUSALEM | This image was taken about 20 years after the community closed in 1874, when most of the buildings were still intact, including the Ox Barn, Cobbler's Shop, Dairy House, Meeting House, and Seed House and Seed-Drying Houses.

Library of Congress

SHAKER DAM BUILT IN 1832 | The water harnessed by the Shakers powered woodworking equipment (saws, lathes, planers, and so on) and even a cider press.

The Rise and Fall of Tyringham

The Shaker Community in Tyringham, known as Jerusalem by local residents, was formally established in 1792. The spiritual name for the community was "City of Love." Tyringham consisted of three family complexes: the North, Church, and South Family buildings, which were evenly spaced in half-mile increments along Jerusalem Road, overlooking Tyringham Valley. When David Field and Chester Dewey's *A History of Berkshire County* was published in 1829, they reported that these Shakers' "number for several years has been about 100."

The Tyringham Shaker Community was more isolated than Hancock or Mount Lebanon. It remained an agrarian community, particularly noted for its seeds. The Shakers here were particularly effective in building dams to provide power for the community.

In 1858, 23 young adults left the community. The remaining Shakers all left by 1874, moving to the communities at Hancock, Mount Lebanon, and Enfield, Connecticut. The land and buildings were sold, and over the years many of the buildings that existed were lost. The structures that remain are all in private hands.

The best visual record we have of Jerusalem are photographs taken in 1935–1936 that are now part of the Historic American Buildings Survey collection of the Library of Congress, available online at http://memory.loc.gov/ammem/collections/habs_haer/.

BUILDINGS IN THE CHURCH FAMILY COMPLEX OF JERUSALEM, C. 1935 | The building on the right housed the administrative offices for the community.

Historic American Buildings Survey

THE OX BARN

Fortunately, many of the vital Shaker records, a substantial number of priceless artifacts, and a meaningful number of the core buildings at Mount Lebanon and Hancock have been preserved.

The best way to view these treasures involves a daylong journey that begins in Old Chatham, New York, about a half hour west of Lee, easily reached via Interstate 90 (the Mass Pike).

BARN INTERIOR

David J. McLaughlin

JOHN S. WILLIAMS HOME IN OLD CHATHAM

David J. McLaughlin

Shaker Museum and Library

The imminent disappearance of the Shakers was pretty apparent in the early decades of the 20th century, but who had time to worry about the preservation of their priceless heritage during the Great Depression and two world wars? Fortunately, one man did. Beginning in about 1940, John S. Williams (1901–1982) began to visit and develop relations with the surviving members of the Shaker leadership at Mount Lebanon (near where he lived in Old Chatham) and Hancock, just over the border. Ultimately he also forged close relationships with key Shakers in Canterbury, New Hampshire, and Sabbathday Lake in Maine, two other Shaker communities.

Williams began to collect objects from every facet of Shaker life. He obtained some of the finest furniture, baskets, oval boxes, and other artifacts from these communities, as well as the machinery, tools, and equipment they used.

In 1950 Williams established the **Shaker Museum and Library** in Old Chatham, an institution dedicated to preserving and interpreting the Shaker legacy for future generations and presenting a broad picture of Shaker life and culture.

The Museum and Library is open seasonally and (for research) year round by appointment. Its precious collections are well preserved but imperfectly displayed in mid-20th-century buildings that are showing their age. The Museum is now focused on the preservation and adaptation of 10 buildings and 30 acres of the North Family complex at Mount Lebanon, in preparation for building a new museum at that site and moving their entire operation there. They received a Save America's Treasures grant in 2001 to create a master plan for the North Family property and in 2004 they acquired the site.

< THE SHAKER MUSEUM AND LIBRARY | In 1962 the museum acquired a priceless collection of journals, printed material, manuscripts, and historic photographs that had been in the care of the Central Shaker Ministry.

SHAKER CHAIR SHOP

CARPENTRY SHOP AT MOUNT LEBANON

A visit to the existing Museum is a good way to start a day of Shaker discovery. The Museum has an excellent museum store, extensive displays, a particularly knowledgeable staff, and pleasant grounds.

The Shakers at nearby Mount Lebanon had extensive woodworking facilities, and much of their equipment is preserved in the Museum. The Shaker Museum and Library also houses an outstanding Shaker textile collection that includes dresses, cloaks, men's clothing, footwear, bonnets, silks, rugs, household fabrics, dolls, and accessories.

DISPLAY OF SHAKER CHAIRS | The chair collection at the Museum is unparalleled and includes every size and form of Shaker chair.

Mount Lebanon

It is a short 20-minute drive from Old Chatham to New Lebanon, the site of the buildings that remain from the North Family, Church Family, Center Family, Second Family, and South Family at **Mount Lebanon**. These buildings are now occupied by the Darrow School, an independent coed boarding school located at 110 Darrow Road. Route CR13 in Old Chatham leads directly to Route 20. The Darrow School is less than 7 miles to the east (see map).

The Mount Lebanon Shaker Society was the largest and most industrious of the Shaker communities. It operated from 1785 to 1947. The settlement was initially known as New Lebanon, for the town in which it was located, until 1861, when the Shakers got their own post office. In its peak years the community, organized into eight families, totaled some 600 members, several hundred buildings, and over 6,000 acres of land.

The Mount Lebanon community closed in 1947. The buildings and land were broken into sections and sold. Many historic buildings were lost. Fortunately in 1932 a group of Shakers, educational and community leaders in New Lebanon, had founded the Lebanon School for Boys, renamed the Darrow School in 1939, to honor the family that had first settled the land and provided support and leadership to the Shaker community in the difficult early years.

The Darrow School occupies the central site of **Mount Lebanon Shaker Village**, a National Historic Landmark District.

There are several notable structures that can be viewed during a tour, although the interiors are generally not yet open to the public.

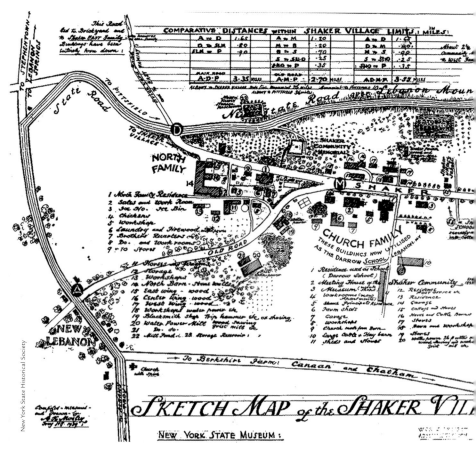

New York State Historical Society

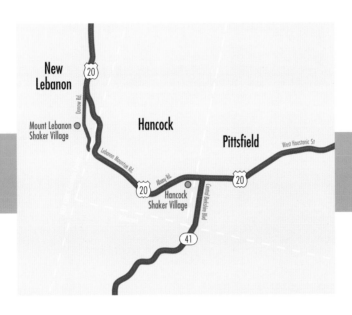

LAYOUT OF MOUNT LEBANON

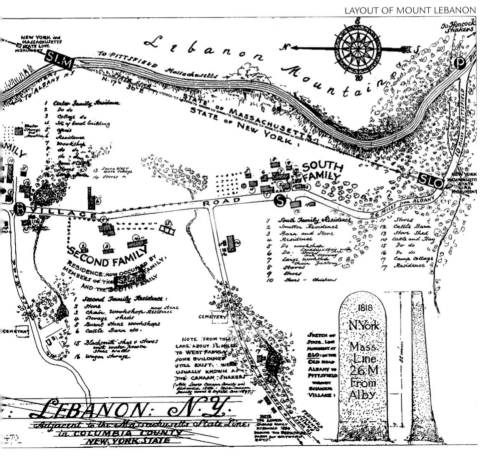

MEETING HOUSE AT MOUNT LEBANON, C. 1932 | A larger second meeting house was built in 1824, which is the building you see today. The vast meeting room (28.4 feet by 63 feet) has no interior supports.

Meeting Houses (1785 and 1824)

The first meeting house at Mount Lebanon, built in 1785, was not only the first Shaker-built building at Mount Lebanon but also the first Shaker meeting house in America. In 1824, the Shakers built a new meeting house with a unique arched-truss roof designed to allow for a large uninterrupted space in the sanctuary for the dancing the Shakers did during their worship. The old meeting house was converted to a workshop. It still stands as the home of Darrow's Head of School.

The Shaker meeting houses had several doors. At the south entrance of the second meeting house at Mount Lebanon, the Sisters entered on the left, Brethren on the right, and the Ministry through the center door. Visitors who attended the weekly public service entered through doors along the street marked "Males" and "Females."

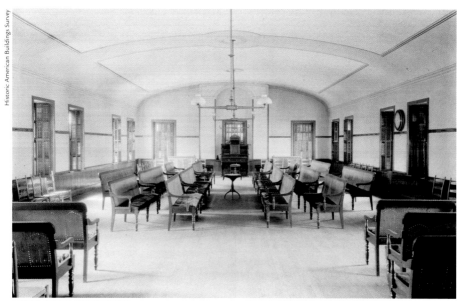

MEETING HOUSE INTERIOR

Great Stone Barn (1859)

The North Family **Great Stone Barn** (1859) was a massive four-story structure that measured 50 feet wide and nearly 200 feet long. In 1972 the barn was totally gutted by a fire, leaving only its four massive masonry walls standing.

Other Notable Buildings

The Sisters' Shop was built about 1852. This building contained a store for sales to non-Shakers and was the center of spinning, weaving, knitting, and bonnet making in this industrious community.

The Shaker Brothers had a multistory workshop, built in 1829. It contained a waterwheel that powered their woodworking equipment as well as the society's laundry (which was in the basement) and a trip hammer in the adjacent blacksmith shop.

David J. McLaughlin

SISTERS' SHOP

Paul Rocheleau

RUINS OF GREAT STONE BARN | This was the largest stone barn in America.

David J. McLaughlin

TANNERY POND

The Shaker Tannery, built in 1834, has been restored and is now the Laflin Whitehead Chapel of the Darrow School. The **Tannery Pond Concerts** held here between May and October offer world-class chamber music at one of the most inviting locations in the Berkshire region. For information see www. tannerypondconcerts.org.

David J. McLaughlin

The full development of the North Family property at Mount Lebanon Shaker Village will take some time, but it is apparent that this site will add significantly to the number of restored former Shaker buildings that will be open to the public and will enhance the presentation of the important contributions made by the Shakers in the Berkshire region. Further information is available at www. shakermuseumandlibrary.org.

< BRETHREN'S WORKSHOP

AERIAL VIEW OF HANCOCK SHAKER VILLAGE

Hancock Shaker Village

Fortunately for all of us, unlike Tyringham, central portions of the **Shaker Village at Hancock**, the third Shaker community in America, have been preserved and are open to the public. The complex covers 1,200 acres along Route 20.

This is a living museum that contains a farm and animals, period gardens, and a discovery center where young visitors can practice Shaker crafts and even "milk" the replica of a cow.

The museum contains most of the important buildings that were part of the Church Family complex that had survived up to 1960. The South Family was dissolved in 1849 and the West Family in 1867, followed shortly by the North Family.

SHEEP ON THE MUSEUM GROUNDS

BRICK DWELLING HOUSE | The second and third floors housed the sleeping areas, where two to four members retired each night into their own rooms, the Brethren on the east and the Sisters on the west. >
David J. McLaughlin

The middle years of the 20th century were difficult for the Shakers as the population declined. During this period several important buildings were demolished, including the Meeting House in 1938 and the Shaker Store in 1958.

In 1960 a group of local citizens organized to purchase the remaining buildings and land and set to work creating the extensive "museum" that you experience today. There is ample parking just to the west of the Village, along Route 20. Access is through a modern Visitors Center, erected in 1972. This building has rest rooms, a café, and a large, inviting store.

Be prepared to walk the grounds. If you have children in tow you will find that they make a beeline for the first animals they see.

The grounds of Hancock Shaker Village have been imaginatively laid out to create an experience of what life must have been like in this tranquil setting. There is an Herb Garden and a mile-long farm and forest trail.

There are 20 original buildings on the 1,200 acres. Most have been restored, though the preservation and restoration work is ongoing.

Brick Dwelling House

Each Shaker family had a communal dormitory-style dwelling which was the center of community life. Some 100 Brothers and Sisters lived in the **Brick Dwelling House**, which contains sleeping quarters, a Believers' dining room, a kitchen, and meeting rooms. The Brethren ate in silence each day at 6:00 A.M., 12:00 noon, and 6:00 P.M. Daily worship was also conducted here.

< VIEW OF VILLAGE FROM GARDEN
Jim McElholm

Other Buildings

The **Sisters' Dairy and Weave Shop** was the first building in the museum to be restored. There was a dairy building on this site as early as 1795. Some time after 1820 a second story was added to hold a two-room weaving loft where the Sisters could busy themselves while waiting for the milk to arrive.

The **Tannery** housed the Shaker shoemakers. In the early years there were vats in the basement in which hides were soaked, rinsed, and leached; a processing room on the first floor where the leather was scraped, smoothed, and softened; and an area in the attic where hides were dried and stored.

By 1875 a commercial tannery in Pittsfield could produce leather more efficiently and cheaply than the Shakers, so this building was converted into a blacksmith shop and a cider room for pressing apples from the Shaker orchards.

Other buildings at Hancock Shaker Village include an 1894 Ice House (restored in 1972), the Shaker Schoolhouse, a Garden Tool Shed adjacent to the Herb Garden, and the Poultry House.

SISTERS' DAIRY AND WEAVE SHOP

BLACKSMITH AT WORK | There are engaging demonstrations of Shaker craftwork at several of the buildings. The blacksmith shop is one of the most popular.

ROUND STONE BARN

Round Stone Barn

The most notable structure at Hancock Shaker Village is the **Round Stone Barn**.

The Round Stone Barn is an architectural gem built in 1826. Its circular design (it is 170 feet in circumference) is unique. Hay was unloaded from wagons into a central storage area on the top floor. The cattle (52 head) were on the next level, hooked to posts. The manure pit was at the bottom, accessible by wagon.

WEAVING

The barn burned in 1864, but the wooden interior and roof were quickly rebuilt. The entire building was fully restored in 1968.

Discovery Center

The **Discovery Center** is a hands-on area where you can explore the Shaker way of life by "doing." There are looms, spinning wheels, and even a model cow to milk. The center also contains a collection of Shaker clothes to try on.

PRETEND MILKING >

"TREE OF LIFE," A SHAKER GIFT DRAWING BY HANNAH COHOON, 1854

Center for Shaker Studies

Hancock Shaker Village has a collection of some 22,000 items—furniture, tools and equipment, household objects, fascinating displays of commercial packaging of Shaker products, and an awesome collection of historic photographs and drawings.

In 2000, access for scholars was expanded with the creation of the **Center for Shaker Studies**. It includes two exhibition galleries open to the public, one of which is dedicated to Shaker "gift drawings."

There was a period in the late 1830s to late 1850s that Believers referred to as the Era of Spiritual Manifestations. During these years some gifted Shakers created inspirational drawings. About 200 of these "gift drawings" have survived. The largest collection of these is at Hancock Shaker Village. Reproductions are sold in the museum's gift shop.

Visiting Hancock Shaker Village

The Village is open year round. During the main season (Memorial Day to mid-October), the hours are 10:00 A.M. to 5:00 P.M. Tours are self-guided. In what the museum refers to as the "guided tour season" (late fall to mid-April), access is tied to guided tours, scheduled for 1:00 P.M. on weekdays and 11:00 A.M. and 1:00 P.M. on weekends. Be sure to call ahead in guided tour season, to be sure a tour is scheduled. The village has a spacious, well-lighted **Museum Store** (open year round) that offers handcrafted Shaker reproductions, some 20 books on the Shakers, fine-art prints, toys, and other intriguing merchandise. The **Florence Gould Café** is open during the peak season. There are frequent special events.

Hancock Shaker Village
1843 West Housatonic Street
Pittsfield, MA 01201
(Proceed to parking lot approx.
½ mile further west on Rt. 20)
413-443-0188
www.hancockshakervillage.org

The Shakers had a saying: "Hands to Work, Hearts to God." Their unique and inspiring way of life is carefully preserved in the Berkshire region. Be sure to devote at least a full day to discovering how richly they spent their time on earth.

ADDITIONAL RESOURCES

The Shaker Experience in America, by Stephen Stein, Yale University Press, 1992, 554 pages. The definitive scholarly study of the Shakers, tracing their history from their origins in England to the late 20th century.

Simple Wisdom: Shaker Sayings, Poems, and Songs, by Kathleen Mahoney, Penguin Press: New York, 1993. Captures the essence of the Shaker philosophy. Includes 45 full-color photographs.

David J. McLaughlin

Hancock Shaker Village: A Guidebook and History, by John H. Ott, 143 pages. This book, written by the former director of the museum, offers a brief history, descriptions of the buildings, and an extensive bibliography.

Testimonies of Life, Character, Revelations, and Doctrines of Our Ever Blessed Mother Ann Lee (Hancock, MA: 1816).

The Shaker Chair, by Timothy D. Rieman and Charles R. Muller, with line drawings by Stephen Metzger, University of Massachusetts Press: Amherst, MA, 1984. A comprehensive and authoritative study of the best-known Shaker product.

Shaker Historic Trail, at www.nps.gov/nr/travel/shaker/ index.htm. The National Park Service's excellent Website, which provides details on 15 Shaker communities, including nine that are open to the public.

A STILL-FUNCTIONING SHAKER DAM

CENTRAL BERKSHIRE TOWNS

Richmond, Lanesborough, and Dalton

These days the residential towns that surround Pittsfield are linked to the Berkshires' largest city by major state highways: Richmond immediately to the south, along Route 41; Lanesborough, the next town to the north of Pittsfield, along busy Route 7; and Dalton to the east, reached via Route 9. They each have a rich and quite diverse history and each is well worth exploring for its own special attractions.

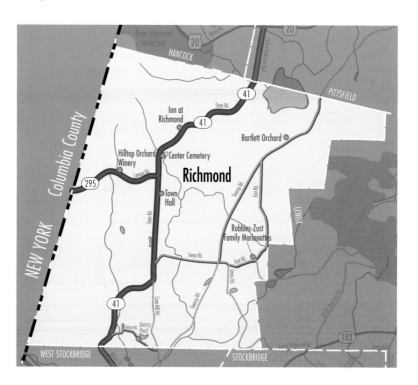

Richmond

Richmond was settled in 1760 and incorporated in 1765. This scenic town, known today for its rural ambience and progressive zoning, was an important center of Berkshire iron making in the 19th century. What started out as a smelting operation at Richmond Furnace, in the southwestern part of town, evolved into the **Richmond Iron Company**, which produced 12,000 tons of iron each year and employed about 700 men in 1885.

SPRING IN RICHMOND >
Paul Rocheleau

BATTLE OF *MONITOR* AND *MERRIMACK*

MANAGER'S HOUSE

The company mined several ore beds in Richmond and in West Stockbridge. There were Richmond Iron Company furnaces in Richmond, in the Van Deusenville section of Great Barrington, and in Cheshire.

Some of the iron went to the South Boston Gun Works, a facility that produced large guns for the *Monitor* class of ironclad warships.

Virtually all the forests around Richmond were cut and the trees used to make charcoal, essential for the iron-smelting process. Ultimately specially constructed wagons (which looked like "corn cribs on wheels," according to the local history) were sent into the mountains to bring back charcoal to the furnace.

The Richmond Iron Works closed in 1923 because of the development of the Bessemer process and competition from Midwestern ore beds, which had better access to coal and cheaper transportation costs. The former company manager's office has survived as a private residence.

< THE RICHMOND FURNACE | This large stone structure was completed and went into operation in 1829. It operated for about 100 years.

Historic Structures

One treasured legacy of the town's long prosperity is the housing stock, which includes a large number of well-preserved antique homes of all types, from early "salt box" style homes and two-story center-chimney colonials to handsome late 18th- and early 19th-century Georgian structures.

One stately Georgian was named **Goodwood** after the ancestral seat of the Duke of Richmond. It was built in 1792 by Pierson/Goodrich and purchased by Rev. Henry Willes Dwight as a wedding present for his wife, Mary Sherrill.

It is a pleasure to randomly turn down a side road in Richmond and discover a well-sited house tucked into the woods. This is a particularly pleasant experience at the peak of the fall foliage season.

*The main house at the **Inn at Richmond** (802 State Road), a charming B&B on Route 41, was built by Isaac Cook between 1774 and 1776. A barn on the property, originally part of the Shaker community at Hancock, was moved here in the 1930s. www.innatrichmond.com |*
413-698-2566

COLLINS – EDWARDS HOUSE, 1774

GOODWOOD

HOUSE IN FALL

NORTHEAST SCHOOLHOUSE, BUILT IN 1781

RICHMOND DEPOT IN 1857, BY JERUSHA PORTER WILLIAMS

A charming drawing of how the Richmond Depot section of the town looked in the middle of the 19th century has survived.

This is a community that cares about its past and its present. **The Richmond Civic Association** was founded in 1947 and the **Richmond Land Trust** in 1989. The town has had an **Historical Society** since 1992.

The Historical Society now owns the **Northeast Schoolhouse**, one of the town's remaining district schoolhouses. At present, access to the interior has to be scheduled, with the primary emphasis on educational groups. The schoolhouse, which has been renovated several times, is located at 961 Osceola Road Extension.

Cemetery Carvings

Just south of the Richmond Inn, along Route 41, is the **Center Cemetery**, which contains a number of late 18th-century tombstones carved with a unique form of "soul effigies." It was common in New England to decorate tombstones with "representative" images of the deceased, winged angels and other figures. The practice began to die out after the 1800s and the Berkshires region, which was settled much later than the rest of Massachusetts, has relatively few of these carved tombstones.

The Richmond carvings are distinctive. They resemble 20th-century cartoon characters. Michael Bathrick, who has identified 35 gravestones in Berkshire County decorated with what he calls "Lulu carvings," attributes them to two Richmond carvers who emigrated from the Connecticut Valley, where this style originated. Mr. Bathrick's study of the carvings is online at www.berkshireweb.com/plexus/graveyards/rip.html.

Don't miss a stop at one of the Richmond cemeteries. Over 70 percent of all of these special carvings are in Richmond—19 at the Center Cemetery, 10 in the Northeast Cemetery of Richmond, and 6 in the Cone Hill Cemetery.

David J. McLaughlin

< GRAVESTONE IN CENTER CEMETERY

CURTAIN AT TOWN HALL | The local artist who painted this scene in the 1920s was Albert Sterner.

Excursions and Discoveries

Although Richmond's **town hall**, built in 1923, is rather ordinary, it contains a massive hand-painted curtain that captures the spirit and beauty of the town. The Richmond Grange staged plays here in the early decades of the 20th century.

There are two orchards in town. **Bartlett's Orchard** (575 Swamp Road) was founded in 1947. This 52-acre orchard is still owned and managed by the Bartlett family. There is an appealing farm stand that offers locally grown vegetables, bakery goods and country gifts. You can pick your own apples from Labor Day to Columbus Day. Be sure to see the cider press, which you can view through glass windows. Visit www.bartlettorchard.com for more information.

Hilltop Orchards (508 Canaan Road - Route 295) not only offers delicious apples at its 200-acre property (pick your own apples, pears, and plums), but the complex contains the first farm winery in the Berkshires, **Furnace Brook Winery**. The entrepreneurial owners offer cross-country skiing in the winter months and celebrate the renewal of spring with an Apple Blossom Bash in May. For further information, check www.hilltoporchards.com or phone 800-833-6274.

A great place to find pumpkins is **Clark's Clover Hill Farm** at 81 State Road.

Richmond Pond is a center of summer fun for the town residents. This 226-acre manmade pond contains the town beach (on the

northwest shore) and a boat ramp. There is a Girl Scout camp (Camp Marion White), summer cabins, and some homes along the shore. The pond is stocked and trout fishing is particularly good.

Richmond still has a rural feel. This is a town where you want to wander the back-country roads.

SUMMER FUN

The Performing Arts

The Music Works in the Berkshires was organized as the community-based Richmond Performance Series in 1985. Under the artistic direction of Mark Ludwig, the group presents world-class chamber music at convenient locations throughout the region. In addition to the classics, MWB commissions and premieres new works. They also provide artist residencies and collaborate with the Berkshire Music School, the Berkshire Institute for Lifetime Learning, public television station WMHT, and Bard College at Simon's Rock to support music education and appreciation. To learn more, visit www.musicworksberkshires.org or phone 413-698-2002.

THE PUPPETS

David J. McLaughlin

A very different form of entertainment is offered by the Richmond–based **Robbins–Zust Marionettes**, a talented group of puppeteers who have performed for families, churches, schools, and groups all over the Northeast since 1971. Using an extensive collection of their own handcrafted puppets, they perform the classic tales that appeal to children (and all the young at heart), from *Cinderella* and *Beauty and the Beast* to *Winnie the Pooh*. Robbins-Zust has scheduled performances in July and August at the Guthrie Center in Great Barrington. See www.berkshireweb.com/zust/ or phone 413-698-2591.

A Hidden Gem

In 1995 the Richmond Land Trust and the Berkshire Natural Resources Council were given 128 acres of very special Berkshires land that lay in Richmond and West Stockbridge. Lenox Mountain Brook flows over the property through **Stevens Glen**, tumbling down a 40-foot drop and over a series of cascades through a narrow gorge. Stevens Glen was a premier sightseeing attraction in the late 19th century and early 1900s. In about 1884 the farmer who owned the land at that time, Romanzo Stevens, began to build a series of bridges and platforms from which you could view the falls ... for 25 cents a head. The elite of the carriage trade from Lenox, Stockbridge, and Pittsfield would flock here to enjoy nature and picnic. There was even a covered dance pavilion until it collapsed in 1919.

Access to Stevens Glen is on Lenox Branch Road, 1.5 miles from the center of West Stockbridge, near the Richmond–West Stockbridge border. The entrance is on the north side of the road. For further information on this and other special properties in the area, see www.bnrc.net.

David J. McLaughlin

ALONG EAST ROAD

Lanesborough

In 1741 the General Court of Massachusetts granted a 6-square-mile block of wilderness to Samuel Jackson and 75 others from the Framingham area. The first three settlers arrived about 1754 to settle "New Framingham," first known as Richfield, but were driven out by marauding Indians during the waning years of the French & Indian Wars. The first meeting of settlers was held in 1759 at a fort erected during the hostilities. **Lanesborough** was incorporated in 1765.

Today Lanesborough is beautifully sited in a well-watered valley created by the hills and mountains of the Taconic and the Hoosac spur of the Green Mountain ranges. Historic Route 7 leads directly to the town center.

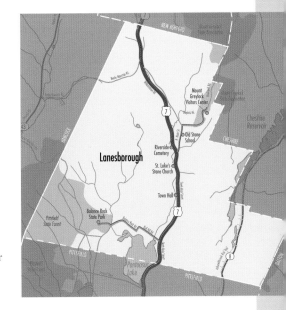

Paul Rocheleau

LOOKING NORTH ON PONTOOSUC LAKE | This 480-acre lake is shared with Pittsfield. This image was taken from the park on the south end of the lake.

As you cross the Pittsfield–Lanesborough border, Route 7 passes along the shores of **Pontoosuc Lake**, offering an enticing view of this splendid lake and mighty Mount Greylock in the distance.

Pittsfield State Forest extends into the southwest portion of Lanesborough, where a natural curiosity, a 165-ton, 25-foot-tall limestone boulder, is balanced precariously on bedrock. Early photographs show that it was an irresistible palette for graffiti in the 1800s and still is today.

Balance Rock State Park is about 2 miles to the west of Route 7 (see map).

BALANCE ROCK

Courtesy North Adams Library

David J. McLaughlin

SITE OF FIRST AND SECOND MEETING HOUSES

The Town Center

The Lanesborough **town hall** and **library** are located along Route 7. A monument notes the critical role played by Jonathan Smith, "a plain farmer of Lanesborough," whose speech of "good sense and good feeling" persuaded the Massachusetts Convention to ratify the Federal Constitution in February 1788. It is easy to forget how difficult it was to reach a consensus on this basic foundation of our government. The vote in Massachusetts was 187 to 168 in favor of ratification.

On the east side of the road (known as South Main Street as it passes through the center of town) is a prominent marker of the town's early history. A tablet affixed to the original marble steps (from the marble quarries of Lanesborough) marks the site of the First and Second Meeting Houses of the **First Church of Christ**, which was organized on March 28, 1764.

Lanesborough is noted for its architecturally distinctive churches. When the government was documenting historic structures throughout the country in the 1930s, both the **First Baptist Church of Lanesborough** (built in 1827–28) and **St. Luke's Episcopal Church**, a handsome stone Gothic-style building erected in 1836, were included.

VILLAGE CHURCH OF ST. LUKE'S

Both churches are still standing. The Baptist Church is now the **Fellowship Bible Church** (11 Summer Street). The original St. Luke's Church, now referred to as the **Old Stone Church**, still stands on the west side of North Main Street. It contains one of the oldest hand-pumped organs in the country, a black walnut Johnson organ installed in 1862.

Because the Old Stone Church is not heated, a modern Saint Luke's was built and services are held there the rest of the year.

OLD STONE CHURCH | St Luke's Episcopal Church was one of one of the first Church of England parishes in the Berkshires. Services are still held here in the summer months. >

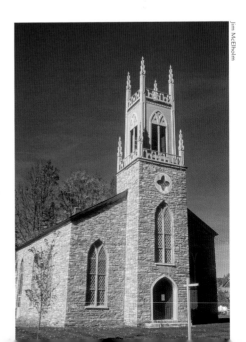

Jim McElholm

ALONG ROUTE 7 NORTH OF TOWN CENTER

SOME SAYINGS OF JOSH BILLINGS

"A dog is the only thing on earth that loves you more than he loves himself."

"Silence is one of the hardest arguments to refute."

"Be like a postage stamp. Stick to one thing until you get there."

"Men mourn for what they have lost; women for what they ain't got."

"The best way to convince a fool that he is wrong is to let him have his own way."

"There is no revenge so complete as forgiveness."

Along North Main Street and Old Williamstown Road

A little over a mile north of the town center is the **Talcott Cemetery**, where Lanesborough's most famous son is buried. Henry Wheeler Shaw (1818–1885), the noted 19th-century humorist known as **Josh Billings**, was born in Lanesborough. The accompanying box will regale you with some of the pithy sayings for which he became famous.

Just beyond Talcott Cemetery the road forks. Route 7 (which is named Williamstown Road at this point) continues to the north-

northwest. This portion of historic Route 7, from the upper half of Lanesborough through mountainous New Ashford (see Chapter 16), is one of the most scenic highways in the Berkshires.

There is a great view of **Mount Greylock** from Route 7.

VIEW OF MOUNT GREYLOCK FROM ROUTE 7

North Main Street, which continues directly north as Route 7 begins to veer to the northwest at the junction, connects with Rockwell Road, which leads to the **Mount Greylock Visitors Center** and on to the summit.

North Main Street is quite scenic. **Brookside Farm** is on the west side of North Main Street.

One of the town's original one-room schoolhouses, known as the **Stone School**, is located along here, at 732 North Main Street. This substantial limestone structure has been fully restored and now functions as a gallery and B&B.

The building served as a school from 1832 until 1950.

BROOKSIDE FARM

STONE SCHOOL GALLERY

STONE SCHOOL IN 1885

ROCKWELL ROAD TO MOUNT GREYLOCK

Mount Greylock

Lanesborough is located on the southern foot of Massachusetts' highest mountain. All the access roads to Mount Greylock are closed during 2008 and 2009 for upgrading and repair, but the Visitors Center remains open.

MOUNT GREYLOCK VISITORS CENTER

The mountain was largely deforested by the late 1800s. Concerned citizens and civic leaders organized the Greylock Park Association in 1885 and purchased 400 acres at the summit. In 1898 the site (by then expanded to 800 acres) was given to the state and formed the nucleus of the first state park in Massachusetts. It now covers 12,500 acres.

An early settler named Ephraim Bradley once farmed the land on which the Visitors Center now sits. **The Bradley Farm Trail** passes by orchards that the family originally planted.

Do stop into the Visitors Center, which has a wealth of material available on the trail structure, wildlife, and just about every aspect of Greylock. The last time I was there a gentleman asked if there had ever been an airplane crash on the mountain, and the ranger quickly found a report that documented seven plane wrecks, beginning in 1943, when a Navy twin-engined Grumman Subchaser crashed and killed the pilot and copilot. The largest loss of life was in a 1971 crash of a Piper Cherokee that killed all the members of a family, including their two dogs.

The **Appalachian Mountain Club's** Western chapter is located in the Berkshires (http://amcberkshire.org). The club is a reliable source for trail maps, camping supplies, and naturalist programs.

Dalton

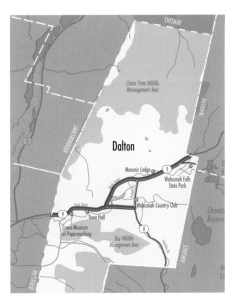

In 1739 the enterprising Oliver Partridge of Hatfield (who we'll meet again in Chapter 12) surveyed the area that ultimately became Dalton and was impressed with its ample water and inviting landscape. When he and his associates lost their grant of acreage along the Ashuelot River in New Hampshire (it was "voided" in 1743 as a result of the settlement of the Massachusetts–New Hampshire boundary), Partridge elected to obtain rights to the area in the Berkshires initially called the "Ashuelot Equivalent."

By 1755 Ashuelot had its first settlers, and the town soon prospered. An early source of income was supplying nearby Pittsfield with wood and timber from three "horse-powered" wood mills. In 1778 a petition for a separate town was submitted, but it wasn't approved until 1784.

The town was eventually renamed for Tristram Dalton, who at the time of its incorporation was speaker of the Massachusetts House of Representatives.

In the first history of Berkshire County (1829), David Dudley Field observed that "few towns in the County are more industrious … throughout the year." That remarkable work ethic, the location of Dalton along a robust

stretch of the Housatonic River, and the good luck to have enlightened and talented founders of the town's paper mills has created a special place that stands out among the 19th-century mill towns of New England. **Dalton** is a town with clean rivers, a still vibrant manufacturing base, substantial public buildings, a robust community spirit, and a lifestyle that continues to have a rural quality. The population grew more steadily than most Berkshire towns, peaking at 7,505 in 1970 and averaging about 6,900 since then.

DALTON TOWN OFFICES

David J. McLaughlin

In the 19th century Dalton had a diverse manufacturing base with textile mills, a shoe company, and equipment manufacturers, but through most of its history its leadership in papermaking has driven the local economy. In 1801 Zenas Crane and his partners, Henry Wiswell and Daniel Gilbert, established the first paper mill west of the Connecticut River. The business that became **Crane & Company**, now in its seventh generation of family ownership, is the oldest manufacturing business in the Berkshires, renowned worldwide for the quality of its 100 percent cotton papers.

Historic Crane buildings still grace the grounds of the company campus and the community.

CRANE & COMPANY | In 1879 the company won a contract to supply the paper on which U.S. currency is printed, and it is still the exclusive supplier. All Crane papers are still made in the mills alongside the Housatonic River.

MODEL FARM | Once a Crane family residence and model farm, this building is now used for meetings and conferences.

MODEL IN CRANE MUSEUM

Crane Museum of Papermaking

In 1844 the company built a handsome stone mill that was used to wash and sort rags. This building, which is on the National Register of Historic Places, was converted to a museum in 1930, originally called the Pioneer Museum.

This historic structure, with its many-paned windows, colonial chandeliers, oak beams, and wide oak floorboards, is now the **Crane Museum of Papermaking**. The interior resembles the Old Ship Church in Hingham, Massachusetts.

The museum tells the story of papermaking from Revolutionary times, naturally emphasizing the Crane papers used so broadly in currency, bonds, stock certificates, and upscale stationery. There is an interesting scale model of the vat house of the first Crane mill.

One of the more interesting features of the museum is the collection of artist renderings of "money," on display in the museum's gallery.

The museum is open Mondays through Fridays from early June through mid-October and admission is free.

MUSEUM

I LOVE MONEY, BY YVETTE GUITTER

Crane Museum of Papermaking
30 South Street
Dalton, MA 01226-1751
413-684-6481
www.crane.com/navcontent.aspx?navname=
aboutus&deptname=museum

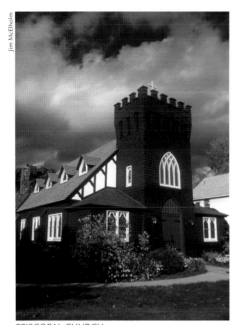

EPISCOPAL CHURCH

WAHCONAH COUNTRY CLUB

Exploring Dalton

Driving around Dalton, one is struck by the extent and quality of the infrastructure.

The inviting **town library** is part of the brick town office complex. Substantial churches line Main Street (Routes 9 and 8 in the center of town): St. Agnes Roman Catholic Church (489 Main), the Church of Christ First Congregational (514 Main), the United Methodist Church (755 Main), and Grace Episcopal Church (791 Main). The First Church of Nazarene, organized in 1965, is at 165 North Street, which is what Route 9 is called after it veers north and begins to ascend into the hills of Windsor.

The **Wahconah Country Club** (20 Orchard Road) is a semi-private country club established in 1930. In consistently ranks in the top 100 public-access golf courses in New England.

A community like Dalton has many civic organizations, youth groups, and social clubs, most with a rich history. The Knights of Columbus Council 411 was formed in 1899 and the **Mason's Unity Lodge** in 1897.

Naturally, both the American Legion and the Veterans of Foreign Wars are active in Dalton, which has supplied service men and women for all the nation's conflicts; 174 served in WWI, 501 in WWII, and 252 in the Korean War. Two Dalton men died in the Vietnam conflict.

Wahconah Falls State Park

The 104-acre **Wahconah Falls State Park** is located at the eastern edge of Dalton, right off Route 9, just before the town line of Windsor. A brook of that name tumbles over several small tiered falls and then cascades about 40 feet into a deep pool. You can hear the "roar" of the falls in the spring, but this is an inviting spot at any time of year. A moderately difficult ½-mile loop trail is a particularly popular place to hike.

< UNITY LODGE | At one time the Globe Lodge in Hinsdale covered seven towns. In 1997 it relocated to the Masonic Building at 45 North Street in Dalton, which is also the home of the Unity Lodge.

IN TRIBUTE TO THE WOMEN OF DALTON
WHO SERVED IN THE ARMED FORCES OF
THE UNITED STATES OF AMERICA
✝
RESPECTFULLY DEDICATED BY
THE DALTON HISTORICAL COMMISSION
MAY 31, 1999

David J. McLaughlin

WAR MEMORIAL

Richmond, Lanesborough, and Dalton have all retained their unique character. Stop and enjoy another dimension to the experience we call "the Berkshires."

ADDITIONAL RESOURCES

Richmond, Massachusetts, 1765–1965, The Story of a Berkshire Town and Its People, by Katharine Huntington Annin, Excelsior Printing Co.: North Adams, MA, 1964, 214 pages. One of the most literate town stories in print, but it only covers the years up until 1964. Well illustrated and indexed.

The Story of a Wilderness Settlement: Lanesborough, Mass., 1765–1965, by Frances S. Martin, Pittsfield, MA: Eagle Printing and Binding Company, 1965. The published history of Lanesborough, done at the time of the Bicentennial.

A Bicentennial History of Dalton, Massachusetts, 1784–1984, by Bernard Drew, ed., Dalton Bicentennial Committee, 1984. A thorough, professional history of this important center of papermaking.

Dalton and the World War: Being the Story of the Service Rendered Their Country by the People of Dalton, Massachusetts, in the World War of 1917–1918, by Benjamin F. Sullivan Post No. 155 of the American Legion, 1922. A special book that honors those who served in the Great War.

THE HILL TOWNS
Hinsdale and Peru, Windsor and Savoy

The Berkshire hill towns covered in this chapter began as small, self-sufficient farming communities settled after the end of the French & Indian War. Windsor and Partridgefield (which included present-day Hinsdale and Peru) were both incorporated in 1771, Savoy in 1797.

In the first history of Berkshire County, published in 1829, David Dudley Field described the residents of Peru as "industrious, temperate, moral people … farmers mostly [who produce] considerable quantities of rye, corn and oats in favorable seasons." Windsor was notable for its "dairying and the raising of sheep." While he reported that Savoy's land was "too broken for cultivation," he noted that the farmers there "raise stock and keep considerable dairies." Peru, Windsor, and Savoy were also important sources of lumber in the 19th century.

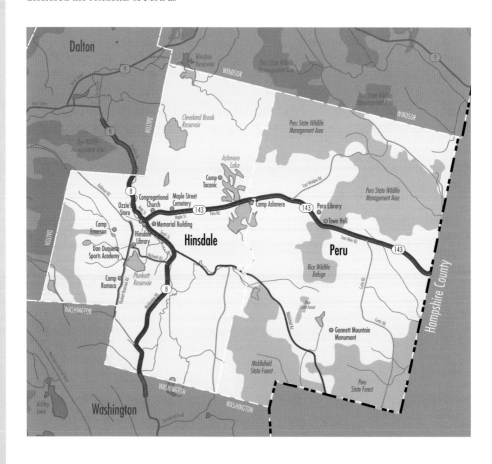

LAKE SCENE

David J. McLaughlin

Hinsdale was a farming community whose principal business was "the dairy and raising of cattle" until Merino sheep were introduced about 1810. It was then that the farmers switched to the "care of sheep," which, Field observed, "affords a very handsome profit."

However, because of its access to ample water power from a branch of the Housatonic River, Hinsdale already had a "woolen factory and 2 clothier's mills" in 1829. With the arrival of the Boston and Albany Railroad in 1842, connecting Hinsdale with Pittsfield and the major Massachusetts towns to the east, Hinsdale flourished as an important manufacturing center and railroad depot.

Today these hill towns offer unique opportunities. Hinsdale embodies the wonderful architectural legacy of a prominent hill town that used its wealth to create enduring public buildings. The other three towns, which retain their rural character and small-town atmosphere, provide a sense of life in days gone by.

Our journey begins in Hinsdale, easily reached from Pittsfield and Dalton via Route 8, which leads directly to the center of town.

Hinsdale

Hinsdale was incorporated as a separate town in 1804 and enjoyed considerable growth and success in the industrial era. The town was named for the Rev. Theodore Hinsdale, whose sons and then other successors ran the woolen mill from 1836–1930. The mills are long gone now, and Hinsdale is best known today for its scenic lakes and countryside. The town is quite popular as a summer resort and residence. The population surges in the summer months, and the largest employers are the town's six summer camps.

Life still revolves around the historic village center that contains a number of significant properties.

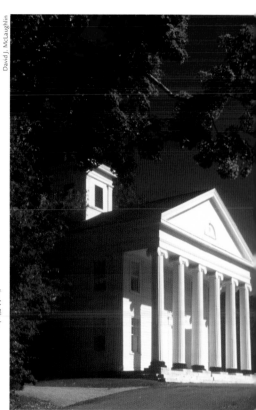

HINSDALE YOUTH CENTER | The Hinsdale Academy building now serves as the town Youth Center. It was carefully restored in 1963 under the leadership of the Lions Club.

Town Center and Historic Buildings

The **First Congregational Church of Hinsdale** was organized in 1795, when the town was the West Parish of Partridgefield. The handsome Christopher Wren-style church, dedicated in 1799, was based on the design of the Old South Church in Boston.

One of the most distinctive buildings in Hinsdale started life as the **Hinsdale Academy**, founded in 1849. This large Greek Revival-style building, with six tall fluted columns mounted on stone slabs, sits on a prominent knoll near the center of town. The building was patterned after the Maplewood Institute in Pittsfield.

FIRST CONGREGATIONAL CHURCH | This historic meeting house was originally erected on Schoolhouse Hill, further east on Route 143, and was relocated to the present site in the center of town in 1857.

David J. McLaughlin

HINSDALE LIBRARY

The residents of Hinsdale also enjoy a library designed by one of the leading church and civic building architects of the post-Civil War era. Leopold Eidlitz (1823–1908) of New York City designed this largely Tudor-style building, which has steep slate roofs. The library was completed in 1866.

The **Hinsdale Library** (58 Maple Street) is open six days a week. Check their extensive Website for hours and other details at www. hinsdalelibrary.org.

On the lawn of the library is a distinctive war memorial with an interesting history. The cannon that sits on top of the monument is a Model 1857 Napoleon "12 pounder" field gun, manufactured in Boston in 1864. It was used in the battle of Port Hudson, Louisiana, during the Civil War. The memorial was dedicated in 1923 and fully restored in 2006.

Jim McElholm

WAR MEMORIAL | The historic cannon was donated to the town as a result of efforts by a Hinsdale native, Francis E. Warren, who won the Medal of Honor for action during the Battle of Port Hudson. Warren went on to become governor of Wyoming and the first U.S. Senator from that state.

OZZIE'S

You will find plenty of historic homes in this town. One of my favorites is a stone house (481 Michaels Road) originally built in 1792.

Hinsdale Grange (No. 19) is the oldest surviving social organization. The **Grange Hall**, erected in 1909 by the Sons of Temperance, was purchased by the Lions Club in 1981 and now serves as the Hinsdale Community Center.

Hinsdale still has several stores, a service station, and an eatery, Ozzie's Steak and Eggs, at 26 Maple Street.

< 1792 HOUSE

Maple Street Cemetery

The gently rolling hills of the **Maple Street Cemetery** in Hinsdale contain the grave and memorial to a Revolutionary War soldier who played a critical role in the early days of the American Revolution.

The story of how the colonies were warned about the beginning of hostilities with the British has been the subject of much research and even more debate. The facts seem to be that two post riders, Paul Revere and William Dawes, were the first to sound the alarm. However, they were captured after riding only about 20 miles. On April 19, 1775, while the Battle of Lexington and Concord was underway, a member of the Committee of Correspondence assigned other post riders to set out in several directions to warn "all friends of American Liberty" that the Revolutionary War had begun. One of those men was 23-year-old Israel Bissell. Bissell escaped capture and continued to sound the alarm for almost five days, riding 345 miles—all the way to Philadelphia—on a succession of horses.

Later, Israel Bissell fought heroically in the Revolution, then became a sheep farmer, first briefly in Windsor and then for the rest of his life in Hinsdale, where he died. He is buried in the Maple Street Cemetery, where the D.A.R. erected a plaque in his honor.

The story of Israel Bissell's ride is an entertaining tale whose popularity increases with the publication of every scholarly article arguing over the facts. Clay Perry, a Berkshire Eagle columnist, even penned an alternative to Henry Wadsworth Longfellow's famous poem, *The Midnight Ride of Paul Revere*. It begins:

Listen my children to my epistle

Of the long, long ride of Israel Bissell

Who outrode Paul by miles and time

But didn't rate a poet's rhyme …

ENTRANCE TO MAPLE STREET CEMETERY

ISRAEL BISSELL'S GRAVE >

DAN DUQUETTE SPORTS ACADEMY SIGN | The academy was founded in 2004 by Dan Duquette, the former general manager of the Boston Red Sox.

A Center for Summer Camps

The picturesque lakes, clean air, and convenient location of Hinsdale not only attract many summer visitors; they led to the creation of more summer camps than any other Berkshire town. Camp Ashmere (1915), Camp Taconic (1928), Camp Romaca (1929), Camp Danbee (1950), Camp Emerson (1968), and the latest facility, the Dan Duquette Sports Academy (2003) have given boys and girls from all over the Northeast a special taste of the Berkshires.

The **Dan Duquette Sports Academy** (101 Michaels Road) is a unique new facility on the shores of Plunkett Lake, designed for training young athletes.

This impressive complex has four baseball fields, four lighted outdoor basketball courts, and a sand volleyball court. Its weeklong programs focus on boys and girls in the 8–18 age brackets and accommodate both overnight and day campers. For additional information, see www.duquettesportsacademy.com.

BASEBALL FIELD

David J. McLaughlin

The Lakes of Hinsdale

Hinsdale has three large bodies of water, all of them manmade: Plunkett Reservoir, Cleveland Brook Reservoir, and Ashmere Lake, as well as a portion of Windsor Reservoir in the Northwest corner of the town.

One of the most picturesque ponds is **Plunkett Reservoir**, a 73-acre beauty that is stocked with trout each year.

< ENTRANCE TO CAMP ROMACA | The puzzling name of this camp was created from the first few letters of the initial words of its original name, Rose Dale Manor Camp for Girls.

PLUNKETT RESERVOIR   David J. McLaughlin

David J. McLaughlin

LAKE ASHMERE

Peru

Peru lies immediately to the east of Hinsdale, reached directly by going east on Route 143. A causeway passes over Lake Ashmere, which runs along the eastern border of Hinsdale. There is a nice view of the lake from the south side of Route 143, looking toward the hills of Peru, where a fire lookout tower on Hickingbotham Road looms over the landscape.

The lake was named by William Cullen Bryant (see page 44), who came through the Hinsdale railroad station each year, then traveled overland to his boyhood home and summer residence in Cummington. Leonard Swift's fascinating book, The *Heritage of Hinsdale*, tells the story of how the famous poet and *Saturday Evening Post* editor was asked to suggest a name for what was then known as Plunkett Reservoir. He suggested Ashmere, a combination of *ash* (for the trees which lined the shore) and *mere*, one of his favorite suffixes (his primary residence in New York was named Cedarmere).

In colonial days Peru was an isolated rural village whose history began with a Massachusetts auction of nine townships in 1762. Township No. 2, which included most of present-day Peru and Hinsdale, was purchased by Oliver Partridge and Elisha Jones. It was first settled in 1764.

When the town was incorporated in 1771 it was named Partridgeville, after Oliver Partridge, but most residents considered this name too long. After considerable debate over the proper name, Partridgeville was changed to Peru in 1806. According to Peru's Bicentennial History, the pastor of the Congregational Church, the Rev. John Leland, suggested that name because "like the Peru of South America [this is] a mountain town and if no gold or silver mines are under her rocks she favors hard money and [her new name should] begin with a P."

There were Indian trails through the mountains when the first white settlers arrived; many of these were gradually widened to create paths to accommodate carts and wagons. In 1797 the Third Massachusetts Turnpike (a toll road extending from Northampton to Pittsfield and ultimately the New York border) came through Peru, connecting the town to the mills and other facilities of Massachusetts. Peru's dense forests were a major source of lumber, and the town had three sawmills. Peru was also a big source of maple syrup. In this busy era, the population of Peru soared to a peak of 1,361 residents in 1800. A stagecoach line connected Peru with Hinsdale, Dalton, and Pittsfield.

The still active **Congregational Church** is the most significant building in town. The society was organized in 1770.

The church, built to replace an 1806 structure that burned, formally opened on February 16, 1896. Its steeple houses a 1,300-pound bell. Legend has it that the roof is a continental divide of sorts. Rain falling on the right side is destined for the Connecticut River watershed, while the left side drains eventually into the Hudson.

Peru, at an elevation of 2,295 feet above sea level, has the highest town center in Massachusetts.

The small **Peru Library**, open two days a week, is staffed by a knowledgeable librarian.

The social and economic center of town was the **Creamer Store**, which also housed the post office. This well-sited "store on Peru Hill" was often featured in early Berkshire books.

The store owner, Frank G. Creamer, was apparently a real go-getter. Historians have

STORE ON PERU HILL, FROM *PICTURESQUE BERKSHIRES, 1895*

documented that in addition to operating the store, he was, at various times, postmaster (for 28 years), tax collector, town treasurer, town clerk, selectman, pound keeper, fire warden, library trustee, justice of the peace, assessor, auctioneer, and horse trader. Sadly, the old Creamer store no longer exists. The building was purchased in 1973 and relocated to Moodus, Connecticut, to be part of a museum village.

PERU CONGREGATIONAL CHURCH AND TOWN LIBRARY   David J. McLaughlin

234

World War II Crash

The most dramatic event in Peru's history occurred on a Sunday evening in the summer of 1942. August 15 was a particularly foggy night in the mountains. An Army transport plane en route from Fort Bragg, North Carolina, to Camp Edwards in Providence, Rhode Island, veered off course in the fog and crashed into 2,200-foot Garnet Peak.

Peru, like many of the hill towns during WWII, had an aircraft warning observation post (on Middlefield Road), manned around the clock by volunteers. Mrs. Mattie Bishop, who was on duty that evening, notified the authorities of the crash. Rescue workers made their way to the site of the flaming wreck. There were three survivors, but 13 paratroopers and the three-man crew died in the crash.

The residents of Peru erected a five-foot cobblestone memorial at the site of the crash in 1946 to honor the men who lost their lives here while in the service of their country. It is inspiring to see American flags still flying over 60 years later at this very remote site, a good hour's hike from civilization.

Enjoying the Outdoors in Peru

Much of Peru is preserved woodlands. The Peru State Wildlife Management Area, Peru State Forest, and much of Middlefield State Forest cover almost half of the town's land area.

One site that draws outdoor enthusiasts from all over is the **Dorothy Francis Rice Sanctuary for Wildlife**. In the late 1920s Oran and Mary Rice established the 176-acre sanctuary in their daughter's memory. This serene reserve contains a pond and habitat trail and is considered one of the best and least crowded birding places in Massachusetts. The sanctuary has over 40 nesting species of birds. The well-groomed trail system is also perfect for cross-country skiing in the winter months. The entrance is on South Road, about a mile from Route 143. The New England Forestry Foundation has managed the site since 1974. Their website provides further information at www.neforestry.org/forestry/forestdetail.asp?id=24.

For a special treat, drive along Peru's wonderful back-country roads.

GARNET HILL MEMORIAL

David J. McLaughlin

SCENIC VIEW >
Paul Rocheleau

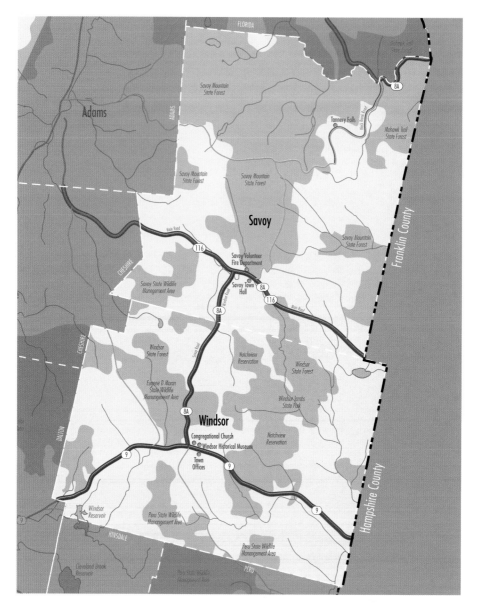

Windsor

The next town on this journey is **Windsor**, the adjacent town to the north, whose center is about 10 miles from Peru. You can make your way there on back-country roads and enjoy the scenery (see map). Windsor can also be reached from Dalton on State Routes 8A and 9.

Windsor is a once-remote hill town that thrived for many years as a dairy, sheepherding, and lumbering center. There were 10 operating sawmills in Windsor at the beginning of the 19th century. The population peaked at 1,108 in 1810 but then declined over the rest of the century as the timber ran out and residents moved to other towns with better soil, train service, and higher-paying manufacturing jobs.

Since the 1970s, however, this hill town's scenic beauty, friendly family atmosphere, abundant land, and vastly improved road access to Dalton and Pittsfield have attracted many new residents. Over half the homes in Windsor have been built since 1970.

The town was initially incorporated in 1771 as Gageborough, in honor of Gen. Thomas Gage, then the British governor of Massachusetts. But after all things British became detested during the American Revolution, the name was changed to Windsor in 1778.

The biggest business here was the Windsor Cheese Co., which was organized by farmers in the vicinity and in whose two-story facility milk was made into cheese.

The cheese factory dates to 1811 and operated into the early 1900s. The business shut down in the winter and dances and suppers were held in the building.

As you enter the town of Windsor you'll see a cluster of buildings along Route 9: a general store, the town hall and town offices, the Congregational Church, and right next to the church, a museum.

WINDSOR PIE SALE

ARTIST DEPICTION OF WINDSOR CHEESE FACTORY | This drawing is in the collection of the Windsor Historical Society.

Windsor's **general store** still stands, though not in the original building. For about 100 years the store was owned and operated by the Estes family. As was the practice in these small towns, the post office and later the telephone exchange were part of the store complex. The original store was struck by lightning and destroyed in 1919. In 1943, the replacement, too, was destroyed by fire. The current building was built soon after the second one burned.

There is a charming model of the early 20th-century store in the town museum.

The picturesque **Congregational Church** is located along Route 9.

There are several historic cemeteries in Windsor where you can discover gravestones of Revolutionary War soldiers like Ephraim Minor, "Esquire" Walker, and Stephen Hume.

David J. McLaughlin

TOWN OFFICES AND CONGREGATIONAL CHURCH OF WINDSOR | The Congregational Church was organized in 1772. The present building was erected in 1847.

David J. McLaughlin

MODEL OF WINDSOR GENERAL STORE

Darlene Bordwell

BUSH CEMETERY IN WINDSOR STATE FOREST

WINDSOR HISTORICAL MUSEUM

David J. McLaughlin

Windsor Historical Museum

Windsor has a fascinating repository of town memorabilia housed in a classic hill farmhouse that became the **town museum** in 1975. The main building dates to 1876. It was donated to the town by The Trustees of Reservations and relocated from the southeast corner of Savoy Hollow and Shaw Roads to its present site, just east of the Congregational Church.

There are displays of early sleds and farm equipment on the lawn outside. The building, which was restored over several decades by volunteers, contains a full-scale replica of a 19th-century kitchen. The spacious, well-lighted interior effectively displays the period furnishings and many artifacts collected by the Historical Commission over the years.

The most captivating and unique items in this spacious farmhouse museum are three-dimensional scenes of early town industries, most of them constructed by Olive Volsky. They depict the industrial activities that took place in Windsor in the 19th century, including charcoal making, the operation of a spruce oil distillery, ice cutting, and talc mining. The museum is open during the summer months, but if you are driving along Route 9 at any time of year and see a sign for a pie sale, be sure to stop. The ladies of Windsor not only make great pies (I favor the apple ones); the sale is usually held in front of the museum, and someone is sure to give you a tour.

EXTERIOR DISPLAYS

Notchview

The rural Berkshire towns are still laced with stone walls and cellar holes of abandoned farmhouses. In the final decades of the 19th century much of this farmland was consolidated into large estates, like the 3,000-acre **Notchview Farm** in Windsor, assembled by Lt. Col. Arthur D. Budd. This elevated property (most of it above 2,000 feet) was bequeathed to the Trustees of Reservations in 1965 and added to in 1993 with the 93-acre Smithers Woodland Preserve.

In the winter months, as the Trustees Website notes, "Notchview is one of Massachusetts' premier Nordic cross-country ski destinations." There are 30 kilometers (19 miles) of cross-country ski trails, a third of which are back-country trails.

The highest point in Windsor is Judges Hill, 2,297 feet above sea level. The views from Windsor on a clear day are incredible. You can see the Catskills to the southwest, Mount Greylock and the Green Mountains of Vermont to the north, and Mount Tom and Mount Holyoke to the east. In the early decades of the 20th century, a sightseeing bus traveled from Williamstown to Pittsfield over a route called the Berkshire Trail. The trip up Peru Road in Windsor, with a stop to admire the view, was the highlight of the journey.

CROSS-COUNTRY SKIING

Notchview
Route 9
Windsor, MA 01270
413-684-0148
www.thetrustees.org/prages/345_notchview.cfm

BIRDS MEAT WAGON DIORAMA

David J. McLaughlin

Other Outdoor Attractions

Windsor State Forest (at River Road in the northeast quadrant of town) contains a captivating waterfall at Windsor Jambs Brook, named by the early settlers because the rock formations suggested the stone jambs of a fireplace. The cascading falls plunge through a gorge with 75-foot-high perpendicular granite walls that rise on both sides. The Westfield River meanders through the forest. There is a wooded picnic area and a 100-foot-long sandy beach for swimming. The forest is open from sunrise to sunset, year round.

Wahconah Falls is technically part of the State Park of that name in Dalton (see page 222), but the falls themselves are actually in the southwest corner of Windsor, easily reached off Route 8A/9. This is a great picnicking area. A series of small pools along Wahconah Falls Brook are popular for wading. Incidentally, this is a wonderful area for fall foliage viewing.

A popular spot in town is the 48-acre **Windsor Pond**, easily reached by taking Windsor Pond Road south from Route 116/8A near the town lines of Savoy, Windsor, and Plainfield (in Hampshire County). This natural pond is quite deep, averaging 21 feet, and good for fishing. While the shoreline is heavily dotted with homes, the pond is open to the public if you bring your own boat. There is a boat ramp at the east end of the pond.

Savoy

There are two ways to reach the center of **Savoy**. One is to take Route 8A North from Windsor, which leads to the center of town. An alternative, one of my favorite ways to enter the Berkshires, is to take Route 116 West (reached off Interstate 91), which wends through the picturesque towns of Conway, Ashfield, and Plainfield, then enters the Berkshires through Savoy.

Northern Berkshire Township No. 6 was auctioned to Able Lawrence in 1765, but the area wasn't actually settled until 1777. It was incorporated 20 years later. Savoy, which rests on rocky mountainous land situated on the southern slope of the Hoosac Mountains, was aptly named for a region in the French Alps.

This is a beautiful area, much of it protected in state forests and wildlife sanctuaries. The 11,000-acre **Savoy Mountain State Forest** has over 60 miles of trails and two scenic ponds (North and South Ponds) where you can picnic, fish, and swim. Four campsites at South Pond have log cabins available for rent year round.

Spectacular natural features in this forest include **Bog Pond**, with floating bog islands, and **Tannery Falls**, which cascades through a deep chasm, finally plunging over a precipice to a clear pool below (best visited in the spring when the water flow is at its best). There is a large "balanced rock" near the falls, a granite boulder left after the glaciers retreated following the Ice Age. The Massachusetts Department of Conservation and Recreation has an extensive Website with all the details at www.mass.gov/dcr/parks/western/svym.htm.

In the 19th century, Savoy was heavily wooded and at one time had 16 sawmills. It was never really suited for agriculture, but sheep were successfully raised here during the years when the Berkshires area was a textile powerhouse. The Civilian Conservation Corps (CCC) reforested much of Savoy with Norway and blue spruce in the 1930s, and Savoy is now even more heavily forested than it was in colonial days.

David J. McLaughlin

SIGN NEAR THE TOWN LINE OF SAVOY ON ROUTE 116

The population peaked at 861 souls and gradually declined as the timber was harvested and sheep farming became less viable. The population today is back to almost 800 as roads to Pittsfield and Adams have improved.

Because the Mohawk Trail (Route 2) cuts through part of northern Savoy and the town boundaries are prominently signed, some visitors assume that they have "seen" Savoy if they have traveled along the trail. In fact, as the 1874 *Gazetteer of Massachusetts* noted, "the principal village and best lands are in the southerly part of town."

TANNERY FALLS

Henry Dondi

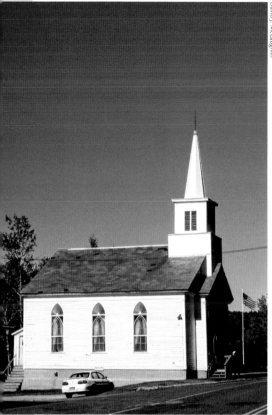

The Savoy Volunteer Fire Department is a prominent landmark as you enter town. Savoy is the kind of small town that has always sent a high proportion of its young men to fight the country's wars. Seventy-one men from Savoy fought in the Civil War, and nine were lost in that bloody conflict. In the photograph shown here, a sign on the outside of the fire station honors two of the current generation of young men with wishes for "Good Luck in Iraq."

The Savoy firefighters can be counted on to participate in virtually all the major parades held each year in Berkshire County.

The **Sovereign Grace Baptist Church of Savoy** is sited prominently along Route 116. It is a worthy successor to the first Baptist church organized here over 200 years ago, in 1797.

Brier Chapel, built by members of the Advent Society around 1863, is now used for events, including concerts and lectures. Governor W. Murray Crane donated the chapel bell, which still hangs on its original rope.

SOVEREIGN GRACE BAPTIST CHURCH, SAVOY

MARCHING IN LEE FOUNDERS' WEEKEND PARADE

SAVOY FIRE DEPARTMENT

It was the Berkshire Hills which lured Longfellow, Hawthorne, Melville, and the other literary greats of the 19th century to this region. The hills still beckon. Make time to enjoy them!

ADDITIONAL RESOURCES

Town of Windsor 200th Anniversary, published in 1971 by the Windsor Bicentennial Committee, 128 pages. This book is organized into series of concise, well-written descriptions of the historic structures, villages, societies, and events that constitute the history of the town.

The Heritage of Hinsdale: An Anthology, Leonard F. Swift, Editor, Quality Printing Company: Pittsfield, MA, 2005, 194 pages. This engaging book includes profiles and stories of early residents (gathered from many sources) and offers an insider's perspective on the places, events, and institutions of this significant town. It's printed on glossy paper that does justice to the black-and-white photographs that accompany the text.

A Bicentennial History of Peru, 1771–1971, Peru History Committee, 1971, 44 pages of text plus another 44 pages of photographs. Here is a useful source of information and anecdotes on this fascinating windswept town, the highest in the state of Massachusetts.

A History of the County of Berkshire, Massachusetts, In Two Parts, written by the Reverend Chester Dewey (Part the first being a general view of the country) and David Dudley Field (Part the second being an account of the several towns), Pittsfield, 1829. This first history of Berkshire County is a primary source document of 468 pages.

DISCOVERING ROUTE 8
Cheshire and Adams

This journey takes you north along Route 8, a scenic corridor that passes directly through Cheshire and Adams.

Both towns were important industrial centers in the 19th century. The first company in Western Massachusetts to install water-powered looms was a Cheshire cotton mill. High-quality sand suitable for glass making was plentiful, and the first plate glass made in the United States was produced in Cheshire in 1853. Cheshire and Adams were both major suppliers of lime. Adams was an industrial powerhouse, the center of textile manufacturing in the Berkshires.

While today neither town has major cultural institutions, they have a fascinating history, great scenic beauty, and, in the case of Adams, a handsomely preserved downtown whose spiraling steeples give testimony to one of the most ethnically diverse populations in Massachusetts.

RUINS OF FARNAM CHESHIRE LIME COMPANY >
Lucia Saradoff

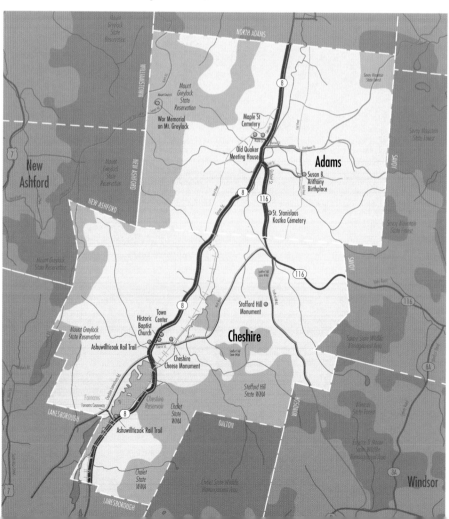

David J. McLaughlin

CHESHIRE TOWN HALL

Cheshire

Cheshire was settled in the 1760s by Baptists from Rhode Island. They named the hill where they settled New Providence Hill (later renamed Stafford Hill). The town was incorporated in 1793 as Cheshire, a name that was chosen, according to the 1885 town history, "because the town was developing into so fine a grazing and dairying county, like Cheshire in England." Cheshire has a particularly uneven boundary, with some 25 "corners." This is because "in laying out the town ... the religious views of the settlers [were considered] taking the farms of the Baptist families into Cheshire and leaving the Presbyterians in Lanesboro."

The early immigrants were descendants of those who had followed Roger Williams to Rhode Island in 1636 in a quest for religious freedom. Cheshire has had a reputation for tolerance and religious diversity throughout its history.

Begin an exploration of Cheshire with a walk along the Ashuwillticook Rail Trail. Shortly after you cross the southern boundary of the town, turn left (west) off Route 8 onto Farnam's Causeway (see map).

Ashuwillticook Rail Trail

In 1846, the Pittsfield & North Adams Railroad built a rail line to connect the two cities, with plans to extend service into Vermont. The Boston & Maine Railroad, the last of a series of owners, operated the line between 1981 and 1990, when service was abandoned. The **Ashuwillticook Rail Trail** was created by converting 11.5 miles of the rail corridor into a 10-foot-wide paved path that passes through wooded hills and marshlands and, in a particularly glorious stretch, runs along the Cheshire Reservoir. The Reservoir itself was built in 1869 by flooding 1,000 acres of land. It is one of the largest lakes in Berkshire County and is a popular spot for kayaking and canoeing in summer and ice fishing in winter.

The Rail Trail currently connects Lanesborough, Cheshire, and Adams, with proposals to extend it south to Pittsfield and Great Barrington and north to North Adams and Williamstown. This universally accessible paved trail is popular for walking, jogging, biking, and rollerblading.

There is also access to the Trail (and parking nearby) at Berkshire Mall Road in Lanesborough, at Church Street in Cheshire, and behind the Visitors Center in Adams. The Farnam's entrance brings you to the most scenic part of the Trail.

David J. McLaughlin

SIGN FOR RAIL TRAIL

SCENIC TRAIL NEAR FARNAM'S ENTRANCE

David J. McLaughlin

VIEW OF MILL | The original Farnam's mill was made of wood and destroyed in a fire. This concrete, steel, and sheet-metal structure was erected in 1921–1922.

Farnam's

Farnam's was a large lime manufacturing complex operated in the Cheshire Village of Farnams between 1875 and 1968. Well before then, farmers in the area had quarried the abundant local limestone on a small scale, producing lime (largely used for fertilizer) by burning the rock in simple kilns. Just after the Civil War twin brothers who had survived the battle of Gettysburg, Alfred S. and Albert Farnam, began a venture to manufacture lime on a commercial scale. The *Berkshire County Gazetteer* reported that in 1885 A. S. Farnam's & Bros. employed 20 men and manufactured 30,000 barrels of lime a year.

VIEW OF QUARRY

You can see the massive former mill on the far side of the reservoir, set back only a few yards from the shoreline.

Rock was hauled from a quarry behind a mountain to the north, broken into pieces, then burned at the millworks in multistory kilns (at the peak of operations there were 21). The kilns were loaded from the roof of the new mill by means of a small-gauge railroad. The track extended to a rooftop loading system.

After the lime cooled it was put in barrels and shipped throughout the Northeast. Cheshire was famous for its "Blue Label" plaster, used extensively in New York City.

In 1929 the business (by then the company was known as the Farnam Cheshire Lime Co.) was acquired by U.S. Gypsum, which operated the facility until 1970, when the mill was permanently closed. In *Working the Stone*, their engaging story of the hundred-year history of this business, Paul Metcalf and Lucia Saradoff describe the mill today as "an indoor wilderness, a dusty brick and iron desert, a curving inner landscape." Fortunately the critical features of this hauntingly beautiful property have been preserved from development.

Incidentally, just south of Farnam's, on Route 8, there is an enticing "pick your own" farm.

Whitney's Farm Stand (1775 South State Street/Route 8) offers a wide selection of produce and bedding plants. This is the place to find perfect Berkshire pumpkins in the fall.

There is a petting zoo, café, and many attractions for the entire family.

SELECTING YOUR PUMPKIN

Jim McElholm

Jim McElholm

< CHESHIRE BAPTIST CHURCH
This church was built in 1794.

In 1792 a vigorous young Baptist minister moved to Cheshire. Rev. John Leland (1754–1841) was a forceful advocate of the separation of church and state. Leland, a gifted speaker and natural promoter, worked as an itinerant preacher in Virginia during the American Revolution. He knew Thomas Jefferson and James Madison. Cheshire was the only town in the Berkshires to support Thomas Jefferson for president. When Jefferson won, Leland developed a plan to honor him and get some positive publicity for Cheshire. At his suggestion, all Cheshire dairy farmers contributed one day's mill production to make a 1,250-pound cheese. The cheese was so large (four feet in diameter, 18 inches thick) they had to use a cider press to mold it. Never one to miss an opportunity, Rev. Leland accompanied the cheese on its journey to Washington, D.C. It was moved on a six-horse sled to the Hudson River, then shipped by boat to the nation's capital and presented to President Jefferson on New Year's Day. Leland preached at every port along the way.

In 1940, the town erected a concrete replica of the cheese press to celebrate this historic event and as a monument to John Leland. (A bronze portrait of the Rev. Leland, in profile, is attached to the sculpture.)

The **Cheshire Cheese Monument** is located on Church Street across from the Cheshire Post Office.

You will find a few interesting small businesses along Church Street, including **H. D. Reynolds General Merchandise**, circa 1844, which still sells penny candy. A short walk from there is the handsome Cheshire **town hall**, built in 1898.

Historic Downtown

As you approach the center of Cheshire (Route 8 is named North Street in town) you will see the **Baptist Church** (32 North Street) at the intersection of Route 8 and Church Street, the town's principal thoroughfare. The Second Baptist Church was organized here in 1789 (the first Baptist church was on Stafford Hill).

There were originally four churches in Cheshire: the Baptist, Catholic, Methodist, and Unitarian Universalist Churches. All were built on the town's main street, hence the name Church Street.

CHESHIRE CHEESE MONUMENT >
The sculptors of the monument were George Haskins and Edward J. Farris.
David J. McLaughlin

254

BATTLE OF BENNINGTON

STAFFORD HILL MONUMENT

Stafford Hill

One of the early settlers of Cheshire was Joab Stafford, who commanded the Silver Greys, a company of Berkshire troops that fought in the Revolutionary War. Col. Stafford, along with several other Cheshire men, played an important role in the **Battle of Bennington**, one of the decisive early victories in the long struggle for independence. On August 16, 1777, New Hampshire, Vermont, and Massachusetts militiamen killed or captured over 900 of a mixed force of German mercenaries (from Brunswick), Canadians, Tories, and Indians.

In 1927 the Massachusetts Sons of the American Revolution erected a monument to commemorate the battle and the early settlers of Cheshire. The **Stafford Hill Monument** is a fieldstone replica of a tower erected in Newport, Rhode Island.

Stafford Hill Road, in the northeast quadrant of Cheshire and easily reached from Route 116, offers a commanding view of the valley. The view looking north toward Adams is particularly scenic.

VIEW FROM STAFFORD HILL

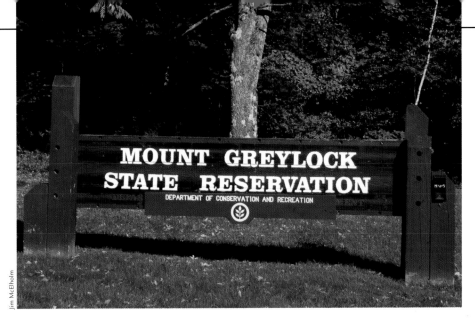

Jim McElholm

Appalachian Trail

Those interested in a more extensive outdoor excursion in the Cheshire area can hike the **Appalachian Trail**. Cheshire is one of the few remaining "sanctuary" towns along the trail. The Cheshire post office offers a way for "through-hikers" to exchange information, send mail, and receive personal shipments of food and other supplies.

The Appalachian Trail crosses Route 8 at Church Street. The northern route will take you to Mount Greylock State Reservation, where there are 70 miles of trails. To the south, a short side trip from the top of the ridgeline will bring you to **Cheshire Cobbles**, a series of white-quartzite ledges. On a clear day there is a great view of Mt. Greylock from here.

Continue north along Route 8 approximately 3 miles beyond the center of town and just past the state police barracks. This area is known as **Cheshire Harbor**, so named because a number of the homes here were used as stops along the Underground Railroad. The Rail Trail also passes through this area along the east side of the highway.

Jim McElholm

TWO MOUNTAIN BIKERS ON GREYLOCK

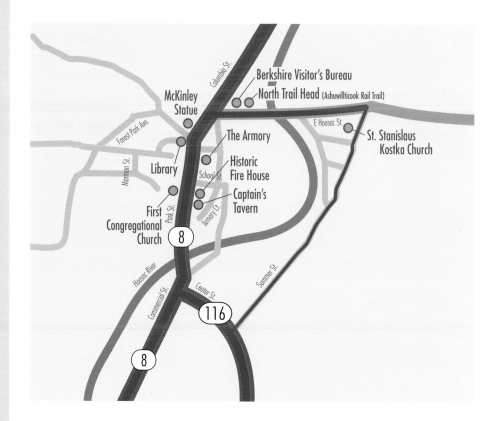

Berkshire Visitor's Bureau

North Trail Head (Ashuwillticook Rail Trail)

McKinley Statue

Columbia St.

E Hoosac St.

St. Stanislaus Kostka Church

Forest Park Ave.

The Armory

Library

Historic Fire House

School St.

Marman St.

Captain's Tavern

First Congregational Church

Park St.

Armory Cr.

8

Hoosac River

Center St.

Summer St.

Commercial St.

116

8

INCORPORATED 1778

WELCOME TO ADAMS

David J. McLaughlin

Adams

On June 2, 1762, the general court of Massachusetts auctioned off nine townships in the northwestern part of the county. Township No. 1, East Hoosac, was sold to Nathan Jones for £3,200. By 1778 the township had enough settlers to be incorporated as the town of **Adams**, named for the patriot Samuel Adams, who would later become governor.

As the 1876 "Landowner Map" drawn by F. W. Beers shows, Adams included South and North Adams for its first 100 years. In 1878 North Adams was incorporated as a separate town. (In 1895 it would adopt a city form of government and become the second city in Berkshire County.)

Adams is one of the best laid-out and best preserved former mill towns in Massachusetts, a Victorian-era delight.

1876 MAP OF ADAMS BY FREDERICK W. BEERS >

NORTH ADAMS

BRAYTONVILLE

TROY & GREENFIELD R.R.

Greylock Mills
North Adams Wooten Mfg Co
Ford

Gallup Houghton & Smith
Dryout
Wooten Co
Beaver Mill
Strout Store

C.M.Perry
B.F.Robinson
SCHOOL
B.F.Robinson

Stone Quarry

J.M.Chase Sr. Co.
Saw Mill
D.Wells

A.C.Patterson
J.W.Eddy

Stone Quarry
Hotchkin's & Co.
Dr.G.C.Lawrence
Lime Kilns

A.W.Richardson
F.E.Colegrove

HOOSAC TUNNEL

G.M.Mowbray's
Nitro Glycerine Works

SCHOOL

A.Walden & Son
H.R.Arnold
A.Walden Res.
SCHOOL
Cem.

Mrs.Kimball
Mrs.Jennings

B.F.Robinson

B.F. Robinson

ADAMS
Scale 160 Rods to the inch

O.Tinney Res.

Miss Tanner

C.A.Howland

THE SADDLE

A.W.Richardson

S.E.Dean

H.Anthony

T.J.Fowler

J.Richmond

Mrs.Flynn

YLOCK PEAK
Ft above tide Water

Lime Kilns
Whipple

Renfrew Mfg Co
Cotton Mill

D.Cole

J.L.Follott

D.Earnum

A.M.McGrath

J.McClement
F.Arnold
H.Reynolds

J.Dudley
E.Hathaway Est.

E.Neary

J.Staples

J.Sculley

A.Hall
F.Ballou Res.

S.Tinkey

D.D.Allen

J.Anthony

J.E.Thomas
W.B.Sh.
G.W.Brown

J.E.Thomas

A.M.Sherman

SOUTH ADAMS

A.Bowen

J.Dudley
C.Ballou
SCHOOL
B.Seddler
F.Hathaway
G.Perow
J.Dean
Geo Saunders

Dunham Est.
D.Jenks

B.P.O.

L.F.Williams
E.Sherman
E.Briggs

G.W.Sherman

H.Anthony

C.Palmer

J.Goldthwaite

J.Carter
H.A.
J.Bowen

H.Anthony

MAPLE GROVE

B.F.Phillips

A.W.Sayles

W.Richmond & Bro.

C.Richmond

E.Miller Res.

J.Briggs
H.Byrt
SCHOOL

D.F.Burlingame

ARNOLDSVILLE

Wm. Steele
Mrs. F. Jenks
J.Jenks

J.Brown

S.Loud

C & C Jenks

FIRST CONGEGATIONAL CHURCH OF ADAMS
This is the only wooden church in Adams still in use.

Historic Park Street

Route 8 north will take you directly to the inviting downtown of Adams, whose current appearance was shaped during the last decade and a half of the 19th century, a boom time in the cotton industry. In 1883 the town hall was built at the corner of School and Park streets, opposite the First Congregational Church.

At this time the commercial center of town was to the south, along Center Street (Route 116). Over the next 15 years most of the significant buildings you see today were built along Park Street (that stretch of Route 8 from the Hoosac River and intersecting with Center, extending north to McKinley Square).

The capable Adams Historical Society has created a walking tour of historic **Park Street**, described online at http://adamsma. virtualtownhall.net/Public_Documents/ AdamsMA_Historical/walktour.

There are several significant structures along Park Street. The current **Adams town hall** (8 Park Street) was originally built in 1907 as the home of C. T. Plunkett, one of several Plunkett family mansions at this end of Park. A veterans memorial to those who gave their lives in war graces the lawn.

The **First Congregational Church** (42 Park Street) has been prominently located on Park since it was built in 1868. The Parish House and Parsonage, to the south of the church, were built in 1895.

The **Park Street Fire House**, on the National Register of Historic Places, was built in 1891 for the town's volunteer fire company, **Adams Alert Hose Co. No. 1**, founded in 1876. For the fascinating history of Alert Hose Co. No. 1, now located on Columbia Street, see their extensive Website: http://adamsalerts.com/index.php.

ALERT HOSE CO. NO. 1 | A perennial parade favorite, the Alert Hose Co. No. 1 march in a distinctive Prince Albert-style buff-and-white period uniform.

If you get hungry during your tour of Adams, have lunch at the **Captain's Tavern** (formerly the Miss Adams Diner) at 53 Park Street. There has been a diner at this location for over 70 years. This current structure, prefabricated in a diner factory, dates to 1949.

The **Armory of Company M** (39–45 Park) is modeled after a Norman medieval castle. It was built in 1914.

The **Adams Free Library** (92 Park), which also houses the **Adams Historical Society** on a portion of the second floor, was built in 1897 as a library and Civil War memorial. President McKinley laid the cornerstone of this building on one of his visits to town.

The library has an extensive newspaper collection dating back to 1844. Further details and the variable times the library is open, seven days a week, are available at http://adamsma. virtualtownhall.net/Public_Documents/ AdamsMA_Library/index.

The **Berkshire Visitors Center** is just off Park on 3 Hoosac Street. This state-of-the art facility has an interactive exhibit on Berkshire Country, plenty of brochures and maps, and a particularly knowledgeable staff.

David J. McLaughlin

ADAMS FREE LIBRARY | The buff-colored brick of the library building is trimmed with marble quarried at the former Adams Marble Co.

MCKINLEY STATUE | The statue, unveiled on October 10, 1903, was sculpted by August Lukeman.

McKinley Square

An inviting feature of downtown Adams is a spacious green known as **McKinley Square**, anchored by a prominent statue of William McKinley (1843–1901), the 25th President of the United States. Throughout his political career McKinley strongly supported legislation and tariffs which helped the U.S. cotton industry. He was friends with the Plunkett family, which owned the Berkshire Cotton Mfg. Co. (known as the Berkshire Mills) and visited Adams three times.

After McKinley was assassinated while standing in a receiving line at the Buffalo Pan-American Exposition in 1901, Adams erected this statue of the slain president.

A handsome Roman Catholic Church, **Notre Dame des Sept Douleurs**, was erected by the French-Canadian community of Adams on what is now the square in 1887. Ten years later, in 1897, the Irish and German residents of the town erected **St. Thomas Aquinas Church** (2 Columbia Street), visible just beyond Notre Dame. These churches were merged into a joint parish in 1998.

Important upcoming events in town are often noted on a sign next to the McKinley statue. Watch for the **Greylock Ramble** sign which advertises an annual hike up Mount Greylock each Columbus Day. The event draws upward of 1,000 participants of all ages.

Mount Greylock

The highest mountain in Massachusetts looms over Adams and is central to its identity. **Mount Greylock State Reservation** covers much of the western quarter of town. The prominent **Veterans War Memorial Tower**, erected on the summit, is actually in the town of Adams.

The memorial (built in 1931–32) is a 93-foot-tall shaft with eight observation openings. The beacon at the top reaches 70 miles. The tower was formally dedicated in 1933 in a ceremony broadcast nationally on NBC.

There are several hiking trails you can take to the summit of Mount Greylock from Adams. The **Cheshire Harbor Trail** (about 2.6 miles) is the easiest and shortest route. It connects with Rockwell Road and the Appalachian Trail, which leads to the summit. The trailhead for Cheshire Harbor is at West Mountain Road. **Gould Trail** (at the same trailhead) is a more strenuous hike. The **Bellows Pipe to Ragged Mountain Trail** (accessed at Gould Road in Adams) is a moderate to strenuous hike. All of these hikes can easily take five to six hours and you should be in good physical condition

to make them. Full details and maps of these trails are online at www.mass.gov/dcr/parks/mtGreylock/downloads/suggestedhikes.pdf.

As noted previously in our discussion of Mount Greylock in Chapter 10, the main access roads to Greylock are in Lanesborough and North Adams. These roads will be closed until late in 2009.

Jim McElholm

ON MOUNT GREYLOCK

Jim McElholm

WAR MEMORIAL TOWER | The tower was designed by Boston-based architects Maginnis & Walsh and is made of granite quarried in Quincy. It bears the inscription "they were faithful even unto death."

FRIENDS MEETING HOUSE C. 1935

Historic American Buildings Survey

Friends Meeting House

The most historic house of worship in Adams is the **Friends Meeting House**, which was built over the years 1782–1786, about 15 years after a group of Quakers settled in what was then known as East Hoosac. Adhering to the Quakers' code of simplicity, the meeting house was built with very little ornamentation and left unpainted. Many of the early Quakers are buried in the open area in front of the meeting house, in unmarked graves.

The Quaker Community had a total of 40 families in Adams in 1819, their peak year. The last official meeting was held in 1842. The Meeting House is located in Maple Street Cemetery (see map).

Susan B. Anthony

The most enduring Quaker family name in Adams is Anthony. Susan B. Anthony (1820–1906) was born in Adams in a Federal-style house on 67 East Road. The **Susan B. Anthony Birthplace** (soon to be opened as a museum) is an important symbol of the woman's suffrage movement.

There is a monument to Susan Anthony along Park Street, near the Hoosac River Overpass. A festival celebration is held in her honor each summer. The event includes a biathlon, a street fair, guided historical walking tours, and the three-day Adams Agricultural Fair.

Other Attractions

There isn't a better town in the Berkshires than Adams in which to enjoy Victorian architecture. Be sure to drive or walk along Summer Street between Route 116 and Hoosac Street. The southern stretch is lined with beautiful Victorian-era homes. This is part of a National Register Historic District which includes some 70 historic buildings.

St. Stanislaus Kostka, another Catholic church built in 1902 by the Polish community, is at the southeast corner of Summer and Hoosac streets (25 Hoosac Street). Its towering spires help shape the profile of downtown.

St. Stanislaus Kostka Parish is the only religious organization in the United States that managed to get the leaders of the Communist Party inside a church. In 1952, when the church was renovated for its 50th anniversary, they commissioned several new stained-glass windows. One window featured Fr. Maximilian Kolbe, a Franciscan who died in Auschwitz in 1941 after offering his life in exchange for that of a condemned prisoner. Fr. Kolbe was canonized in 1982. On the opposite side of the church is a stained-glass window that includes the image of Bishop John Cieplak defending his faith at a Bolshevik show trial held by Lenin, Trotsky, and Stalin. The two windows remind Polish people of the historic struggle to achieve and maintain their independence.

David J. McLaughlin

A VICTORIAN BUILDING

Kelly Lee

ST. STANISLAUS KOSTKA

David J. McLaughlin

VIEW OF FORMER MILL TOWERS

As you drive around Adams you begin to appreciate its industrial heritage. In Adams the former mills, many of which have been converted to housing, preserve the essential character of the town. The tower of **Mill No. 1** is quite visible and now serves as a marker for an upscale housing complex.

Textile finishing was the major industry in Adams, but local mills also turned out shoes, machinery, rugs, brass and aluminum castings, and, in the 20th century, electrical goods. Most of the manufacturing jobs are long gone.

The year 1958 marked the end of 150 years of textile manufacturing in Adams. That year the Berkshire-Hathaway Company announced that it was shutting down Mill No. 4, the last operating cotton mill in Berkshire County. This decision, incidentally, was made four years before a young man named Warren Buffett acquired control of the company and transformed it into one of the most successful investment vehicles of all time. Berkshire-Hathaway ultimately exited the textile business entirely in 1985.

There is one remaining mill in Adams. **Specialty Minerals** mines and processes limestone for calcium carbonate, used in antacids and food supplements, as well as paper whiteners and other industrial purposes.

Adams' transformation from an industrial powerhouse to a smaller town with a largely service-based economy has been painful. Adams doesn't have a magnet attraction like MASS MoCA, but the town's inviting downtown, historic architecture, affordable housing, and convenient location are attracting a new generation of residents. In 1885 Hamilton Child marveled at Adams's "picturesque scenery" with the "highest point of land in Massachusetts, old Greylock, towering over the town … and the Hoosac River twisting its serpentine course through a rich valley of great beauty." This setting is still here to marvel at and enjoy. The Adams experience should continue to improve and expand with restoration of Armory Court, renovation of the Jones Block and Renfrew Field, the expansion of the Ashuwillticook Rail Trail, and realization of the Greylock Glen project.

Any visitor who wants to see some of the best of 19th-century American architecture in two friendly, unspoiled Berkshire towns should schedule a journey of discovery to Cheshire and Adams.

ADDITIONAL RESOURCES

History of the Town of Cheshire Berkshire County, by Ellen M. Raynor and Emma L. Petticlerc, 1985, 214 pages (reissued by Heritage Books in a facsimile edition, 2002). Covers the years 1767–1884. No images. Informative sections on religious life, agriculture, and manufacturing. Devotes a chapter to the Rev. John Leland.

In This Valley: A Concise History of Adams, Massachusetts, by Eugene F. Michaelenko, 2000, Adams, MA, 49 pages. A coherent and useful summary of the town's history.

The Forging of a New Mill Town: North and South Adams, Massachusetts, 1780–1860, by Timothy Coogan, New York University, 1992. A scholarly study that contrasts Adams with other Massachusetts mill towns.

Adams, Massachusetts, Its Historians and Its History, An Object Lesson, by Charles F. Adams.

Bedbug Hollow: Tales of the Past from the German Neighborhood in Adams, Massachusetts, by Doris DeLugan. An engaging tale of life in one of the many ethnic neighborhoods of Adams.

Working the Stone, by Paul Metcalf and Lucia Saradoff, San Diego: San Diego University Press, 2003. An engaging book that tells the natural, social, and industrial history of the Village of Farnams in the Town of Cheshire. The focus is on the Farnam Bros. Lime Works and the people of Farnams.

MINING AT SPECIALTY MINERALS   Darlene Bordwell

ALONG THE MOHAWK TRAIL

Florida, Clarksburg, and North Adams

This journey is a little different from the others described in this book in that it begins with the story of a road.

America's late 19th-century roads weren't made for cars. In the early 1900s, with the support of the League of American Wheelmen (founded in 1880 by bicyclists and bicycle manufacturers, who started the "good roads" movement),

associations were formed all over the country to improve the country's highways. One of the most exciting ideas was to create national auto trails. Between 1911 and 1926, before the United States implemented a numbered highway system, 48 prominent national auto trails were so designated. Each had evocative names and were marked with colored bands on utility poles.

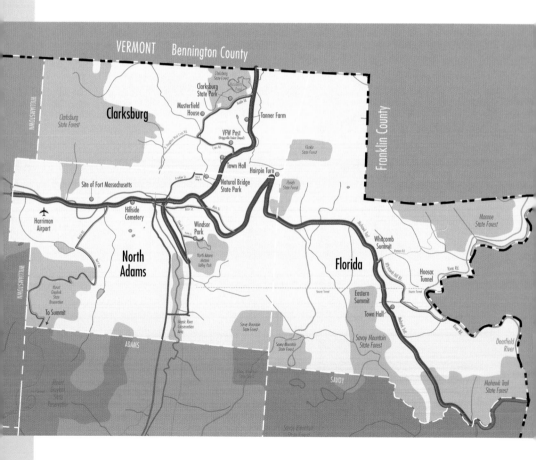

DRIVING THE TRAIL IN 1930S

One of the most popular auto trails in New England was named the Mohawk Trail—that section of Route 2 now extending some 60 miles from the Connecticut River near Erving into North Adams and Williamstown in the Berkshires. The Trail initially ran from Charlemont to North Adams.

The Trail was first proposed by Franklin B. Locke, then city engineer of North Adams, later hailed as the Father of the Mohawk Trail. The road was initially paved with crushed rock laid on top of a layer of oil.

Gift shops, campgrounds, and colorful "trading posts" sprang up along the Trail.

THE MOHAWK TRAIL MARKER | The Mohawk Trail was dedicated on October 22, 1914.

THE BIG INDIAN | This 28-foot wooden Indian chief was erected in 1974 to replace an earlier model. It still draws travelers to the aptly named Big Indian Shop (2183 Mohawk Trail, in Charlemont).

David J. McLaughlin

MOHAWK PARK | The *Hail to the Sunrise* statue in Mohawk Park was erected in 1932 by the Improved Order of Redmen. The fountain was dedicated in 1935.

The sparsely settled, heavily forested western half of the Mohawk Trail is quite scenic. Just beyond the *Hail to the Sunrise* statue in Mohawk Park, on the outskirts of Charlemont, the road snakes along the picturesque Cold River through Mohawk State Forest.

The Trail then climbs steadily over the Hoosac Mountain Range, where observation towers were erected at the best vantage points on the summit and clusters of rustic cabins made this a vacation destination.

This journey covers the towns of Florida, the site of the Eastern Summit and Whitcomb Summit; Clarksburg, which lays claim to the most demanding navigational feature along the Trail; and the important city of North Adams, whose Western Summit provides spectacular views of the Hoosac Valley and the distant hills of Vermont and whose downtown offers a vibrant art scene you don't want to miss.

Paul Rocheleau

FISHING ON THE DEERFIELD RIVER | There is great fly fishing on the rivers in this sparsely settled area, particularly the Deerfield River, which rushes down the steep slopes along the border of the towns of Florida and Monroe. Here there are two "catch and release" areas.

Florida

The town of **Florida** was first settled in 1783. Forty years later there were still only 80 families there, making a meager living from dairy farming and raising cattle and sheep. Florida didn't have any stores or factories, only a tavern and a few sawmills. An early traveler on the carriage road over the Hoosac Mountain wrote: "The town of Florida lies on a bleak, rough mountain top. There are a few good grazing-farms, but grain has a slim chance between the late and early frosts. "

Despite the hostile climate, Florida is the only source in the world of a rutabaga popularly known as the Florida Turnip, which is sweeter than the average turnip.

No one knows for sure why the improbable name of Florida was chosen for the town. It was a name in the news in 1805 when the town was incorporated, 14 years before the acquisition of the state of Florida from the Spanish. One theory I like is that the name was chosen as an act of defiance, since Florida is usually the coldest spot in the state of Massachusetts in the peak winter months.

An audacious undertaking that was to transform this remote town into the epicenter of one of the largest industrial engineering projects of the 19th century began in 1851.

That year the Troy and Greenfield Railroad Co. began to tunnel through 4.82 miles of the Hoosac Mountains as part of an ambitious new rail route that would link Boston and other major population centers in the east with Troy and points west.

Florida became the operating center of a massive effort to create the **Hoosac Tunnel**, a project that would take 24 years to complete and create the longest tunnel in the United States (an honor the tunnel would retain until 1916) and the second longest in the world, after the Mont Cenis tunnel in the Swiss Alps.

The developers expected that new technology would make the dig relatively easy (where have we heard that before?). A 70-ton cast-iron monster known as Wilson's Patented Stone-Cutting Machine began to grind a giant hole into the mountains, then stuck 10 feet into the job. Experts who have examined the design say it would have worked if it had been built using modern hardened steel alloys.

HOOSAC VILLAGE, EAST PORTAL WORK CAMP

270

VIEW OF TUNNEL

The harsh reality was that most of the work was done using hand drills (and later the compressed air Burleigh drill, invented for the project), gunpowder, and nitroglycerine. The Hoosac Tunnel was the first commercial application of "nitro," which proved very unstable. One hundred ninety-six men were killed during the construction, many from unplanned detonations. Most of the workforce (which averaged 800–900 men) were Irishmen, along with some Cornish miners.

The tunnel was officially opened on October 13, 1875. At its deepest point, under the Western Summit, it is 1,728 feet below the surface.

Railroad buffs can drive down to the East Portal from the center of Florida. Whitcomb Hill

Road (see map) winds down the mountain. Turn left on River Road and proceed about half a mile. At the railroad crossing, follow the tracks to the East Portal.

When you stand at the railroad trestle you get the impression that the water here is rushing through a deep gorge. While there actually was a gorge at this spot, excavations from the tunnel were dumped down the side of the river near the tunnel entrance. This filled the gorge and ultimately built up the banks to the present heights.

Though the Hoosac Tunnel is interesting, the most compelling reason to make this side trip is to enjoy the picturesque **Deerfield River**. These days you are much more likely to see a whitewater raft shoot by during the season (April to October) than you are to see a train. Anyone interested in whitewater rafting on the Deerfield should check out Zoar Outdoor (www.zoaroutdoor.com).

Whitcomb Summit in Florida is the highest point (2,173 feet) on the Mohawk Trail. The first roadside cabin complex in America was erected here in 1914 by Charles Canedy, photographer for the *North Adams Transcript*. Today there is a proposal to create a resort (with up to 50 condominium units) on the mountaintop.

In 1923 the Massachusetts Elks Clubs (the Benevolent and Protective Order of Elks, a fraternal order founded in 1868) erected a large bronze statue here to honor the lodge members who died in World War I. The weather was bad on the day of the dedication and the band couldn't make it up the recently paved road, so the national anthem was sung a cappella.

Further along the Trail, after you cross the border into North Adams, the Western Summit offers spectacular views and another gift shop.

< CABINS ALONG THE TRAIL | Most of the early cabins have been replaced by motels, but there are still cabins near the Western Summit of the Trail.

ELK STATUE | The elk statue was created by the Gorham Manufacturing Co. in Providence, Rhode Island. It was designed by Eli Harvey. >
Jim McElholm

Historic American Buildings Survey

MUSTERFIELD HOUSE, BUILT IN 1785

Clarksburg

"Have you visited **Clarksburg**?" is a trick question. While the town center is well north of the Mohawk Trail, the famous **hairpin turn** on the Trail passes through the only part of Clarksburg that is actually on the mountain. The primitive cars used in the early years of motoring over scenic highways had trouble navigating this sharp turn. They also weren't engineered for hills. Many a radiator boiled over trying to get up the slope.

The "turn" became a popular stopping point. A wooden tower and gift shop were erected here in the 1920s, but the building was hit more than a few times by vehicles with bad

brakes, bad drivers, or both. Heavy trucks were a particular menace. When the present building was constructed in 1958 it was turned 90 degrees and some of the rock face was blasted out to accommodate the structure. This is now the site of the **Golden Eagle Restaurant** (1935 Mohawk Trail, 413-663-9834). They are open seven days a week in season and on the weekends the rest of the year.

The hairpin turn was featured in an episode of *Spenser: For Hire*, a TV show that ran from 1985–1988. During the sequence Spenser (played by Robert Urich) and his lady friend spun around the turn at high speed.

HAIRPIN TURN, 1920 POSTCARD

Clarksburg was first settled in 1769. It was incorporated on March 2, 1798, with that name engineered by the numerous Clarks who lived there. In the 19th century Clarksburg had a woolen mill and a wool-carding mill, two grist mills, five sawmills, and three powder mills. An explosion in the powder mill of Edward R. Tinker on June 3, 1869, ended the powder business. The vital records book of the town notes that on June 3, Milo Day, age 35, was "Blown Up in Powder Mill." Tinker had a narrow escape, having just left the building.

Clarksburg has a number of interesting and significant buildings. The **Musterfield House** on Middle Road, built in 1785 (with an addition in 1805), is the oldest house in town. The portico over the front door was added about 1950. The house is of plank construction, with hand-hewn beams marked with Roman numerals and held together with wooden pegs. There is a secret room under the attic that may have been used to hide runaway slaves on the Underground Railroad. In colonial times this building was a tavern.

David J. McLaughlin

MUSTERFIELD HOUSE TODAY

Author's Collection

Panorama from Hairpin Turn, Mohawk Trail.

VFW HALL, FORMER BRIGGSVILLE UNION CHAPEL

You can find detailed drawings and floor plans of this house online as part of the Historic American Buildings Survey at http://memory.loc.gov/ammem/collections/habs_haer/.

Tanner's Farm, on River Road in Clarksburg, just below the Vermont border, was a major dairy farm. The farm is one of the few remaining working farms (they harvest and sell hay) in what was once a large agricultural community.

The **Veterans of Foreign Wars Post 9144** at 144 River Road is located in what was originally the **Briggsville Union Chapel**, built in 1903.

The chapel operated as a nonsectarian place of worship in an era when meeting houses and churches were a center of social life and charitable work. A Ladies' Aid Society met in the Chapel regularly to sew, quilt, and make bandages for the Red Cross.

TANNER FARM TODAY

Clarksburg State Park and Forest

Clarksburg State Forest covers most of the western third of the town. The forest is bordered by Williamstown on the west, North Adams on the south, and Pownal, Vermont, on the north. This 3,1011-acre wilderness is for serious hikers. Four and a half miles of the Appalachian Trail cut through the forest, continuing into the Green Mountain National Forest in Vermont. **Clarksburg State Park**, easily accessible off Middle Road, offers breathtaking views of the Hoosac Range, Mount Greylock, and Green Mountains as you traverse the 9.5 miles of foot trails. This small park of 368 acres has 45 campsites. Mauserts Pond, in the center of the park, is a neat place to picnic, swim, and fish.

Clarksburg State Park
1199 Middle Road/Routes 2 and 8
Clarksburg, MA 01247
413-664-8385

These days Clarksburg is primarily a residential community, favored by many who work in nearby North Adams. The town has revised its bylaws to stimulate industrial development but is committed to preserving its rural character.

If you find yourself stuck in traffic on the Mohawk Trail on a fall day, escape from the other "leaf peepers" by taking Route 8 North and enjoy the views and fall foliage in the quiet hills of Clarksburg, which have some of the most spectacular fall foliage you will find.

MAUSERTS POND   Jim McElholm

THREAD, BY JOSHUA FIELD | Scores of talented young artists have moved to North Adams in the last decade. Joshua Field's studio is in the town's historic Windsor Mill.

MASS MoCA

The idea of creating a contemporary arts center in the vast, vacant industrial complex (26 buildings on 13 acres) that covers almost one third of the city's downtown business district began in 1986. The Williams College Museum of Art (WCMA) from nearby Williamstown was looking for space to exhibit the large works often created by contemporary artists. Under the leadership of Thomas Krens (then director of WCMA), North Adams Mayor John Barrett III, and Joseph C. Thompson, who was named the founding director of the proposed new institution, and with some initial controversy in the community, this bold idea became a reality when the **Massachusetts Museum of Contemporary Art (Mass MoCA)** opened in 1999.

North Adams

In the last 20 years **North Adams** has become a vibrant center of the visual and performing arts, repositioning this classic mill town for the 21st century as a place where new generations can appreciate the creative output of today and the architectural and industrial legacy of 19th-century America.

PANORAMIC VIEW OF MASS MOCA

PROJECTIONS, BY JENNY HOLZER | This MASS MoCA exhibition (November 2007 to Fall 2008) is the first interior light projection of this talented artist staged in the United States. Projections transformed the enormous gallery in Building 5 into an "engaging and provocative meeting place flooded with words, bodies and light," according to a museum press release.

As the design of the complex evolved (the master plan was completed in 1995), it became clear that the scale and versatility of this unique space were ideal for both visual and performing arts, and the mission of MASS MoCA expanded to become "a center that would present and catalyze the creation of works that chart new creative territory." The expanded mission gathered widespread support.

The large posters on the front face of the museum testify to the dynamic and expansive program of an institution whose audacious goal is to "present the best art of our time." The 110,000 square feet of soaring exhibition space allow for the display of paintings, sculpture, and multimedia art that few other museums can begin to match. Moreover, the museum stages over 75 innovative performing arts events each year—music (from folk to jazz to American roots), dance in all its forms, film documentaries, and avant-garde theater.

Kelly Lee

Kelly Lee

ECLIPSE MILL | The four-story Eclipse Mill is now a diverse artistic community with members whose varying skills testify to the rich mosaic of the North Adams arts scene: painters, potters, textile artists, printmakers, musicians, ceramic artists, photographers, a dancer, writers, a paper maker, and a book dealer specializing in art books.

Kelly Lee

The Expanding Arts Scene

In the audacious initial planning for what became MASS MoCA, there was more hope than certainty that creation of the country's largest arts complex in the middle of downtown would be a catalyst for the transformation of North Adams. But today there is evidence all around that a new, younger city is rapidly emerging.

The old mills have been transformed into artist lofts. North Adams State College (founded in 1894 as the North Adams Normal School) became the Massachusetts College of Liberal Arts (MCLA) in 1997 and now offers degrees in the arts. Artists are moving into the area from all over the Northeast, attracted by affordable housing and studio space, an increasingly inviting downtown, and the world-class museums that attract over 100,000 visitors a year. A recent initiative, an Open Studios weekend, involved more than 80 artists.

< ARTIST AT WORK | Paris-based Jean-Noel Chazelle, whose work is exhibited and sold in seven countries, spent three months in North Adams in 2007 at the invitation of gallery owner Kurt Kolok. He paints on large sheets of Plexiglas.

Courtesy of City of North Adams

MOHAWK THEATER

Inviting galleries like the Kolok Gallery (121 Union Street), Gallery 51 (operated by MCLA and located at 51 Main Street), and the Eclipse Gallery (243 Union Street, in the former Eclipse Mill) provide an outlet for a growing artist community.

All kinds of historic structures are finding a new lease on life. **The Porches Inn at MASS MoCA** *(231 River Street) opened in 2001. This boutique inn, built around seven creatively restored Victorian-era worker row houses, has a retro-contemporary décor. 50 rooms. Full services. Year-round heated pool. Across from MASS MoCA. www. porches.com | 413-664-0400*

Eric Rudd, a prominent local sculptor and developer, has turned the former **Unitarian Church** into a showcase and memorial, the **Chapel for Humanity** (82 Summer Street, www.

artchapel.com). The splendid 1938 Art Deco movie showcase, the **Mohawk Theater** (111 Main), is being renovated and will again be a downtown magnet.

North Adams is in a long, painful transition. In its prime—the 1890s into the 1920s—the city was a prominent center of shoe making and textile manufacturing (and later, electronics). The manufacturing jobs that made North Adams a robust manufacturing center for 150 years are gone for good. This is now predominantly a service economy, with a different income mix. The housing stock has deteriorated in too many parts of the city. The road system doesn't route traffic gracefully through the town center. Almost one fifth of the population is over age 65. Despite these handicaps, today's visitor will discover a city on the move.

Kelly Lee

ERIC RUDD SCULPTURES IN CHAPEL FOR HUMANITY | The former church contains over 150 life-size figures sculptured by Eric Rudd. The center is open during the summer, Wednesdays to Sundays, from 12:00 to 5:00 P.M. Admission is free.

David J. McLaughlin

MAIN STREET

Downtown

Begin an exploration of downtown by walking along the city's historic **Main Street**. Two buildings designed by the noted Victorian architect Marcus Fayette Cummings command attention. The **Blackinton Block**, at the corner of Holden and Main streets, features an ornate Italianate brick structure. The second

Blackinton Block, facing Main Street, has a fortress-style roof parapet.

Since 1947 the city has celebrated the arrival of fall with an extravaganza known as the **Northern Berkshire Fall Foliage Festival**, a week of imaginative events—races, children's events like the Phantom Leaf Hunt, dinner dances, an Arts Festival and Craft Fair, and others. This culminates in the Fall Foliage Parade (held on the Sunday before Columbus Day), where marching bands and clever floats keep upwards of 30,000 spectators entertained. For details, visit www.fallfoliageparade.com.

The city offers other "happenings" throughout the year, including Winterfest, the last Saturday in February; the Northern Berkshire Food Festival, held the third Sunday in June; the Mayor's Downtown Celebration on the third Wednesday in August; an Open Studios weekend in mid-October; and the favorite of every kid in the Northern Berkshires, the Eagle Street Beach Party, where one of the downtown streets is closed off and filled with sand.

Courtesy of City of North Adams

FLORIDA TURNIP FLOAT IN 2007 FALL
FESTIVAL PARADE

CIVIL WAR SOLDIERS MONUMENT >

As you explore Main Street, keep watch for the **Monitor Monument**, which celebrates the city's industrial past. This marks the location of the North Adams Iron Co., where in 1861 pig iron was smelted for the armor plates on America's first ironclad ship, the *U.S.S. Monitor.*

At the head of Main Street is **Monument Square**, in the center of which stands the city's Civil War Soldiers monument, dedicated on July 4, 1874, the same year that North Adams was incorporated as a town. The statue was created by Charles Niles Pike, a North Adams native and Civil War veteran. The marble statue sits on a pedestal of brown freestone. In 1913 former President Theodore Roosevelt made a campaign speech here, running for the Presidency on the Bull Moose Party ticket.

Just beyond Monument Square is the **North Adams Public Library** (74 Church Street), a stunning Second Empire-style building, built in 1867–69 to be the home of textile baron Sanford Blackinton (1797–1885). In 1896 the mansion was donated to the city as a gift from the city's first Mayor, Albert Charles Houghton, and renovated to serve as the city library in 1897.

In 2003–4 the library completed a new eastern wing, which enabled the expansion of its collection.

Robert Behr

NORTH ADAMS PUBLIC LIBRARY | The Blackinton Mansion was also designed by Marcus Fayette Cummings. Considered one of the finest examples of Second Empire-style architecture in New England, it contains a spectacular crystal chandelier and three marble fireplaces imported from Italy.

A great way to explore historic North Adams is to participate in one of the free **walking tours** that local historian Paul W. Marino leads from June to mid-October. They begin on selected Saturdays at 2:30 P.M. His tours are informative and engaging. For details, check the extensive city Website at www.northadams-ma.gov, call 413-207-1344, or email historyman@copper.net.

Kelly Lee

Kelly Lee

SMITH HOUSE AT MCLA | Two of the three buildings survive from the days when this was the North Adams Normal School, later North Adams State College. The Smith House served for years as the residence of the school's president but is now used for receptions and visitor housing.

Massachusetts College of Liberal Arts

An important source of youthful energy (and employment) in this city is the four-year liberal arts college known since 1997 as the **Massachusetts College of Liberal Arts** (MCLA; main campus at 375 Church Street). The school began in 1894 as the North Adams Normal School, the first educational institution in the Berkshires dedicated to training teachers. For over a century the school's close identification with the city was reflected in its name. Between 1932 and 1960 the school was known as the State Teachers College of North Adams and then, until this latest change, the North Adams State College.

MCLA describes itself as "a public college with a private atmosphere."

THE WESTERN GATEWAY HERITAGE STATE PARK

David J. McLaughlin

Jim McElholm

DISPLAY IN VISITORS CENTER

Western Gateway Heritage State Park

In 1985 the state of Massachusetts created an urban park, the **Western Gateway Heritage State Park**, in the former Boston and Main freight yard to celebrate the building of the Hoosac Tunnel and the importance of the railroad in the development of our country. North Adams was indeed the "western gateway"; over half of the train traffic to and from Boston came through this city. Six of the historic buildings, such as the B&H Freight House, are on the National Register of Historic Places. Incidentally, this is the only Heritage State Park in Massachusetts still functioning successfully.

The heart of the park is the Visitors Center (Building 4), which incorporates the former Hoosac Tunnel Museum. A 30-minute documentary tells the history of the Hoosac Tunnel. There are fascinating exhibits that include a vintage floor scale that was used to weigh loads of up to half a ton (and will hold any number of kids anxious to do something).

The Northern Berkshires Creative Arts (Building 1; 413-663-8338) organizes art workshops for children, teens, and adults and stages a summer art camp. They do a

remarkable job of helping integrate art into the community.

The park includes the **North Adams Museum of History and Science** (Building 5A), a museum created in 2001 to chronicle the history of the city and the Northern Berkshires. The large (400 member plus) North Adams Historical Society, with roots that go back to a women's Monday Club established in 1895, created the museum and maintains and periodically updates its extensive exhibits. The museum is open year around—four days a week (Thursdays, Fridays, and Saturdays from 10:00 A.M. to 4:00 P.M. and Sundays from 1:00–4:00 P.M.) from May through December, and on Saturdays and Sundays from January through April. For additional details, see www.geocities.com/northadamshistory/.

The **Freight Yard Pub** in the complex (Building 3) is open throughout the year. A gallery displays works by area artists. During the summer months there are concerts, walking tours, and other special events.

Western Gateway Heritage State Park
9 Furnace Street, Route 8
North Adams, MA 01247
413-663-6312

Natural Bridge State Park

There is both a natural and a manmade white marble wonder just north of the city on Route 8 (the road to Clarksburg). The only natural white marble bridge in North America is the centerpiece of the **Natural Bridge State Park**, established in 1985. This was the site of a marble quarry for almost a century and a half (1810–1947).

The manmade wonder is a dam built using the quarry's white marble. It spans Hudson Brook, which cascades through the 48-acre park.

Mount Greylock

Notch Road, one of the two major access roads to **Mount Greylock**, is easily reached from Route 2 west of the center of North Adams. Until late 2009 all the roads into Mount Greylock State Reservation will be closed for repair to attain better access and safety improvements, as is Bascom Lodge (built between 1833 and 1838) and the 93-foot Veterans Memorial Tower (see page 261 in the Adams section).

The view from the summit of Mount Greylock is unsurpassed, and we all look forward eagerly to the anticipated completion of the project by October 2009. In the interim, the hiking trails to the summit will be open, but you should call ahead and confirm access. In general these are trails suitable only for experienced hikers.

NATURAL BRIDGE

THE VIEW FROM MOUNT GREYLOCK

Other Excursions

Cascade Trail (reached at the end of Marion Avenue) follows Notch Brook to a cascading waterfall. This easy hike is an in-town gem. Parts of the trail require walking along the rocks.

On the east side of the city, **Windsor Lake** is a pleasant, small (17-acre) pond with good public access. You can launch canoes or car-top boats from a gravel ramp (no motors allowed). This is a popular place to fish for trout from April through June. There is also decent swimming. Historic Valley Campground, adjacent to the park, has 100 campsites. Both the lake and campground are operated by the city. There are free concerts at the lake every Wednesday at 7:00 P.M. in the summer (bring a lawn chair or blanket).

Hillside Cemetery, the oldest municipal cemetery in North Adams, contains the graves of many of the city's notables from all walks of life. If you are lucky enough to be around when Paul Marino holds a Hillside Cemetery Walk, you can enjoy a fascinating tour of the stonework and significant monuments. Look for the gravestone of John Henry Haynes, a noted archeologist and early photographer. It is a replica (a duplicate in size and shape) of the Black Obelisk of the Assyrian King Shalmaneser III and is registered with the Smithsonian Institution through Washington, D.C.-based Save Outdoor Sculpture. The aptly named Hillside Cemetery is particularly picturesque after a snowstorm.

DAM IN NATURAL BRIDGE STATE PARK

Darlene Bordwell

HILLSIDE CEMETERY

Jim McElholm

WINDSOR LAKE

The ongoing creative collaboration of MASS MoCA, the Clark Art Institute, and the Williams College Museum of Art has made the Northern Berkshires a "don't miss" center for the arts. The continuously improving infrastructure has enabled a new generation to discover the affordable delights of this former mill town and given visitors a score of reasons to arrive in the Berkshires by way of the Mohawk Trail and stop to explore North Adams.

ADDITIONAL RESOURCES

MASS MoCA: From Mill to Museum, by Joseph Thompson, Simeon Bruner, and John Heon, edited by Jennifer Trainer, photography by Nicholas Whitman, 2000. The development of MASS MoCA, richly illustrated.

History of North Adams, Massachusetts, 1749–1885, by W. F. Spear, North Adams: Hoosac Valley News Print, 1885. The early settlement and development of North Adams and the history of its institutions.

The Forging of a New Mill Town: North and South Adams, Massachusetts, 1780–1860, by Timothy Coogan, New York University, 1992. This Ph.D. thesis compares the industrial society of Adams (which then included North Adams) with that in other cities of the Northeast, particularly Lowell, Massachusetts.

Steeples: Sketches of North Adams, by Joe Manning, Flatiron Press: Torrington, CT, 1998 (second edition), 249 pages. This book contains captivating interviews with a cross-section of mostly "ordinary" people who know the city and the events that have shaped it. Generously illustrated with vintage and contemporary black-and-white photographs.

Disappearing into North Adams, by Joe Manning, Flatiron Press: Lawrence, MA, 2001, 368 pages. Manning's second book on the city he has adopted. Covers the period from the 1960s (when a massive urban renewal program began) to 1999, the year that MASS MoCA opened.

Last Agony of the Great Bore, by F. W. Bird, Boston: E.P. Dutton and Company, 1868 (second edition). An engaging story of the trials and tribulations of the 19th-century "big dig."

History of the Hoosac Tunnel, by Orson Dalrymple, North Adams, 1880. An early comprehensive history of the tunnel.

North Adams, Massachusetts: Tunnel City, by Charles H. Possons, Glens Falls, NY, 1890. A study sponsored by the North Adams Board of Trade.

http://graylocke.tripod.com/monumentsquare/index.html. An extensive and fascinating Website that tells the full history of North Adams' Monument Square.

STEPHEN HANNOCK'S 8' × 12' 2005 PAINTING OF THE HOOSIC RIVER IN THE NATIONAL GALLERY OF ART | The full title of this stunning work is *A Recent History of Art in Western Massachusetts: Flooded River for Lane Faison* (MASS MoCA #12). S. Lane Faison Jr. (1907–2006) was a renowned art scholar and head of the Art History Department at Williams College, a friend and mentor to artist Stephen Hannock. >

"THE VILLAGE BEAUTIFUL"

Williamstown

Henry N. Tague, who opened the Greylock Hotel in **Williamstown** in 1912, coined the phrase "Williamstown, the Village Beautiful" when he promoted the hotel in *The Gul*, the Williams College Class of 1915 yearbook. This nickname continues to be an apt characterization of this very special Berkshire town.

As the home of prestigious Williams College, Williamstown is an intellectual and creative powerhouse. Ever since the Sterling and Francine Clark Art Institute opened in 1955, Williamstown, which already had one of the best college art museums in the country, has been a dynamic center of the visual arts. There are enough well-preserved historic buildings in Williamstown to keep a history buff interested

for days. *A Walk Along Main Street*, published by the town Historical Commission, offers a self-guided walking tour. The town not only has the sophisticated restaurants, inviting shops, and performing arts one would expect of an elite college town; the scenic countryside is certain to lure you outdoors, where a network of carefully preserved farms, hiking trails, and parks is within 15–20 minutes of the town center.

Williamstown is in the northwest quadrant of Berkshire County, less than an hour from the southern Berkshires and easily reached on historic Route 7. It is some 20 minutes south of Bennington, Vermont. The Mohawk Trail (Route 2) also leads directly to Williamstown from the east.

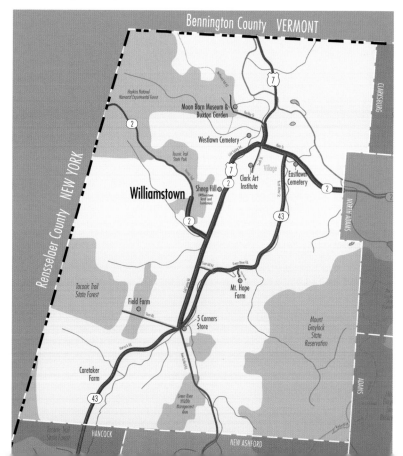

WILLIAMS COLLEGE SCENE

Early History

Williamstown was settled during a brief lull in the French & Indian Wars, when it had the ungainly name of West Hoosuck Plantation. Sixty lots of about 11 acres each were sold between 1751 and 1752. Almost a quarter of the lots were purchased by soldiers at nearby Fort Massachusetts, which was established in 1745 to guard the frontier.

Captain (later Colonel) Ephraim Williams, Jr., who commanded all the frontier forts and stockades from the Berkshires to the Connecticut River, bought two of these lots. Williams was killed in 1755 during the battle of Lake George, before he could settle in the area, but he bequeathed funds for the founding of a local free school with the stipulation that the hamlet be incorporated and renamed.

In 1765, West Hoosac was incorporated as Williamstown. The free school opened in 1791 and became **Williams College** in 1793. This prestigious liberal arts college has an undergraduate population of about 2,100 (coed since 1970). The town and college have grown together in general harmony. Ivy-clad buildings lie along the Main Street originally laid out two and a half centuries ago.

AN AERIAL VIEW OF WILLIAMSTOWN

David J. McLaughlin

FORT WEST HOOSAC SIGN

*The **Williams Inn**, conveniently located in the center of town at 1090 Main, offers 21st-century accommodations and attentive service on a site near where a 1756 stockade and blockhouse stood. Information on the inn is available at www. williamsinn.com | 413-458-9371* INN

The remnant of the village green that ran the length of Main Street in colonial days is now a small grassy area called **Field Park**, located across from the Inn. The area was given this

name in 1878 for its principal benefactor, Cyrus Field (1819–1892), who laid the first transatlantic cable. The park contains a replica of the type of "regulation" house the first settlers would have constructed.

Markers in the park show the location of the community's first (1768–1798) and second (1798–1866) meeting houses.

After the end of Indian hostilities (formalized in 1763 with the Treaty of Paris), Williamstown grew rapidly, initially as a center of dairy farming, sheepherding, and wool production. During the colonial era and well into the early decades of the 19th century, trade centered on the towns to the west, keeping Williamstown bustling. In the 1820s at least 30 wagons a day passed between Williamstown and Troy, New York. There was a even a proposal, in 1827–28, to build a canal extending from Cheshire through Williamstown to the Hudson River, but the steam locomotive put a stop to canal building.

1753 HOUSE, A 1953 RECONSTRUCTION | This house is a careful 1953 reproduction of several of the early homes built in West Hoosac between 1752 and 1753. It was constructed using only techniques and tools from the period. An order of the General Court, adopted on January 17, 1750, required that each settler build a house of at least 18 feet by 15 feet. Typically, as the family grew, a second unit of the same size was built at the home's gable end.

Jim McElholm

With the arrival of the railroad (which reached the town in 1859) and the Industrial Revolution, farming began to decline. Thankfully, the amount of water power in Williamstown limited the extent of manufacturing, and the few sizable operations—two textile mills and a twine factory—are long gone. The textile mill housing still stands on Hall and Arnold streets, as does the building that was the mill store, St. Raphael's Church (built in 1899 and now listed for sale) and the railroad station. This area is part of the town's historic district.

Artifacts from Williamstown's manufacturing past are part of a superb collection of photographs, documents, and objects preserved in the **House of Local History**, located inside the **David and Joyce Milne Public Library** at 1095 Main Street.

The House of Local History was founded in 1941. Its treasure trove of artifacts, documents, and photographs are professionally displayed in spacious, well-lighted galleries.

There is a special room set aside for children. This contains period clothing and other artifacts that engage youngsters in a special way.

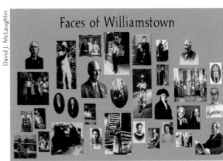

FACES OF WILLIAMSTOWN

CHILDREN'S ROOM

House of Local History
David and Joyce Milne Public Library
1095 Main Street
(at Intersection of Routes 2 & 7)
Williamstown, MA
413-458-2160
www.milnelibrary.org/hlh.html

DISPLAY OF EARLY FARM EQUIPMENT

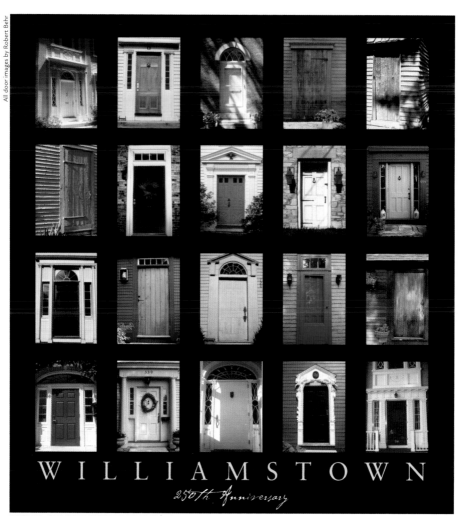

All door images by Robert Behr

WILLIAMSTOWN

250th Anniversary

POSTER OF HISTORIC DOORWAYS | The poster was designed by Beth Carlisle Design. Printed by Excelsior Printing.

Visitors are surprised to learn that Williamstown once had a successful soft-drink operation. **Sand Springs**, about 2 miles north of town, was used by the Indians of the Five Nations as a campground and source of healing water. The town history reports that "students and tutors of Williams College visited the Springs … for baths." After Greylock Hall–Sands Spring Hotel, built on the site in 1870, burned to the ground in 1886, Dr. S. L. Lloyd set up a sanitarium there in 1893, bottling and selling water. Flavorings were added, and Sand Springs Ginger Ale was a pioneer in the soft-drink business. The Springs are now the site of a spa and family fitness center.

Williamstown has an extensive number of antique homes. A beautiful poster of historic Williamstown doorways, available at the House of Local History, will encourage anyone with an interest in period homes to seek out these well-preserved treasures. The poster above was developed in 2003 to celebrate the town's 250th anniversary.

The House of Local History is typically open Monday through Friday between 10:00 A.M. and noon, but hours can vary and it is wise to call ahead.

RESIDENCE OF WILLIAMS COLLEGE
PRESIDENTS, BUILT 1802

Among the Williamstown historic homes you
don't want to miss is the **Samuel Sloan House** at
936 Main, which has housed the presidents of
Williams College since 1858.

For those who like to live their history, a
certified historic structure, the **Col. Benjamin
Simonds House**, built about 1770, has been
beautifully restored and is filled with tasteful
antiques. *This authentic Georgian Colonial is now*
River Bend Farm, *a four-bedroom B&B at 643
Simonds Road (Route 7 north of Williamstown).
Col. Simonds was one of Williamstown's founders
and a soldier at Fort Massachusetts. For further
information, see http://windsorsofstonington.com/
RBF/ or phone 413-458-3121.*

Another historic structure is the **Nehemiah
Smedley House** at 530 Main, built by one of
the original Proprietors of the town in 1772.
It operated as a tavern for a time. Benedict
Arnold spent the night of May 6, 1775, here,
on his way to join Ethan Allen in taking
Fort Ticonderoga in the early days of the
Revolutionary War. Bread was baked here to
supply troops who participated in the Battle
of Bennington.

Many of the major institutions of Williamstown
are located along or just off Main Street,
including its superb summer theater.

COL. BENJAMIN SIMONDS HOUSE, C. 1770

NEHEMIAH SMEDLEY HOUSE, 1772

FROM A 2007 PRODUCTION OF NOEL COWARD'S *BLYTHE SPIRIT*

Courtesy Williams Theatre Festival

The Performing Arts

The **'62 Center for Theatre and Dance**, 1000 Main Street, is the home of the renowned **Williamstown Theatre Festival (WTF)**.

This Tony Award-winning center offers both classic and new plays each summer on three stages as well as a late-night cabaret, readings, workshops, and other special events. WTF also provides training programs for aspiring actors and opportunities for those interested in set design and theater management to intern with professional designers, directors, and administrators.

The **Williamstown Film Festival** was founded in 1998. This nonprofit organization was set up to honor film classics, explore new film technologies, and celebrate present-day filmmaking through seminars and other events that involve actors, writers, directors, and producers. More than 35 filmmakers are in residence during the annual event. The films are screened at the Images Cinema, a distinguished site for art and independent films year round. For information, see www.williamstownfilmfest.com.

The **Williamstown Jazz Festival** (formerly known as Jazz Town) is a weeklong festival held during the height of the "Mud Season," in April. Lectures, dances, competitions, and concerts are held during this "happening." The festival is sponsored by the Williams College Department of Music, the Williamstown Chamber of Commerce, MASS MoCA, the Clark Art Institute, and other institutions. For information, see www.williamstownjazz.com.

> **Williamstown Theatre Festival**
> '62 Center for Theatre and Dance
> 1000 Main Street
> Williamstown, MA
> 413-597-3400
> www.wtfestival.org

David J. McLaughlin

THOMPSON MEMORIAL CHAPEL | The remains of Col. Ephraim Williams were moved from Lake George to Williamstown and reinterred in the chapel at the time of its dedication. A war memorial lists the names of all Williams College men who died in the Civil War, World Wars I and II, Korea, and Vietnam.

Jim McElholm

CONGREGATIONAL CHURCH | This was originally a Romanesque Revival-style church, built of brick. In 1914 the church was redone in the neoclassical style, modeled in part on the First Congregational Church in Old Lyme, Connecticut (which itself is a 1910 reconstruction of the 1817 meeting house designed by Samuel Belcher).

David J. McLaughlin

CIVIL WAR MONUMENT IN FRONT OF GRIFFIN HALL

Along Main Street

Just beyond the President's house on the north side of Main Street is the **Congregational Church** (906 Main), the town's third meeting house, completed in 1886.

Williams College commencement exercises were held in each successive Congregational Church from 1795 until 1912, when the college's Chapin Hall was completed.

Thompson Memorial Chapel, at 860 Main, is a signature building built in 1903–04. The west transept window, dedicated to Williams alumnus and U.S. President James A. Garfield, was created by the famous 19th-century stained-glass artist John LaFarge. It was first installed in the Stone Chapel across the street.

Griffin Hall, at 844 Main, was constructed in 1828, originally the Brick Chapel when it was designed by the college's third president, Edward Dorr Griffin. It was relocated to the northeast in 1904 to align it with the Thompson Memorial Chapel.

HOPKINS OBSERVATORY

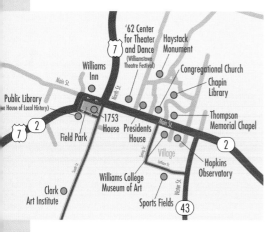

On the south side of Main Street, **Hopkins Observatory**, at 829 Main, is the oldest existing astronomical observatory in the United States. Professor Albert Hopkins and his students built the observatory between 1826 and 1828 from stone they quarried on East Mountain.

The observatory was originally located in the center of the quadrangle; it was placed in its present location in 1961. The building now houses the Milham Planetarium and the Mehlin Museum of Astronomy. There are shows on Tuesdays and Thursdays at 7:30 P.M. during the summer months.

Art Museums

Williamstown is the location of two major art institutions.

Williams College Museum of Art (WCMA) is located at 15 Lawrence Hall Drive, west of the observatory. WCMA, one of the finest college art museums in the country, was founded in 1926. There are over 12,000 objects in the museum's permanent collection, which focuses on contemporary art and the art of world cultures.

The neoclassical rotunda in the oldest part of the museum was originally the Williams College Library. The museum was expanded significantly beginning in 1981. Designed by the noted architect Charles Moore, the expansion added a dramatic three-story atrium that connects the original building with a four-story addition.

In 2001 WCMA, with funds from the Museum Fellows, friends, and museum endowments, commissioned artist Louise Bourgeois to create an outdoor sculpture to celebrate the 75th anniversary of the museum. This striking piece, *Eyes*, which consists of nine elements, lines the walkways at the front entrance to the museum.

EYES, BY LOUISE BOURGEOIS

Courtesy WCMA

WCMA ROTUNDA | The rotunda was designed by architect Thomas Tefft in 1846.

WCMA is open Tuesdays through Saturdays from 10:00 A.M. to 5:00 P.M. and Sundays from 1:00 to 5:00 P.M. It is closed on New Year's Day, Thanksgiving, and Christmas.

Williams College Museum of Art
15 Lawrence Hall Drive
Williamstown, MA
413-597-2424
www.wcma.org

Arthur Evans

CLARK ART INSTITUTE ORIGINAL BUILDING

On May 17, 1955, the **Sterling and Francine Clark Art Institute** opened in Williamstown. Robert Sterling Clark (1877–1956), the grandson of the cofounder of the Singer Sewing Machine Co., was born into a life of privilege and wealth. He used his considerable fortune to assemble a diverse, high-quality art collection. He and his French wife, Francine Modzelewska Clark (1876–1960), intended to create a museum in Manhattan to house their collection, but concern about a nuclear attack led him to "scout upper New York and possibly even the Berkshires" for a less vulnerable location. The family had ties to Williams College and Clark quickly settled on Williamstown.

The world-renowned Institute's greatest strengths lie in 19th-century European and American painting, especially the French Impressionists. The museum also contains an extensive collection of English silver, master drawings and prints, and, more recently, early photography.

In 2001 the Clark completed a master plan for the evolution of the museum in the 21st century. The Japanese architect Tadao Ando, known for designing serene interior spaces and for modernist buildings that complement the natural beauty of the land, is designing a new facility for the campus. The landscape architectural firm of Reed Hilderbrand Associates will design the exterior grounds and gardens.

Sterling and Francine Clark Art Institute
225 South Street
Williamstown, MA 01267
413-458-2303
www.clarkart.edu

CLARK BILLBOARD

The Clark is renowned for promoting new approaches to understanding works of art. It offers gallery tours for children and adults, stages studio art classes, and holds outdoor family festivals. The museum has an extensive performing arts program that ranges from outdoor band concerts to chamber music. Its publications include the annual *CAI: The Journal of the Clark Art Institute*, an extensive number of books on the museum's collections, exhibitions, and conference proceedings; and free electronic publications posted on its Website. The large Museum Store has over 2,000 offerings.

The Clark Art Institute is open year round, from 10:00 A.M. to 5:00 P.M. daily during July and August and on Tuesdays through Sundays the rest of the year. The museum is closed on Thanksgiving, Christmas, and New Year's Day.

Other Williams College Attractions

There are other notable college attractions near the center of Williamstown.

The **Chapin Library,** at 26 Hopkins Drive, is on the second floor of Stetson Hall, behind Thompson Chapel. This library, which opened in 1923, contains original copies of the four founding documents of the United States: the Declaration of Independence, the Articles of Confederation, the Constitution, and the Bill of Rights. (Only the National Archives in Washington has a similar collection of these four key documents.) On Independence Day each year the Library sponsors an open house for viewing of the rare documents and readings by actors from the Williamstown Theatre Festival.

The lowest level of Stetson Hall, incidentally, contains the archives of band leader Paul Whiteman. The collection includes over 3,500 original scores and a complete library of music of the 1920s.

A multiyear renovation of Stetson Hall will close the Library until 2011. Interim arrangements are being made for a limited collection to be housed in the historic Southworth Schoolhouse (corner of Southworth and School streets). For the

latest information on access, visit www.williams.edu/resources/chapin/welcome.html.

One afternoon in August 1806, five Williams College students met in a grove to talk and pray together. When a storm came up, they sought refuge in the lee of a haystack. During their spirited discussion, they pledged to dedicate their lives to the welfare of people across the seas. This led to the formation of the American Board of Commissioners for Foreign Missions. The **Haystack Monument** was erected in 1867 in a section of the Williams College campus named Mission Park (see map), to honor the start of the American Foreign Missions Movement.

HAYSTACK MONUMENT

Robert Behr

David J. McLaughlin

SIGN AT CORNER OF MAIN AND SPRING STREETS

Downtown

The commercial center of Williamstown is located along Spring and Water streets, where an array of boutiques, antique shops, art galleries, and restaurants beckon.

Parking can be a challenge at the height of the season, so if a stroll into town is feasible from where you are staying, this is preferable.

Cemeteries

Williamstown has several spacious, well-maintained cemeteries that offer a tranquil setting and an opportunity to learn more of the town's history. **Westlawn Cemetery**, just west of the town center on Main Street, was laid out in 1766.

It contains the **Sprague Family Chapel**, which is decorated with Art Nouveau ironwork with leaf and floral motifs, as well as colorful stained-glass depiction of an angel.

The initials stand for Robert Chapman Sprague (1900–1991), founder of Sprague Electric Co., an industrial powerhouse in early 20th-century North Adams in the buildings that now house MASS MoCA.

IRONWORK, SPRAGUE CHAPEL

Darlene Bordwell

David J. McLaughlin

Eastlawn Cemetery, east of the town center and just off Route 2, was created in 1842. The stone fence at the entrance was built in 1899. The Sherman Burbank Memorial Chapel, built in 1935, is available at no cost for memorial services.

Many of the town residents who served in the armed forces of the United States are buried in this cemetery, including William Henry Seeley (1853–1932), one of the youngest soldiers to serve in the Civil War. He was not yet 12 years old when he enlisted in the 25th Regiment on January 10, 1865.

Southlawn Cemetery in South Williamstown contains the graves of many of the area's early settlers.

WESTLAWN CEMETERY >
David J. McLaughlin

VETERANS' GRAVES AT EASTLAWN

SHERMAN BURBANK MEMORIAL CHAPEL

David J. McLaughlin

Excursions

During any visit to Williamstown, allow time to enjoy the outdoors. While most Berkshire towns have one or two special places to hike and enjoy nature, Williamstown can keep you busy for days.

Hopkins Memorial Forest (entrance at 271 Northwest Hill Road) is located in the Taconic Hills in the northwest quadrant of Williamstown, spilling over into adjacent Pownal, Vermont, and Petersburgh, New York. This 2,600-acre reserve originally consisted of many small farms, which were consolidated between 1887 and 1910 by Col. Amos Lawrence Hopkins, the son of Mark Hopkins, President of Williams College from 1836 to 1872. The forest was established in 1934 and is managed by the Williams College Center for Environmental Studies. There are 15 miles of nature and cross-country trails here.

Buxton Garden is a one-acre farm garden designed to have flowers blooming in the spring, summer, and fall. The **Moon Barn Museum** on this site has a fascinating collection of farm machinery and tools, historic photographs, and other memorabilia.

NATURE HUT

For information, see www.williams.edu/CES/hopkins.htm or phone 413-597-4353.

Sheep Hill Farm, at 671 Cold Spring Road, consists of 50 scenic acres. It is the site of Sunnybrook Farm Dairy, which Art and Ella Rosenburg operated for over 50 years. In the 19th century, sheep were raised here, and the prominent hill behind the well-preserved farmhouse has been called Sheep Hill for over a century. Since 2000, Sheep Hill has been the headquarters of the **Williamstown Rural Land Foundation**, a private, nonprofit land conservation trust. The Foundation was established in 1986 with a mission of "protecting the rural character of Williamstown."

Sheep Hill is open to the public year round for hiking, birding, picnicking, and cross-country skiing. The farmhouse is loaded with exhibits.

This is a very kids-friendly venue that stages imaginative special events: firefly hikes, star gazing, full-moon snowshoe outings, bird and butterfly walks. The view from the top of Sheep Hill is one of the best in the Berkshires. For further information, see www.wrlf.org/events.html.

Another special place in Williamstown is **Field Farm**, an enchanting 316-acre nature preserve with mixed hardwood and pine forest, freshwater marshes, open meadows, and (in the Caves Lot area at the north end of the farm) small streams that disappear into underground channels carved into the limestone bedrock. There are over 4 miles of (moderately difficult) trails.

SHEEP HILL POSTER

FIELD FARM | The Main House was designed in 1948 by Edwin Goodell. The Folly was designed by Ulrich Franzen in 1966. Modern sculptures, including works by Herbert Ferber and Richard M. Miller, are located in the garden.

This magical spot, a property of The Trustees of Reservations property since 1984, has two architecturally distinctive houses that illustrate post-World War II architecture. **The Folly**, *the Guest House at Field Farm at 554 Sloan Road, offers upscale accommodations (five rooms) to the lucky few, who get to enjoy a view of Mount Greylock. For more information visit http://guesthouseatfieldfarm. thetrustees.org/pages/650_about_the_guest_house. cfm or phone 413-458-3135.* **INN**

Williamstown was the center of agricultural research early in the 20th century. **Mount Hope Farm** was a renowned experimental farm started in 1910, ultimately extending over 1,300 acres. Mount Hope was successful in using genetic principles to increase crop yield (primarily potatoes, then still a major Berkshires crop) and to boost the productivity of poultry. The farm is now owned by Williams College and isn't open to the public at the present time.

One of the most picturesque trails up Mount Greylock is **Money Brook Trail**, a 9.7-mile, five-and-a-half hour hike that begins on Hopper Road in Williamstown. The trail passes a beautiful waterfall, then joins the Appalachian Trail to the summit.

MONEY BROOK TRAIL

STORE AT FIVE CORNERS | The second story and the Greek Revival portico were added in 1830.

Scenic South Williamstown

South of Williamstown, where Route 7 intersects with Route 43, there are remnants of an 18th-century settlement, called the **Five Corners Historic District**. A cabin was built here in 1762.

The **Store at Five Corners** at this site, originally a tavern built in 1770, is said to be the oldest continuously operated country store in the United States. The first South Williamstown Post Office was located here.

This is a great place to stop and refresh yourself. The store has a full-service delicatessen and sells gourmet specialties from around the world.

Green River Farms, 2480 Green River Road in South Williamstown, is a reliable source of farm-grown vegetables, bedding plants, and a wide variety of apples. It has an inviting farm animal petting area with miniature horses, Shetland sheep, pygmy goats, llamas, donkeys, piglets, bunnies, ducklings, and chicks. Visit www.greenriverfarms.com for more information.

Caretaker Farm (1210 Hancock Road) in South Williamstown has been operating as a family-owned organic vegetable farm for over 35 years. It is a Community Supported Agriculture Farm (CSA) where members purchase a share of the annual harvest. The farm is pioneering solar-powered electric fencing and livestock feeders and plans to ultimately generate its own electricity for barn lighting and vegetable refrigeration.

As you head south on Route 7 you will pass another recommended Accommodation with a Past. *The* **1896 House**, *an upscale B&B offering six luxury suites in a restored historic barn; a popular eatery, the 6 House Pub; and two tasteful motels, all set amidst 17 acres of gardens, water landscapes, romantic footbridges, and a duck pond.*

GREEN RIVER FARMS

CARETAKER FARM

Williamstown should be on the itinerary of every visitor to this region. The Village Beautiful has a knack for showcasing the best of the Berkshires. Innovative art exhibitions, well-staged festivals, and the beauty of the countryside reward every visit with something special to remember.

INSCRIPTION ON HOPKINS MEMORIAL STEPS, WILLIAMS COLLEGE

ADDITIONAL RESOURCES

Williamstown: The First Two Hundred Years, 1753–1853, Robert R. R. Brooks, Editor, Williamstown MA: The McClelland Press, 1953, 458 pages. One of the most comprehensive and readable town histories available. The book benefits from a thorough review of town records and area newspapers and the involvement of dozens of researchers and advisors.

Origins in Williamstown, by Arthur Lathan Perry, New York City: Scribner, 1894, 631 pages. A useful source of the town's beginnings, including details on Fort Massachusetts, the American Revolution, and early town characters. Generously illustrated. Reprinted in 1992.

HIGH COUNTRY

New Ashford and Hancock

We conclude our journeys through the Berkshires with a visit to two small Berkshire towns that lie south of Williamstown: New Ashford and Hancock.

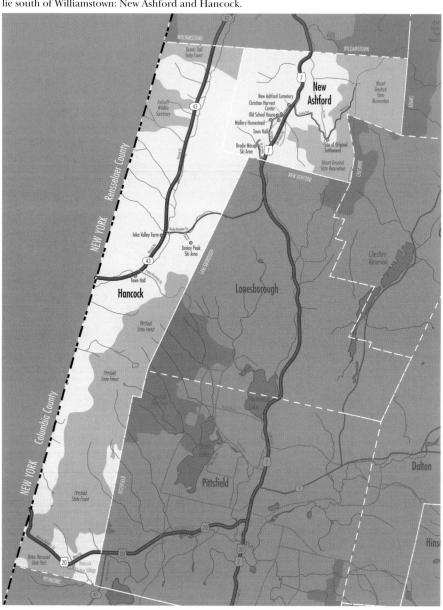

SITE OF ORGINAL SETTLEMENT

New Ashford

The land surface of **New Ashford** is quite mountainous. The Taconic range on the west and Mount Greylock on the east tower over the small town, which is located within a picturesque gorge. Route 7 snakes its way through the town from Williamstown to Lanesborough. This is a scenic area of great natural beauty.

Settlement of New Ashford began in 1762. The colonists initially located their houses on the slopes of the highest mountain in Massachusetts. Greylock Road, a sharp turn off Route 7, wends its way up Mount Greylock (ultimately connecting with Rockwell Road, one of the main access roads to the summit). A log cabin-like monument, about a mile and a half from Route 7, marks the approximate site of the original settlement.

Almost half of the land area of New Ashford is incorporated within Mount Greylock State Reservation.

For some 35 years, the **Brodie Mountain Ski Area**, in the southwest quadrant of New Ashford, was an exciting place to ski, offering a vertical drop of 1,250 feet and runs of up to 2.5 miles. Its nickname was "Kelly's Irish Alps," named for its founder, Jim Kelly, who gave the slopes names like Killarney and Shamrock. Now closed, the area is the site of the proposed Snowy Owl Resort. The annual St. Patrick's Day Snow Party drew thousands. Sadly, the

resort couldn't compete with the larger, better capitalized New England resorts and was sold in 1999 to nearby Jiminy Peak in Hancock. In 2002 the property was sold again to a condominium developer.

The center of New Ashford is easily reached by turning west off Route 7 onto Mallery Road, named after one of the founding families of New Ashford. The **Mallery house** burned to the ground a century or so ago, when clothes were hung near the fireplace to dry and caught fire. The fireplace has been restored and marks the site of this historic homestead, which dates back to about 1770.

MALLERY HOMESTEAD MARKER

VIEW OF NEW ASHFORD VALLEY >
Paul Rocheleau

David J. McLaughlin

1792 ONE-ROOM SCHOOLHOUSE | In 1920, after women won suffrage, the first American woman (Phoebe Jordan) to cast a vote in a national election did so here. The polls opened in New Ashford at 12:01 A.M., earlier than any other town on the East Coast. With only a handful of people to vote, voting was completed within minutes and results submitted to the state.

The town hall of New Ashford and two historic buildings are also located on Mallery Road.

One of the oldest **one-room schoolhouses** in the country, dating to 1792 (and showing its age), sits across from the town hall.

The **New Ashford Church**, adjacent to the old schoolhouse, was built in 1828 as a nondenominational house of worship. There was never a permanent minister, but the church was often used for Methodist services. It served the community for 120 years but was closed and boarded up in the 1950s. The former church was reopened as the Christian Harvest Center in 1994.

CHRISTIAN HARVEST CENTER | The center is now used for concerts, community events, and weddings.

STEEPLE WITH LUCKY FIVES

Members of the community were asked to pay for the original church by pledging money for its construction. The major subscriber turned out to be a gambling man who required that his favorite number be incorporated in the overall design. If you stand outside the church and look up you will see the number 5 incorporated in the design all around the bottom of the steeple.

The **New Ashford Cemetery** sits at the end of Cemetery Road, rising over Route 7.

NEW ASHFORD CEMETERY | The early cemetery records were lost in a fire, so many of the old markers have not been identified.

Jim McElholm

FALL DISPLAY ALONG MALLERY ROAD

The town of New Ashford is a small community whose population peaked at 390 in 1800. When David Dudley Field and the Rev. Chester Dewey published *A History of the County of Berkshire* in 1829 there were two sawmills, a grist mill, and a quarry where marble was excavated and cut into blocks for shipment to the Hudson River. These days this is a residential community for individuals who like to be in the country. Most commute to the larger towns north and south of New Ashford.

Route 7 between Lanesborough and Williamstown is one of the most scenic stretches of highway in the Berkshires. I try to make this trip in the fall whenever I can. The heavily forested hills of New Ashford are a delight when fall colors are at their peak.

Next Page Photo by Jim McElholm

Jim McElholm

FALL COLORS

Hancock

Hancock is a long, narrow town that extends from the border of Williamstown to Richmond in the south. The two main roads, U.S. 43 and U.S. 20, cut through the town and connect Hancock closely to New York State, which borders the entire 16-mile length of the town. In colonial days Hancock was wider than its present 2 miles, but it lost some of its choicest land to New York State when the Massachusetts–New York boundary was finally settled in 1787.

The portion of Hancock that is familiar to most visitors is **Hancock Shaker Village**, in the south,

which lies along Route 20. We covered this important living museum in Chapter 10, "The Shaker Experience."

The center of Hancock actually lies along Route 43, easily reached from Route 7 on Brodie Mountain Road.

Starobin Pond is a picturesque spot located about a mile north of where Brodie Mountain Road joins Route 43.

The **old town hall**, built in 1850, sits in quiet isolation along Route 43.

STAROBIN POND

Jim McElholm

Two principal attractions draw visitors to the center of Hancock.

Ioka Valley Farm, founded in 1936 by Robert and Dorothy Leab and still run by the Leab family, is an inviting, family-friendly farm set in a lovely valley. (*Ioka* is an Indian word meaning *beautiful*.) The founders were early pioneers in scientific, conservation-minded farming and, until 1996, operated a dairy farm. The Leabs now concentrate on producing healthy products and on what they call "agri-entertainment." Ioka Farm offers high-quality natural, hormone-free beef, "pick-your-own" berries, pumpkins and squash in the fall, Christmas trees to cut for the holidays, and plenty of authentic maple syrup and maple sugar products. Kids love the hayrides, pedal tractors, and petting zoo, where they can meet the farm's friendly pigs, sheep, and goats. The farm's Main Barn Calf-A serves homemade pancake meals mid-February to early April, during the peak of the maple syrup season.

Ioka Valley Farm is located on Route 43 in Hancock (413-738-5915). Before you go, check out what produce is available and what rides are open by phoning or visiting their Website at www.taconic.net/~iokavalleyfarm/.

There are picturesque barns and other country delights to discover in Hancock.

Hancock is also the location of **Jiminy Peak Mountain Resort**, the largest full-service ski and snowboarding resort in southern New England.

Jim McElholm

FALL DISPLAY

Jim McElholm

ENTRANCE TO JIMINY PEAK

Jim McElholm

RED BARN IN HANCOCK

318

SKIING AT JIMINY PEAK

< WINTER SCENE

In addition to 44 trails (18 lit for night skiing) and nine lifts, Jiminy Peak has a snowboard park, a mountain coaster, and plenty of hot tubs. There is 93 percent snowmaking coverage of the trails.

The resort with two adjacent condominium developments is open year round. Fair-weather attractions include a two-story rock-climbing wall, a Euro-bungee trampoline, an alpine slide on which you can zoom down the mountain on a bobsled, miniature golf, mountain biking, and scenic chairlift rides (on the weekends) up the mountain.

The resort also promotes Jiminy Peak as a meeting and conference site and an appealing place to have a wedding, particularly a large one; the facility's extensive facilities can accommodate groups of up to 400.

Jiminy Peak is located at 37 Corey Road (just off Brodie Mountain Road) in Hancock; phone 413-738-5500. The Resort has an extensive and useful Website: www.jiminypeak.com.

SUMMER FUN

The once-remote towns of New Ashford and Hancock are now easily within reach, just off Route 7, one of the most scenic roads in the Berkshires. These communities have their special charms. Hancock is a year-round destination for the outdoor enthusiast and families planning an excursion their children will enjoy. This is 21st-century Berkshire County, with a growing number of condominiums, many organized as timeshares. New Ashford involves a trip to a quieter past, a town whose historic buildings and old cemetery provide a glimpse of what life was like in the early days of New England.

MOUNTAINS IN RAIN AND SUN >
Paul Rocheleau

JIMINY PEAK COMPLEX IN FALL

Acknowledgments

Researching a book of the scope and complexity of *Inside the Berkshires* involved hundreds of individuals and scores of institutions. I am particularly indebted to the staff members of the area's outstanding museums and performing arts institutions, who provided essential images and shared future plans. I received a great deal of help from town officials and historical society members who helped identify obscure historic structures, assisted me in finding lesser-known attractions, and facilitated access to places not open to the public.

I would like to acknowledge the local experts on whom I counted for inside knowledge and advice and who generously took the time to supply facts, research century-old events, provide historic images, and review copy. In addition to the dozens of indispensable town contacts, I am particularly indebted to Barbara Allen, Curator of the Historical Collection of the Stockbridge Library Association; Kathleen Reilly, Supervisor of Local History & Melville Collections at the Berkshire Athenaeum; Amy Lafave, Reference Librarian at the Lenox Library; Nancy Burstein, Curator of the House of Local History in Williamstown; Katharine C. Westwood, Special Collections Librarian at the North Adams Library; Norma Purdy of the Berkshire Historical Society; Will Garrison, Historic Resources Manager of the Trustees of Reservations; and the prolific author and noted historian Bernard Drew. Several authors of important Berkshire books generously shared their expertise and reviewed chapter drafts, including Cornelia Brooke Gilder (*Houses of the Berkshires*), Lucia Saradoff (*Working the Stone*), John D. Sisson (*A Pictorial History of New Marlborough*), Leonard Swift (*The Heritage of Hinsdale: An Anthology*), and James R. Miller (*Early Life in Sheffield, Berkshire County, Massachusetts: A Biography of Its Ordinary People from Early Times to 1850*). Among the subject experts who went out of their way to help were Jerry Grant of the Shaker Museum and Library in Old Chatham; Christian Goodwoodie, Curator of Collections at Hancock Shaker Museum; Dorothy Napp Schindel, Museum Director Becket Land Trust Historic Quarry; and railroading experts Thomas Delasco and Robert Podolski.

I am especially indebted to Clarence Fanto (columnist, contributing writer, and general expert on all things Berkshire) who generously agreed to review the final manuscript and whose suggestions were invaluable.

This image-intensive book benefited from the talents of a number of professional photographers: Jim McElholm of Single Source worked with me in the early planning and image acquisition and did important contract photography for Pentacle Press. The preeminent Richmond photographer, Paul Rocheleau, gave us access to his images and responded to several special requests. Kevin Sprague of Studio Two, who supplies images and graphic help to dozens of leading Berkshire organizations, was especially helpful in providing captivating images of performances and scenic locations. We also benefited from the stunning images of professional photographers Darlene Bordwell, David Dashiell, Arthur Evans, Marta Fodar, Kelly Lee, Stephanie Motta, Cheryl Sachs, and H. David Stein. Three talented members of the Berkshire Camera Club supplied images: Robert Behr, Cesar Silva, and Henry Dondi.

Several contemporary artists gave us permission to include images of their work in the book, including Stephen Hannock, Melissa Lilly, Joshua Field, Jenny Holzer, and the sculptor Andrew DeVries.

I am particularly indebted to the key members of the team that helped create *Inside the Berkshires*: Laren Bright (323-852-0433), my friend and long-time collaborator, who helped shape the end product from start to finish and wrote the cover copy; Cindy Wilson (904-826-1672) and the talented graphic artists of Cindy Wilson Design (particularly Kat Radicioni, who designed the maps, and Stephen Heymann, who laid out the book); and Darlene Bordwell (www. DarleneBordwell.com), whose editorial and photographic services we have used for several years.

— David J. McLaughlin

Index

Jim McElholm

Jim McElholm